I0820119

90 SECONDS TO MIDNIGHT

90 Seconds *to* Midnight

A HIROSHIMA SURVIVOR'S NUCLEAR ODYSSEY

CHARLOTTE DECROES JACOBS

Potomac Books
An imprint of the University of Nebraska Press

 Potomac Books is an imprint
of the University of Nebraska Press.
Manufactured in the United States of America.

For customers in the EU with safety/GPSR concerns, contact:
gpsr@mare-nostrum.co.uk
Mare Nostrum Group BV
Mauritskade 21D
1091 GC Amsterdam
The Netherlands

Library of Congress Control Number: 2024047437

Designed and set in Arno Pro
by Lacey Losh.

For

Owen

Colin

Savannah

Gigi

Hallie

Dillon

Ezra

Mira

Contents

Part 3. The Quest

Illustrations

Abbreviations

ABCC	Atomic Bomb Casualty Commission
ICAN	International Campaign to Abolish Nuclear Weapons
ICRC	International Committee of the Red Cross
IPPNW	International Physicians for the Prevention of Nuclear War
JFS	Japanese Family Services of Metropolitan Toronto
NATO	North Atlantic Treaty Organization
NGO	Non-governmental Organization
NPT	Treaty on the Non-Proliferation of Nuclear Weapons
OEWG	Open-Ended Working Group
TPNW	Treaty on the Prohibition of Nuclear Weapons (Ban Treaty)

Note on Japanese Names

The Japanese convention in which the surname precedes the given name is used until the start of the twentieth century, after which Japanese names are presented in Western order—given name before surname.

90 SECONDS TO MIDNIGHT

Prologue

When she reached the base of the mountain, she found an army training ground the size of two football fields packed with thousands of dead and dying. The air reeked of burnt flesh. What she saw stunned her: strips of skin hanging like ribbons, bones sticking out, stomachs burst open, people charred beyond recognition. Earlier that morning a bomb had struck her city just as she was to begin decoding messages for the Imperial Japanese Army. Buried in a grave of rubble, she had miraculously escaped from a burning building, in which twenty-seven of her classmates were incinerated. A soldier urged her and two other surviving girls to flee to the hills above the city. Her name was Setsuko Nakamura; she was thirteen years old.[1]

All she could see in every direction was a bloodbath. An eerie silence was broken by moans and pleas for water. Setsuko didn't call out for her parents or sit at the edge of the field covering her eyes to blot out this scene from hell, waiting for someone to rescue her. Instead, she found a stream nearby. With no buckets or cups to carry water, she directed her two classmates to tear strips from their blouses, soak them in the cold stream, then rush back and place the wet cloths over the mouths of the wounded. As they sucked the moisture Setsuko provided, they gazed up at a mere girl—calm, not terrified—who was focused on their comfort. She managed not to recoil at the blood oozing from gashes on heads and chests, hair singed to stubble, lips so swollen that the water dribbled over them. In some the nose, mouth, and ears appeared to have melted together like lava, eyes peering out from a mass of flesh. Sometimes she couldn't distinguish men from women. People who may have been her neighbors or the local grocer or a revered teacher didn't look human. Some held their intestines in their hands. A mother cradled a small, blackened mass.

Setsuko scanned the training ground, searching for a doctor or nurse. She found none. The three girls continued to run back and forth to the stream. What else could they do? When the dark clouds lifted, fierce sunlight seared the already blistered bodies. Setsuko couldn't move fast enough to quench the crowd's collective thirst. All around her a multitude of stricken people seemed to be waiting for their agony to end. Yet even in the last second of their lives, as she offered water, they looked at her and murmured, "*arigato*" (thank you). The staring gaze of death followed.[2]

At dusk the three girls sat on the hillside, watching their city, Hiroshima, burn. They remained speechless, their grief incomprehensible. Setsuko thought briefly about her family, but the possibility that they had met the same fate as those around her was too painful. How could Setsuko not be paralyzed with grief when at dawn she saw nothing where Hiroshima used to be? Although she was just a young teen, from somewhere deep inside her emerged a strength that propelled her forward and willed her to hold on. So when the sun rose on August 7, 1945, she stood up, surveyed the unimaginable carnage on the ground below, and pressed on.

Out of the ashes of Hiroshima emerged a young woman who had lost almost everything except her indomitable will. She would vow to her family and classmates slaughtered by the first atomic bomb: never again. She would go on to speak on the world stage and command the attention of international leaders in her lifelong quest to abolish nuclear weapons. It was an arduous journey, and the odds were against her. Setsuko Nakamura was born into a family of samurai origin. Meaning "those who serve," samurai embraced a code of conduct emphasizing devotion to the common cause and fearlessness in the face of the enemy.[3] These tenets contributed to her fortitude and a spirit that would guide her actions throughout life. This is her story.

Part 1

BEFORE

1 The Heart of a Samurai

> The sense of honor, implying a vivid consciousness of personal dignity and worth . . . characterize[s] the samurai, born and bred to value the duties and privileges of their profession.
>
> —Nitobe Inazō, *Bushido, the Soul of Japan*

No one knows the exact origin of the samurai. In AD 787, as Japanese soldiers crossed the Kitakami River on their way to subdue the indigenous people in northern Honshu, the barbarian cavalry swooped down from the hilltops and drove Emperor Kanmu's army into the water. Weighed down by their armor, over a thousand infantrymen drowned. The barbarians, unsurpassed in mounted archery, proved difficult to overcome. Imperial military leaders concluded that, instead of building an army from conscripted farmers, they needed to develop superior warriors, as had the barbarians, trained from a young age in horsemanship, archery, and the art of the sword. This decision generated a feudal warrior caste, thought to be ancestors of the samurai. These warriors gained further significance when the emperor began granting members of the imperial family large landed estates. With less than a quarter of Japan's land suitable for farming, local chieftains attempted to seize their property. The lords appealed to the imperial court for protection. In response it appointed deputies from among the warriors to safeguard them—the samurai. Pledging fealty to their lords, they received a steady income and land grants in return. This military elite gradually grew in number and strength. Eventually they came to rule the country.

Toward the end of the twelfth century, Minamoto no Yorimoto, one of the greatest samurai heroes, assumed the title of shogun—"commander of troops"—and established the first military government in Japan, the shogunate. With that the emperor lost his political power and was reduced to a mere figurehead. Under Minamoto's rule, preeminent samurai warlords, *daimyo*, formed powerful domains, consisting of vast private estates with associated clans. Armies of lower-rank samurai, retainers who vowed loyalty, defended them. Despite a symbiotic relationship with the shogunate, clashes arose among daimyo, which led to years of civil war. Throughout this extended era of conflict, daimyo erected large castles for protection as they extended their dynasties. In 1589 Lord Mōri Terumoto, grandson of a great warlord, began to build a castle on the Otagawa River delta, in an area he named Hiroshima. At the turn of the century, a powerful military family, the Tokugawa, gained control of the country.

Under the Tokugawa shogunate, prosperity and political stability prevailed for 250 years, known as the Edo period. Its first shogun, Tokugawa Ieyasu, appointed several hundred daimyo and directed them to govern their semiautonomous domains by civil means instead of military force. Whereas samurai had defended their daimyo's lands in times of war, during these peaceful years, they served as administrators for the estates, keeping watch over the commoners, including farmers, artisans, and merchants. To distinguish themselves from the commoners, samurai wore two swords—one long, one short—and a top knot. Constituting about 6 percent of the population, samurai and their families had a high literacy rate. *Bushidō* (the way of the warrior) defined their unwritten code of conduct, which emphasized honor, discipline, and fearlessness in the face of the enemy.

By the mid-1800s, the peaceful existence of the Tokugawa dynasty was coming to an end. Japan, composed of four main islands and over three thousand small islands, had been isolated by and large from the outside world and remained a feudal state. That changed in 1853, after Commodore Matthew Perry steamed into Edo Bay (renamed Tokyo Bay) and delivered a letter from President Millard Filmore, demanding that Japan open its main ports to international trade. Six months later Perry returned with ten heavily armed ships and secured an agreement. This exposure to the outside world, along with peasant uprisings due to widespread destitution, precipitated a civil war. With the defeat of the last shogun, political power was returned to the emperor, ushering in the Meiji Restoration of 1868.[1]

In the new regime, orchestrated in large part by young samurai, fifteen-year-old Emperor Mutsuhito remained a figurehead. As the new rulers began to modernize Japan, they knew they must terminate the feudal system, which meant waiving the privileges of their own class. Daimyo returned their domains to the emperor, who divided the country into prefectures. Samurai lost income and property. They could no longer be distinguished by their swords and topknots, previously worn in public. Several thousand were disinherited. "In a sense," a historian wrote, "the samurai abolished themselves."[2]

During the Meiji Restoration, the government created universal education and required military conscription for every male over twenty, consisting of three years of active duty followed by four years in the reserves. They built railways and modern factories and opened banks to provide investment capital. Western clothing and hairstyles were introduced. With its first prime minister, a constitution, and the establishment of the Diet, Japan transformed from a feudal warrior state into a parliamentary government. Despite its dissolution, the old samurai class still retained its social status. The code of conduct—*bushidō*—had been ingrained in the moral constitution of its members. Now referred to as *shizoku,* they held leading positions as educators, government employees, scholars, and businesspeople.[3]

As did most samurai families, the Nakamuras suffered financial losses during the Meiji Restoration. Setsuko's grandfather, Nakamura Yataro, was born in the mid-1800s. As the eldest son, he bore responsibility for his parents and siblings, as well as extended family. When the new governor of the Hiroshima Prefecture, Senda Sadaaki, announced plans to invigorate the city, Yataro saw an opportunity to be of assistance. Upon arriving in Hiroshima, the governor had found no proper harbor; visitors had to anchor their boats in the bay and wade ashore. Senda undertook the construction of Ujina Port in 1884. This costly project required raising substantial funds, and Nakamura Yataro played an important role in that undertaking.[4] As a result, Hiroshima became a vital port for the exportation of manufactured goods.

Meanwhile, a marriage had been arranged for Yataro. His wife, Sasaki Tama, came from a family of equal standing, which professed a famous samurai warrior among its ancestors.[5] Her customary duties included managing their household, bearing children, and caring for her in-laws. As indications of wealth and rank, Tama's dowry included exquisite, lacquered writing boxes, jewelry chests, and ornate furniture. She maintained the mien of a samurai wife, dressed and coiffed in the traditional way. Strict and demanding, she insisted on proper education and cultural training for her four sons and two daughters. The Nakamuras lived in a traditional Japanese house with a central courtyard and a *kura* (storehouse) behind the home to protect their valuables, which would be passed on to their eldest son.

Setsuko's father, Benkichi, was born in 1883, the second son of Yataro and Tama. According to the Japanese inheritance system, based on primogeniture, his older brother would follow his father as the head of the family, inheriting all their property and undertaking responsibility for the extended family after his father's death. Benkichi, as the second, noninheriting son, had to find his own employment. At school, principals told their students: "First sons, stay in Japan and be men of Japan. Second sons, go abroad with great ambition as men of the world."[6]

As Benkichi approached adulthood, his father's finances once again began floundering, and Yataro looked to North America, where he understood that, if Japanese worked hard, they could make money and return wealthy. The Japanese government was urging workers to immigrate to Hawaii, the United States, and Canada. Furthermore, when Benkichi reached twenty, he would be drafted into military service, unable to contribute much to the family's income. Japan had been at war with China, and its relationship with the Russian Empire was deteriorating. So, in 1899, Nakamura Yataro sent his second son, sixteen-year-old Benkichi, to America.

Benkichi entered North America at Vancouver, British Columbia. At the time an increasing number of Japanese disembarked at Canadian ports, as Canadian Pacific steamships offered more regularly scheduled crossings and better facilities for immigrants than did U.S. ships. Many came from the Hiroshima

Prefecture, where review boards screened emigration candidates to make certain they would uphold Japan's national honor. Before 1900 Canada didn't keep accurate records on Japanese immigrants. Because they could move easily between the United States and Canada under the transit privilege, over two-thirds passed through en route to the States. Benkichi stayed.

As Canada's leading commercial center on the west coast, Vancouver provided ample employment opportunities for issei (Japanese immigrants) on farms and in the fisheries, mines, sawmills, canneries, and logging companies. Japanese shops, groceries, and hotels were springing up along Powell Street in its growing Japanese community. Although most boarding houses were cramped and squalid, some did provide communal baths, laundry service, Japanese food, and friendship.[7]

Benkichi took a job as a *shosei* (schoolboy). These single young men worked as house servants while learning the English language and Canadian customs. Benkichi already knew some English, as it had been required back home, along with mathematics, literature, writing, and religion. For their services shosei received about $1.50 per week, plus room and board. Later Benkichi worked as a railway navvy, short for navigator—a manual laborer on civil engineering projects. Employment on the Canadian Pacific Railway was strenuous, with frequent injuries. Navvies slept in boxcars and subsisted on slim provisions. Despite those conditions, the pay was good—$1.00 to $2.50 per day. Still, he had bigger plans.

After three years Benkichi left Canada. He had become interested in farming, and California's Central Valley appeared to be welcoming. In July 1902 Benkichi moved to Florin, nine miles southeast of Sacramento.[8] When he arrived, the town consisted of scattered hardscrabble farms. By the time he left, it would have one of California's largest Japanese communities and be called "the strawberry capital of the world."[9] Florin had been founded in 1875, its name derived from its vast fields of wildflowers. A handful of white farmers grew wheat and hay in meager amounts on the thin, impoverished soil. With the Chinese Exclusion Act of 1882, they had lost their cheap labor. So in 1898, when four Japanese families settled there and began sharecropping strawberries with some success, the community encouraged more Japanese to move to

Florin. Upon their arrival, issei found a post office, school, several churches, and Sugden's Mercantile.[10]

When he first came to Florin, Benkichi didn't see barren fields of sand and pebbles; he saw acres of land, a precious commodity in his homeland. Anxious to work, honest and diligent, he was just the kind of immigrant this farming community was seeking. Issei provided more than cheap labor, however. They leveled the fields, dug irrigation ditches, and installed pumping machines from local wells, introducing sophisticated irrigation methods that turned the desiccated farmlands into lush strawberry fields. They expanded the production of locally cultivated grapes, the Florin Flame Tokay, and planted strawberries between the rows of vines, increasing the yield per acre. Despite the exhausting work, especially during picking season, when temperatures reached over a hundred degrees, they persevered.

Rising from laborer to tenant farmer, Benkichi worked for and then formed a partnership with Henry Emil Kleinsorge of Sacramento, president of the Western Fruit Company. Before long he served as treasurer for a local businessmen's organization, standing out not only as a result of his entrepreneurial acumen but also because of his appearance. His three-piece suit, along with his fluency in English and decorum, denoted a modern, almost fully westernized man.

In the fall of 1903, Benkichi negotiated to obtain thirty-four acres on Essau and Caroline Gardner's ranch for $2,451.28.[11] When his father, Yataro, and older brother, Daizo, traveled to Florin two years later to check up on his progress, they found he had prospered—cultivating strawberries and grapes and collaborating with an important white man from Sacramento. After Yataro and Daizo returned to Japan, Yataro sent his third son, twenty-three-year-old Hiroshi, to join his brother. He, too, would thrive in California. A shrewd businessman, Benkichi netted $5,000 in 1907, allowing him to purchase more land and a home. And in 1908 he sold his original thirty-four acres for over three times what he had paid.[12] That same year he married Shigeno Masaoka.

For Japanese, marriage was a family concern, not an individual decision. A *nakōdo* (go-between or matchmaker) helped parents choose their offspring's spouse. It's unclear whether Benkichi's marriage had been arranged before he left Hiroshima or through the exchange of photographs between the families after he had emigrated to North America. In either case the *nakōdo* would have informed Benkichi and his parents that Shigeno was born in 1887 into an old samurai family of at least equal standing. Shigeno and her parents would have learned about the success twenty-five-year-old Benkichi had in America as well as his dedication to his extended family. Tall for a Japanese man, Benkichi had prominent cheekbones, neatly cropped hair, and a pencil mustache. He was a man of few words, speaking only when necessary. Twenty-one-year-old Shigeno did not appear as comely as her prospective husband. In seeming disregard for the Japanese beauty ideals of pale skin with shaved eyebrows and red lips painted smaller than natural, she did not embellish her looks with makeup, leaving her eyebrows and lips full. What drew others to her was her personality. Gregarious and of good humor, she would provide a wonderful balance for the somewhat taciturn Benkichi. The two may have been different in appearance and demeanor, but inside Shigeno and Benkichi were the same—adventuresome, hardworking, family-centered, and honorable. It would prove to be a good match.

Shigeno was willing to move from Hiroshima across the Pacific Ocean to a town in the middle of a state called California as the wife of a man she likely had never met. There she assisted her new husband in his farming business and helped develop a Japanese community in a place where people spoke a different language; ate potatoes instead of rice; wore cotton and wool, not silk; and set their own hair. As had Benkichi, Shigeno adopted Western fashion. In a photograph from that time, she wears her hair swept back and piled into a chignon at the crown of her head, based on the Gibson Girl look, topped by a wide-brimmed hat decorated with flowers. She has exchanged her kimono for a long skirt and Edwardian-style blouse with a high collar and puffy sleeves.

Shigeno proved to be as industrious as her husband. While Benkichi recruited over four hundred immigrants to work as pickers, she engaged and supervised the women, mostly new arrivals, who did the cooking. Increasingly, Japanese women from the commoner class were becoming wage earners. Shigeno had never expected to be resourcefully engaged outside the home. She felt a sense of freedom, of achievement, unthinkable for most women from samurai families.

The Nakamuras watched the economy of Florin prosper. Issei converted the barren land into productive and profitable orchards and vineyards. Shipments of strawberries and their famous Tokay grapes totaled up to 280 train cars per season and were shipped across the country from Florin's South Pacific Station. Before long Japanese owned some of the shipping firms; the fruit was packed in baskets made by women in the Florin Basket Company. The proprietor preferred Japanese over white women as they were willing to work fourteen-hour days, seven days a week, adding to the success of the company and the wealth of the community. By 1912 the value of all crops grown on Japanese farms in Florin totaled $557,949, and issei leased or owned almost four thousand acres.[13] They had developed a vibrant community in Florin. There five of the seven Nakamura children were born: in 1909 son Isamu (meaning brave); in 1910 son Susumu (to advance); in 1912 daughter Fumiko (child of literature); in 1915 son Masami (true self); and in 1917 daughter Ayako (child of elegance). In addition Yataro sent his youngest son, Teruya, to live with them.

The Nakamura children, as did other American children born of Japanese parents (nisei), attended Florin Elementary East School, learned English, and wore Western clothing. Teachers described them as intelligent and industrious. An issei couple taught Japanese language and literature in an afterschool program. Shigeno could shop at either of two Japanese groceries and take her sons to a Japanese barber. The Nakamuras joined the Florin Buddhist Church, started in 1896 by ten Japanese immigrants. The membership grew such that in time they purchased 2.5 acres on Florin Road and built a white clapboard church, which became a center of social and cultural life.[14] There Shigeno played the organ, one of her greatest joys.

The Japanese population of Florin continued to increase, estimated in 1915 to be almost nine hundred: 255 farmers, 300 businessmen and basket-company employees, 159 women, and 150 children. The daily labor rate had increased to $2.50 for Japanese workers.[15] Frugal and hardworking, they had started with almost nothing and before long built houses, bought American clothes, and ate American food. The Nakamuras owned their own house and land; Benkichi was among the first in Florin to buy a Model T.

Shigeno looked forward to their weekend trips to San Francisco. While Benkichi attended business meetings with other Japanese immigrants, Shigeno and the children explored the city. Market Street was bustling with motorcars and cable cars. Men wore waistcoats and bowlers; women displayed their tiny, corseted waists and grandiose hats, ornamented with bows, feathers, and artificial flowers. The new city hall dominated the skyline. A walk along Ocean Beach would have given the children their first view of the sea. Strolling in Golden Gate Park, Shigeno might have found solace for any homesickness in the Japanese Tea Garden with its teahouse, Buddhist sculptures, cherry blossom trees, and ponds stocked with koi. In the evenings Benkichi and Shigeno often ate in the hotel dining room. She dressed in Western fashion, wearing gloves and a hat with a decorative veil. Years later she told her daughters how surprised she was when chicken was served, and those sophisticated American women pulled up their veils, peeled off their gloves, picked up the chicken pieces with their hands, and started eating. "Shocking," she said, ending her story with a laugh.[16]

With one of the largest Japanese populations in California, Florin served as a commercial and social center for Japanese from nearby farming communities. But this land of promise did not last forever. White farmers began to feel threatened. Skilled, hardworking, and productive, many issei had become successful proprietors in the fruit, flower, and vegetable business. Fear and jealousy generated anti-Japanese sentiment. It had begun to surface in 1907 with the Gentlemen's Agreement between the United States and Japan, which stipulated that Japan could issue no new passports for Japanese laborers, although wives could still join their husbands in America. As a result, the number of picture brides escalated. These marriages, arranged an ocean apart, based on exchanged photographs, allowed previously single women to immigrate to the United States as wives, further increasing the Japanese population. An article in the *Sacramento Bee* warned, "As soon as a Jap can produce a lease, he is entitled to a wife. He sends a copy of his lease back home and gets a picture bride, and they increase like rats. Florin . . . is producin' 85 American-born Japs a year."[17]

The California Alien Land Law of 1913 prohibited immigrants ineligible for citizenship (including Japanese) from purchasing property, although they could retain what they already owned. How foolhardy: by then shipments of Tokay grapes and strawberries totaled a half million dollars yearly. Whites in Florin complained that Japanese were tricky and dishonest, taking their jobs and land. They feared an overpopulation of immigrant children and intermarriage. "Japanese controlled and owned the town of Florin," the *Sacramento Bee* reported, "and the school built for children of white men is now almost half Japanese."[18] A few years later, Florin's schoolboard segregated its elementary school.

Benkichi Nakamura had thrived in Florin. According to the *Directory of Japanese in Sacramento*, he continued to acquire farmland and began to cultivate tomatoes while starting a fruit broker business on the side. "His extraordinary energy in multiple fields is simply admirable," the directory read.[19] Shigeno cherished her life in Florin as well; they considered it their home. Nonetheless, in 1920 they applied for passports for their five children.[20] There had been a change in the Nakamura family. Benkichi's older brother had suffered an illness that left him disabled. Yataro designated his second son, Benkichi, to be his successor, the future head of the family. Although Benkichi would continue to maintain his businesses in Florin, Yataro insisted that his grandchildren be educated in Japan, where they would learn *bushidō*, the samurai code of conduct, and strengthen the family's bloodline. By Japanese custom, once married, Shigeno belonged to her husband's family. She had no choice but to return.

On November 30, 1920, an announcement appeared in *Nichibei Shimbun*, San Francisco's Japanese American newspaper: "Nakamura Benkichi, a businessman of Florin from Hiroshima Prefecture, held a farewell party at his place from 5 p.m. yesterday, inviting more than one hundred guests, including friends and business customers. There were so many people who gave farewell speeches, and the party was a great success."[21] On December 7 the Nakamuras posted a notice in another San Francisco–based newspaper *Shin Sekai* (New world): "Greetings before going back. Upon our temporary return to Japan, we highly appreciate your kindness to give farewell gifts and to come to see us off while you were busy. Today we departed without accident by *Tenyo Maru*. . . . Please do not worry."[22]

As soon as Shigeno and the five children moved in with Benkichi's parents, he returned to Florin. Having loved her American life, Shigeno found an environment of extreme nationalism in Hiroshima with an emphasis on the preservation of traditional Japanese culture and values along with rejection of Western influence. No one spoke English in the Nakamura household. Shigeno put away her wide-brimmed hat decorated with flowers and her Edwardian-style blouse with puffy sleeves; she no longer played the organ. The happiest chapter in her life had closed.

Benkichi returned to Florin alone, as his successful businesses continued to enhance the finances of his extended family. On February 6, 1922, *Shin Sekai* published an article titled "Top 100 Farmers," which listed California's most successful issei farmers, based on their public reputation. In the category of grapes, Benkichi Nakamura received the second-highest number of votes for "those who introduced their [agricultural] business to Japan and their own people [in the United States] in order to be role models for their juniors."[23]

In the meantime American anti-Japanese sentiment was increasing. The year Shigeno left Florin, picture brides could no longer obtain passports, and the amended Alien Land Law prohibited Asian immigrants from leasing land or holding stock in companies that acquired agricultural land. A year later, in nearby Turlock, armed white vigilantes drove fifty-eight Japanese laborers out of town, threatening them harm if they returned. Graffiti throughout the Central Valley warned, "Japs go home." A highway sign read, "No More Japs Wanted Here."[24] In 1922 the U.S. Supreme Court upheld the prohibition against Japanese immigrants becoming naturalized citizens. Benkichi's last recorded trip between Hiroshima and California was in 1925. He never saw Florin again.

On January 3, 1932, Setsuko (child of integrity) was born.

2 A Cherry Blossom Life

Blossoms of spring are all the more precious
because they bloom so briefly.
–Murasaki Shikibu, *The Tale of Genji*

Throughout Setsuko Nakamura's childhood, Japan was almost continuously at war. In the fall of 1931, four months before her birth, the Japanese army invaded the Chinese province of Manchuria and installed a puppet government. Six days after she was born, a Korean independence activist threw a grenade at Emperor Hirohito's carriage as he left the Imperial Palace. Four months later, during a failed coup, Prime Minister Inukai Tsuyoshi was assassinated. Japan left the League of Nations in Setsuko's second year; two years after that, the Soviet Union declared the fascist state of Japan an enemy. When Setsuko was four, Imperial Japan signed an alliance with Nazi Germany. The second Sino-Japanese War erupted after she celebrated her fifth birthday; it would continue for the next eight years. As she entered elementary school, Japan lost eighteen thousand soldiers battling Soviet troops at the Mongolian-Manchurian border. When she was eight, Japanese troops occupied French Indochina. Despite these ongoing hostilities, Setsuko had happy memories of her early years.

Setsuko was born into a privileged family, members of *shizoku*, the Japanese social class composed of former samurai and their descendants. Her father, Benkichi Nakamura, having prospered in California, owned an entire block of rental properties in Kojinmachi, located in the eastern part of Hiroshima, near the railway station. Their first home was cut in half when the government ordered their street widened to create a broad thoroughfare from the Hiroshima station to Ujina Port, a major military embarkation point. Benkichi moved his family into an adjacent house. Although smaller, the two-story home was of an elegant traditional design, with a tiled roof. Setsuko loved how the rooms seemed suffused with light. Too young to count the number of tatami mats—a measure of the size of a house—she knew it had many. Her mother treasured their ornate *butsudan* (Buddhist alter) and her new organ; her father insisted on lush gardens and a private heated bath with a skylight. In the summertime the family slipped into *yukatas* (cotton kimonos) after their baths and sat in the garden, enjoying the cool evening breeze. While his youngest daughter chased fireflies, Benkichi drank sake.

Setsuko spent much of her childhood playing in their backyard among the pine trees. A miniature representation of nature, the garden contained stones to represent a mountain and a pond to symbolize the sea. The gardener taught her to distinguish between the flowering bushes—red azalea and pink camellia—and showed her how he pruned the maple trees. One morning she found him wrapping rice paper around each peony bud. He told her he was preparing for a weekend garden party. A few days later, just before the guests arrived, the gardener removed the paper. Setsuko marveled at the display of white and pink peonies in full bloom. In summer she climbed the fig tree early in the mornings, sat on a sturdy branch, and savored its cool, tasty fruit.

For years Setsuko felt like an only child living in an adult world. After her grandfather died, her father had assumed his place. In the *ie* (family system) the head of the family managed all of its properties and assured the well-being of its members—elderly parents, brothers and sisters, aunts and uncles, nieces and nephews. Benkichi arranged the family marriages, assisted by his wife, Shigeno, who acted as a *nakōdo* for relatives and others in the community. The sole cloud in Setsuko's otherwise sunny childhood was Grandma Tama Nakamura. Dressed in a silk kimono and coiffured by her hairdresser daily, her father's mother spent her days sitting in one of their living rooms, sipping tea, and looking out at the courtyard. Her conversations with her youngest grandchild consisted of commands, although she occasionally surprised her granddaughter with sweets.[1]

The youngest of seven, Setsuko spent limited time with her siblings. Isamu, twenty-three years old when she was born, studied education and mathematics at Hiroshima Higher Normal School. He was tall, slender, and handsome like his father, yet graced with serenity. Setsuko tried not to disturb him as he sat at a low table in his kimono, facing the inner courtyard, engrossed in his books. After what seemed an eternity, he would stand, stretch, and say he needed a break. Setsuko knew a trip to the beach would follow. As her brother clomped along in his tall wooden sandals, Setsuko raced to keep up with him. Isamu recognized that his youngest sister was clever and imaginative, so he introduced her to *Aesop's Fables* and other classics unfamiliar to most Japanese children her age. Soon after his arranged marriage, Hiroshima University recruited Isamu to teach at an elite boys' school in Seoul. Under Japan's colonial rule, the brightest Korean students were educated for leadership positions. Isamu and his new wife, Michie, both devoted teachers, moved to Seoul. Setsuko didn't know she would never see him again.

Setsuko's second brother, Susumu, was quick-tempered and demanding, like Grandma Nakamura. Militaristic in his demeanor, he frightened Setsuko, so she kept her distance. Susumu had just completed his university education when he was drafted to serve in Korea. Setsuko knew her third brother, Masami, only by the daily prayers her mother chanted. He had died from pneumonia in his teens.[2] Her oldest sister, Fumiko, had emigrated to Los Angeles by the time Setsuko was born. There she married Takekuma "Norman" Takei, who had come to California at age thirteen with his widowed father and brother. Although they lived among immigrants in San Francisco's Japanese People's Town, Norman soon became westernized, playing on the local baseball team. He graduated from a local business college, after which he established a successful dry-cleaning business in Los Angeles. There he was introduced to Fumiko Nakamura. He learned she had been born near Sacramento, yet her grandfather had insisted she be educated in Japan and taught the proper ways of a Japanese wife. They married in 1935 at the Los Angeles city hall.[3]

A year later Setsuko's second sister, Ayako, also traveled to Los Angeles. Upon her return, she brought a measure of excitement into Setsuko's life. A 1937 family photo shows Ayako, "child of elegance," dressed in Western attire influenced by Loretta Young: a floral fitted dress to accentuate her small waist and hips with ruffled cap sleeves; a "picture hat" made of fine white Panama straw, the brim pulled to the side at a jaunty angle; and trendy round glasses with plastic rims. Setsuko stared in amazement as her sister applied makeup and used a curling iron. Ayako showed her fashion magazines, took her to the movie theater, and introduced her to Marlene Dietrich and Claudette Colbert. Shigeno arranged her daughter's marriage to Hitomi Kishida. When they moved to Taiwan, where the Kishida family had a lumber business, Ayako faded from Setsuko's life—but not before she imparted her vitality and daring to her little sister. Six years separated Setsuko and her third sister, Yukiko. She was the antithesis of Ayako in looks and manner. Highly traditional, she insisted on proper demeanor—a behavior not emulated by her younger sister.

Although few of Setsuko's siblings lived at home during her childhood, the house resembled a community center, where aunts, uncles, and cousins gathered. As the leader of his extended family, Benkichi, along with Shigeno, hosted birth celebrations, graduations, and weddings, all of which entailed elaborate banquets. The Nakamura home was considered the *honke* (head family). Behind the courtyard, apart from the main house, stood a large *kura* (storage house), which contained the Nakamura family valuables and mementoes passed down over hundreds of years. Whenever Benkichi and Shigeno hosted an affair, they opened the *kura* with an oversized key, and Setsuko followed them inside.

At first she could barely see; the room was lit by a small grated window. The helmets and decorative swords used by her samurai forefathers frightened her. As her eyes adjusted to the light, Setsuko viewed the family treasures with awe, including stacks of black, lacquered wooden trays, which held special dishes and sake cups for formal banquets; and a large chest, inlaid with ivory, given to Setsuko's great-great-grandmother from a lord's mother in thanks for obtaining milk to feed her infant son during the Great Tenpo famine of the 1830s. Most thrilling were the exquisite jewels her mother had inherited. Benkichi felt confident that the *kura*'s thick dirt walls would protect the family's prized possessions from fire and typhoons.[4]

Among her many relatives, Setsuko adored Aunt Sadayo and Uncle Hiroshi, her father's younger brother, who had joined him in Florin. While there Sadayo had sought her brother-in-law's permission to study fashion in San Francisco. Supportive of industrious women, he had financed their move. Sadayo mastered fashion design, textiles, and merchandising and returned to Florin to open the Futaba Dressmaking Women's Academy. It offered instruction in both Japanese- and Western-style clothing. A successful agent for an agricultural company, Hiroshi had spent much of his time in California learning to play golf and ski as well as enjoying San Francisco's opera. When they returned to Hiroshima, Sadayo opened a fashion school; Hiroshi consulted on the design of Hiroshima's first golf course and, having befriended famed operatic tenor Yoshie Fujiwara in San Francisco, introduced Western opera to the city. Setsuko relished the cosmopolitan lifestyle of her dashing, fun-loving uncle and chic aunt—even though her mother referred to it as *haikara* (high class). And she had a crush on their only son, Henry, the most handsome young man she knew.

When Japan started to become more militarized, Setsuko found an island of urbanity in the presence of her aunt and uncle. At Sadayo's fashion school, students learned how to cut patterns and use the sewing machine, which had created a radical change in women's apparel. Despite shortages, she had been able to obtain fine fabrics such as silk and velvet. When her students needed a model for fitting children's clothing, she volunteered her niece. Setsuko received so many sample dresses in thanks that she thought herself the best-dressed girl in Hiroshima. If Setsuko wanted to see Uncle Hiroshi, she knew she likely could find him at his favorite restaurant, sipping coffee and reading the newspaper, seemingly unperturbed by current events. Setsuko never refused the ice cream he ordered for her, cultivating her lifelong fondness for sweets. Friends would later refer to her as "apple-chan" because of her round, red cheeks.

Above all, Setsuko cherished time with her parents. Growing up as the only young child in a world of adults, she was pampered, especially by her father. Benkichi shared the harmony he found in gardening, the peace he felt drifting in the calm waters of the Seto Inland Sea. He often took her along to business meetings and official functions. In his fifties he still cut a striking figure in his *hakama*, his skirt bearing the family crest, and even more so when he wore his morning coat, a sartorial elegance adopted from the British. Setsuko later wondered why such a distinguished figure in a traditional society took his young daughter along with him to banquets that no other children were allowed to attend. Perhaps as a doyen, he felt proud showing off his precocious child to his business colleagues. Setsuko's parents had a nickname for her—Koshijinchuku (a loin pouch in which samurai kept their tobacco and matches whenever they went outside). It meant she went everywhere with her father. She savored the spread of delicacies and adult conversation at the banquets, and, as an inadvertent consequence, she developed a stamp of intrepidness that one day would facilitate interactions with senior leaders, in particular those of the opposite sex.

Setsuko enjoyed the hours sitting beside her mother, who once again played the organ, singing Japanese folk songs and Buddhist hymns. A devout Buddhist, Shigeno stressed their responsibility to look after the dead souls of her son, parents, and other relatives. Every morning she put freshly cooked rice, sprinkled with sweets or fruit, into a special container. Before the day's activities began, mother and daughter knelt at their family shrine, offered the food to the dead souls, and chanted, tapping out the rhythm on a wooden instrument shaped like a fish. As the wife of the Nakamura patriarch, Shigeno attended to the souls not only of their own deceased family members but also of many who had no relatives to care for them after death. Setsuko watched her mother chant for a long list of people at the Buddhist temple on their death dates and recall their contributions to family and society. Her mother talked to Setsuko about their samurai ancestors with pride and stressed their special duty to care for the commoners.

Setsuko started grammar school eager to learn. She spent six years at Kojinmachi Elementary School, a public school attended by students from all segments of society. For the girl who ate breakfast in a fig tree and modeled velvet dresses, the rigidity dampened her spirit. The day began at eight o'clock with vigorous physical exercise, ending with a brisk run around the building. To enhance fortitude the teacher forbade wearing coats inside the unheated classroom. To learn responsibility the children had to wipe down the blackboard, dust the desks, and mop the floor before their lessons began. Setsuko dreaded the latter task; she had to dip her rag into a bucket of ice-cold water, wring it out, and scrub the surface clean.

She excelled in school, however. Since she found the simple childhood readings boring, her mother supplemented them with magazines that contained articles on history and literature. Her father talked about current events as he read *Chugoku Shimbun*, the daily newspaper. Each year the teachers recognized Setsuko for her academic excellence. Although proud of her daughter's achievements, her mother strived to teach Setsuko humility. When other mothers complimented Shigeno on her accomplished daughter, she was quick to point out some fault, such as calling her a tomboy. Crestfallen at first, Setsuko realized her mother could not accept a compliment; that was not the Japanese way.

Setsuko looked forward to the holidays, especially the New Year's celebration and the Cherry Blossom Festival. Just before Shogatsu (the New Year), her mother supervised the ritual housecleaning, bought new kimonos, and hung pine and bamboo decorations on either side of the front door to draw in lucky spirits. Relatives got together to pound sticky rice and make mochi. On New Year's Eve, they ate bowls of buckwheat "year-crossing" noodles and waited for the Buddhist temple bells to ring 108 times at midnight. Each of their sonorous strokes was believed to absolve 1 of the 108 sins. And on New Year's Day, Setsuko welcomed the colorful envelopes filled with gift money from relatives.[5]

Every spring, from late March to the end of April, Hiroshima transformed into a fairyland when the *sakura* (cherry blossoms) burst forth. Their delicate pinkish-hued flowers adorned the city in tranquil splendor. As soon as they detected the buds with tiny florets on the tree branches, Setsuko's parents counted twelve days until they knew the cherry trees would be in full bloom. On that day Setsuko's mother packed a special picnic of their favorite foods and sake. In the early morning, they climbed Hijiyama Hill, near the central part of the city, where they and most of the community celebrated *hanami* (watching blossoms), a tradition going back at least a thousand years. Setsuko's father spread blankets under the trees, soon to be joined by other relatives and friends. Music and laughter floated through the air. Setsuko thought this the happiest day of the year.[6]

Radiance, tranquility, and the celebration of family—that was what the Cherry Blossom Festival meant to young Setsuko. At the time she did not appreciate its symbolism: in Japanese culture the cherry blossom represents the beauty and fragility of life. After a short period of stunning brilliance, the blossoms start to fall—a visual reminder of how precious and precarious life is. And she did not know that the cherry blossom was a symbol of her ancestors, the samurai. Born to serve, they accepted the inevitability of death; fallen cherry blossoms denoted the end of their ephemeral lives.[7]

Throughout Setsuko Nakamura's childhood, Japan was almost continuously at war. Yet to her, life seemed beautiful, with family picnics, beach outings, velvet dresses, and sweets—a cherry blossom life. A month before her tenth birthday, at 7:55 a.m. on Sunday, December 7, 1941, the Japanese attacked Pearl Harbor. And Setsuko's world changed forever.

3 Raising the Flag of the Rising Sun

May the reign of the Emperor
continue for a thousand, nay,
eight thousand generations
and for the eternity that it takes
for small pebbles to grow into a great rock
and become covered with moss.
–"*Kimigayo*" ("His Imperial Majesty's Reign")

The Rising Sun flag—a crimson disc on a white rectangular background with sixteen red rays emanating from its center—fluttered in the breeze throughout Japan and occupied Southeast Asia. The Japanese believed that one day this flag would light the darkness of the world; Westerners considered it symbolic of Japanese imperialism. At the morning flag-raising ceremony, Setsuko joined her schoolmates in saluting the divine Emperor Hirohito while they sang "*Kimigayo*." She mumbled the parts she regarded as nonsensical. "How could this be scientific?" she asked her mother. "Little pebbles don't grow into great rocks."[1] Shigeno told her daughter to keep her thoughts to herself.

When on December 8, 1941, the Nakamuras heard on the radio that Imperial Japanese aircraft had attacked Pearl Harbor, destroying much of the U.S. Pacific fleet, Setsuko exclaimed, "Wow. The Japanese military is so strong."[2] Her parents did not echo her excitement. Having lived in the United States, they understood the country's power. Her father's face clouded over; her mother said nothing. At 4:10 p.m. the next day, President Franklin Roosevelt, wearing a black armband in mourning for the 2,400 lost at Pearl Harbor, signed a declaration of war against Japan.

Early on, the Imperial Japanese Army achieved considerable success. In January 1942 troops occupied Manila; in February they overtook Singapore, and in March Rangoon and the Dutch East Indies succumbed. Communities throughout Japan celebrated each victory with parades and flag waving. "Doing Without Until Victory! Waste Is The Enemy!" and other such catchphrases bolstered the community spirit while the Japanese people endured increasing hardships.[3] Community councils dictated government policy to the neighborhood associations, which in turn monitored morale and austerity campaigns. Everyone, from children to the elderly, was expected to vow support for the war effort and to live frugally. The government called them "home-front soldiers."[4] Women exchanged kimonos and Western fashions for simple blouses and *mompe* (baggy pants tied at the ankles); cosmetics were banned, and permanent waves were limited to three curls per person. Nonmilitary men wore the national civilian uniform—khaki-colored tunics. The government censored music, jazz in particular, and discouraged the celebration of holidays, which it deemed vacuous rituals.

Most problematic was the increasing food shortage brought on by the depleted rural workforce and paucity of farm equipment, fertilizer, and livestock, leading to the ever-tightening control of food distribution. Setsuko tried to remain positive as want became discomfort, and discomfort became privation. At first she yearned for chocolate; in time she yearned for rice. Two cups of rice per person daily, the government's initial allowance, was reduced to one and a half cups. Setsuko's mother added sweet potato, pumpkin, soy beans, and cracked wheat to increase the volume. The Nakamura household began to change—fewer family banquets, a lighter picnic basket for the Cherry Blossom Festival. Setsuko's father did, however, obtain a supply of sake.

On January 19, 1942, two weeks after Setsuko's tenth birthday, President Roosevelt approved the production of an atomic bomb. Albert Einstein had alerted him in 1939 that scientists performing chain-reaction research found that splitting atoms of the element uranium could release enormous energy, which could be used to develop an exceedingly powerful bomb. Furthermore, Einstein believed the Germans were conducting such research and urged the U.S.

government to do likewise.[5] In the spring of 1941, a group of British scientists with the code name MAUD Committee had concluded that the creation of an atomic bomb was feasible using a critical mass of purified uranium-235. And they confirmed that Nazi Germany had advanced in its experimentation with uranium.[6] President Roosevelt had received the MAUD Report on October 9 of that year. Two months later Japan bombed Pearl Harbor, and Germany and Italy declared war on the United States. With that Roosevelt approved the production of an atomic bomb.

Initially, the Imperial Japanese Army was victorious in all its major military engagements. That changed in the summer of 1942. In June the Japanese fleet lost four aircraft carriers at the Battle of Midway; in August American forces landed on Guadalcanal and, after a bloody, months-long campaign, evicted the Imperial occupiers. Although Japanese citizens were not apprised of these losses, ten-year-old Setsuko began to perceive the heartache brought on by war. The receipt of a red card meant the emperor was calling a young man to join the army and fight for Japan. Recruits from all over the country traveled to Hiroshima, a major military embarkation point, from which they were shipped to the Philippines, Dutch East Indies, Burma, and Malaya. Mothers whose sons had been conscripted stood on street corners, holding up white sashes. They asked passersby to add one stitch of red thread until they obtained one thousand stitches. Soldiers wore the sashes across their waists into battle. Since each stitch meant good luck, the sashes carried wishes for a safe return from one thousand people. Setsuko collected red stitches for her cousins and family friends, and she added stitches for those whom she would never know; she considered it her duty. Even with that protection, many never returned.

Neighborhoods held celebrations to send sons off to war. Setsuko and her parents attended many of these. Before a cousin boarded a ship in Ujina Harbor, family members gathered at a nearby park to say farewell. Despite rationing, they prepared box lunches that contained the best food they could gather. Thirty relatives sat on park benches, toasted the young soldier with sake, and ate a final meal together. This was to be a happy occasion with no tears, yet

Setsuko sensed the sorrow. Although everyone was smiling, she knew many were crying in their hearts.

One evening, while her family was relaxing in their garden, Setsuko heard singing next door. Part of their prior house, cut in half to widen the street, had been converted into a way station for troops. She peeked through the wooden fence and watched as soldiers—some younger than her own brothers—sang and clapped their hands. The house manager spotted her and asked if she would like to join the party. Setsuko enjoyed their songs and listened as they talked about their families. "Where are you from? Do you have children? What are their names?" she asked.[7] Setsuko likely reminded some soldiers of their younger sisters or cousins. Emperor Hirohito had given each of them a special gift of sake for his last night before deployment, for many their last night in Japan. The more sake they drank, the more their conversation turned to dying for the emperor—the supreme privilege. The next day they departed, replaced by a new group of soldiers who sang the same songs and spoke of sacrificing their lives for the emperor.

Groups of women cheered for those leaving by train. They carried placards with slogans such as "Let's Cooperate With Smiling Faces" and "One Hundred Million With One Spirit."[8] Schoolgirls wrote letters of encouragement to soldiers overseas. Sometime later many parents received a parcel that contained a small box. If they shook the box and it rattled, they cried out or dropped to the ground. They knew what they would find inside—ashes and bits of bone. Over two million Japanese men, most in their twenties and thirties, would die during the war. Few families remained unscathed, and in time sorrow touched the Nakamuras too.

Setsuko's oldest brother, Isamu, and his wife, Michie, had been sent to Seoul, Korea, to teach at an elite boys' school. Not long after the bombing of Pearl Harbor, the school informed Benkichi that Isamu had developed a brain tumor. Before he could bring his son back to Japan for surgery, Isamu died. Michie, pregnant with their second child, returned home with her young son and began teaching at Hiroshima Women's Higher Normal School. Setsuko's second brother, Susumu, served in the Philippines and Korea, leaving his wife, Hideko, in Taipei with their daughter. Months passed with no news of his whereabouts.

When the husband of Setsuko's sister Ayako was deployed to Singapore, Ayako returned to Hiroshima with her young son, Eiji, and volunteered to serve as a caregiver for children evacuated to the countryside. Setsuko's third sister, Yukiko, lived with Michie in a nearby city. Yukiko's husband had departed to Manchuria a week after their arranged marriage. Aunt Sadayo and Uncle Hiroshi's son, Henry, was recuperating in a military hospital after an amputation of his injured leg. Setsuko's father was spared. Too old to be drafted into active duty, Benkichi provided leadership for their neighborhood organization.

The Nakamuras did not know how their eldest daughter, Fumiko, was faring. From her last communication, they learned that the Takeis' profitable dry-cleaning business in Los Angeles had allowed them to buy a modern refrigerator and a car, just like middle-class Americans. Their young children—George, Henry, and Nancy—were thriving. Their lives changed abruptly, however, on February 19, 1942, when President Roosevelt signed Executive Order 9066:

> Whereas the successful prosecution of the war requires every possible protection against espionage and against sabotage to national defense material . . . I hereby authorize and direct the Secretary of War . . . whenever he or any designated Commander deems such action necessary or desirable, to prescribe military areas . . . with respect to which, the right of any person to enter, remain in, or leave shall be subject to whatever restrictions the Secretary of War or the appropriate Military Commander may impose in his discretion.[9]

The entire West Coast, home to the majority of Japanese Americans, was designated a "military area." Over 120,000 civilians faced internment in one of ten concentration camps, without due process.

Fumiko and her family were swept up in the net, forced to evacuate their home, taking just what they could carry. As they boarded the Missouri Pacific Railway, a guard attached identification tag "No. 12832-C" to four-year-old George's jacket.[10] Norman told his son they were going to vacation at Camp Rohwer. For days the family saw nothing except barren desert landscape while they tried to find comfortable positions on the train's wooden seats. At last they arrived at the Rohwer Relocation Center in southeast Arkansas. As they got off the train, they felt a blast of hot air; the first thing they saw was a barbed-wire fence.

Camp Rohwer housed eight thousand Japanese Americans, the majority of whom held American citizenship. Nevertheless, the U.S. government considered them potential spies. The five hundred acres of desolate land that constituted the camp were subdivided into numbered blocks. A block housed about three hundred detainees in ten to twelve tarpapered barracks, each of which contained four to six one-room apartments; none had plumbing. The barbed-wire fence, interspersed with guard towers, surrounded the camp.

Assigned to Block 6, the Takei family's living quarters measured sixteen by twenty feet. The room had bare wooden floorboards and was furnished with five cots—no chairs, table, dresser, curtains, or rug. Their neighbors' conversations penetrated the paper-thin walls. They ate whatever food the army provided in the large mess hall; they used a communal latrine. Still, they could laugh that first day when Fumiko unwrapped a large baby blanket in her bag to reveal a forbidden possession: her portable sewing machine, which she had smuggled in past the guards.[11]

The incessant heat and dust, long lines at the mess hall and toilets, and the loss of their homes and personal property for which they had labored, as well as their dignity, added to the inmates' wretchedness. Norman and Fumiko rose above the humiliation. He made stools and shelves from discarded lumber; she found scraps of cloth to braid rugs and sew curtains. Assuming leadership of Block 6, Norman served as a liaison to the camp administration. And with over two thousand children in the camp, George found many playmates and adventures. The Takeis had been imprisoned there eight months when they were told to pack their belongings and report to the railway station. Norman and Fumiko had no idea where they were going; however, they knew their next stop would be more isolated and harsher.

In early 1943, because of increasing concern about potential Japanese American sabotage, the War Relocation Authority required that all adult internees complete a loyalty questionnaire.[12] Question 28 proved particularly problematic. It asked if individuals would swear unqualified allegiance to the United

States and forswear any form of loyalty to the emperor of Japan. Although Norman had grown up in America, he was born in Japan and thus considered an issei (Japanese immigrant), barred from becoming a U.S. citizen by immigration law. If he replied yes to question 28, thus denying the land of his birth, he became a man without a country. So he answered no. Fumiko was designated a nisei, born in America of Japanese immigrant parents. Although an American citizen with American-born children, she refused to deny the land of her parents, siblings, and husband. When Fumiko answered no, she gave up her American citizenship and risked being separated from her children. Internees who either refused to complete and sign the questionnaire or replied no to question 28 were classified as "disloyal." The War Relocation Authority separated these individuals and their families from those marked "loyal." In short order armed guards herded the Takeis onto a train, bound for a facility in northern California, near the Oregon border.[13]

Tule Lake Segregation Center, constructed on a dry lake bed four thousand feet above sea level, held over eighteen thousand dissidents and their families, half of them children. The barbed-wire fences were higher and stronger than those of Camp Rohwer; guards in the turrets carried machine guns, and tanks patrolled the perimeter. A constant biting wind blew sagebrush along the stark landscape.[14] The Takeis were assigned to Block 80. Although their living quarters there consisted of two rooms, Fumiko deplored its location across from the mess hall. Queues formed outside their window before meals; the chatter from hungry children and the smell of stale cabbage pervaded their rooms. Worse yet, the distance to the latrine presented a challenge during the frosty winter weather. Once again Fumiko set about making their two small rooms livable, and Norman became the block leader. They found the atmosphere at Tule Lake far more tense than at Rohwer. Internees included those who voted with their conscience, as had the Takeis, along with political activists, whose spirited rallies led to riots, followed by curfews and tighter restrictions for all the inmates. Yet many felt safer behind the barbed wire, as anti-Japanese sentiment had grown into a frenzy with "exterminate the Japs" campaigns against nisei and issei. Efforts to deport Japanese Americans intensified. "We don't want those Japs back in California," a Congress representative declared. "The more we can get rid of, the better."[15]

By September 1942 the U.S.-led effort to build an atomic bomb had commenced under the direction of Brigadier General Leslie Groves, with the code name "Manhattan Project." The work would be conducted at three highly secure, secret sites. A seventy-square-mile tract in East Tennessee was selected for the electromagnetic pilot plant to purify uranium-235. Straightaway, the U.S. government began the construction of a concealed military base, later known as Oak Ridge, which housed seventy-five thousand. This sprawling instillation did not appear on maps, nor was it mentioned in local newspapers.[16] An even more powerful radioactive element—plutonium—would be produced in Hanford, Washington. Finally, Groves established a laboratory in Los Alamos, New Mexico, where an atomic bomb would be designed and produced under the direction of J. Robert Oppenheimer. In February 1944 Los Alamos received its first shipment of uranium-235 from Oak Ridge.

That fall, after six years of elementary school education, twelve-year-old Setsuko entered middle school. She had competed for acceptance to Hiroshima Jogakuin School, a private institution for young women. From its inception the school had encouraged students to master academics in preparation for a career and fostered a penchant for serving others. Established as a Christian mission school, Jogakuin required daily attendance at the chapel. Setsuko's Buddhist mother did not oppose her application, since the school provided a liberal education and attracted girls from established families. As well, it reinforced her mother's affirmation that, as a samurai descendant, Setsuko had a duty to care for those less fortunate, the commoners. Her father approved too; the school seemed well suited for his precocious daughter.

Setsuko anticipated studying history, English, and music. When she enrolled as a seventh grader, however, she found the educational program altered significantly. These courses had been replaced with more traditional ones, such as proper etiquette for Japanese women. Recent graduates told her that chapel service had periodically come under surveillance by military police, who interrogated the girls afterward: "What do you think? Who is greater—the emperor or Jesus?"[17] A number of Jogakuin's teachers were American missionaries. Some citizens regarded them as spies and tried to shut down the school; a headmaster had been removed with no explanation.

Before long, military duties preempted academic work. The army mobilized all middle and high school students, whether from private or public schools, to serve the war effort. Their classes were suspended. As a member of the compulsory Student Mobilization Program, Setsuko initially worked at a tobacco company, where she packaged cigarettes to be shipped to soldiers in the Pacific Islands. Next she was assigned to a clothing factory, where she checked that each military uniform had buttons in the proper place. In the spring she harvested potatoes; during the rainy season, she planted rice. At the end of a day in the paddies, she peeled off the leeches clinging to her legs. Yet no one complained. "Everything for the emperor," she was told. "You don't want anything until we win the war."[18]

During eighth grade Setsuko felt proud to be selected to train as a decoding assistant for the Japanese military—an honor bestowed on thirty of the most capable middle school girls. She reported to Second General Army Headquarters seven days a week to learn the complicated sequence of numbers that constituted one word. JN-25, the twenty-fifth Japanese Navy code system, provided the most secure communication used by the Imperial Japanese Navy throughout World War II.[19] It consisted of thirty thousand code groups, with new code books introduced at short intervals. Still, Setsuko mastered translating a long series of numbers into a message. The work was highly secretive, accuracy imperative. A small mistake could result in devastation for the troops. Setsuko became quite proficient and was appointed as leader of her team, composed of thirty eighth-grade girls.

As fighting intensified, newspapers and radios announced the successes of the Imperial Army. Decisive defeats were reported as great victories: Japan was winning the war. With time, however, it became apparent that the situation was grim. As goods became scarcer, citizens bore the burden of austerity measures in silence. "No luxuries," they were told, "until the war is won."[20] Pots, pans, nails, bells, and other metal items were melted down to provide material for bullets, bombs, and torpedoes. Citizens gave everything to the government for the glory of the emperor. That included some of Shigeno Nakamura's exquisite jewelry, passed down for centuries and locked in the family *kura*. If she bemoaned her loss, she did so in private.

By the spring of 1945, U.S. submarines had crippled Japan's merchant shipping operations, and food rationing tightened. The allotment per person was reduced further: only one ounce of vegetables and one cup of rice each day and one-half ounce of fish every six days. People stood in line for hours just to buy a small bowl of rice gruel. Many suffered health problems from excessive weight loss. Most of Setsuko's meals consisted of porridge made with rice, chopped carrots, onion, and potato, flavored with soy sauce or miso paste. As the war dragged on, the porridge became thinner and thinner, and Setsuko felt hungrier and hungrier. She knew she should be grateful; some children survived on river reeds, pumpkin stalks, roasted worms, and beetles.[21]

On the night of March 9, 1945, General Curtis LeMay, leading a fleet of 334 B-29 bombers, conducted a raid at low altitude, spraying incendiary bombs across Tokyo. Given the overcrowding of wooden homes and buildings, compounded by the shortage of trained firefighters, the massive conflagration destroyed sixteen square miles. One hundred thousand people died overnight. Throughout the spring and summer, firebombing devastated Osaka, Nagoya, Kobe, Kawasaki, and Yokohama. Targets were expanded beyond military instillations to include large civilian populations.[22]

On April 12 President Franklin Roosevelt died suddenly of a cerebral hemorrhage. It wasn't until after Harry S. Truman took office that Secretary of War Henry Stimson and General Leslie Groves informed him about the Manhattan Project. Stimson told Truman that a presidential advisory group recommended they keep the atomic bomb secret and use it promptly, without warning. After much debate an elite group of military personnel and scientists selected the first target—Hiroshima.

Throughout the war Hiroshima had somehow stood untouched. This mystified Japanese military leaders, since Hiroshima—the tenth-largest city in Japan—was the major staging site for their activities in Southeast Asia and China. Several military installations, a cluster of war industries, and fifty thousand servicemen were located there. Residents became puzzled when they heard that even smaller cities had been bombed. Rumors started to circulate: "Hiroshima produces more immigrants to California; that's why they are grateful," Setsuko heard.[23] President Truman's aunt lives in Hiroshima, others reported, or was it his mother? Some speculated that whoever had drawn the U.S. map of Japan overlooked Hiroshima.[24] Although civilians appreciated their good fortune, most assumed their city would be attacked before long. This created an atmosphere described as *bukimi* (eerie).[25]

The local government ordered more preparatory steps. Although the six tributaries of the Ota River, running north to south, served as natural fire lines, citizens were directed to raze the wooden houses crowded together to widen the streets for more extensive firebreaks. Almost the entire population of middle school girls, as well as boys, was assigned this task near the city center. Japanese soldiers stood guard as the students used simple tools or their hands to tear down structures. The government had no plans for relocating the three thousand displaced families; they had to rely on the kindness of relatives and friends. In anticipation of firebombing, Benkichi's brother-in-law urged him to move the remaining family treasures from the *kura* to his home on the edge of the city. Benkichi resisted. He assumed that the *kura*'s thick walls would protect its contents from fire.

Air-raid warnings punctuated the stillness each night, so Setsuko slept in her clothes. Her father dug a shelter next to their kitchen, a pit in which they had to squat, covered with a lid. Setsuko hated the dark, damp space and cringed whenever the siren blared. Her mother prepared the recommended survival kit, which contained water, roasted soybeans, hard crackers, gauze, and basic medications. The government evacuated fifty thousand to the countryside, among them the elderly and those in poor health. Half were elementary school children, considered old enough to be separated from their families but too young to work. Younger children remained in the city with their mothers.

Setsuko had put away her dresses and wore the mandatory uniform of a white blouse and *mompe*, which allowed her to run faster to reach an air-raid shelter or escape rapidly spreading flames. A photo from 1945 shows a short, sturdy teen, her hair cut bluntly just below her ears. Her look is bold, self-assured. In the event of a bombing raid, she knew how to drop to the floor away from the windows and to cover her eyes tightly with four fingers, using her thumb to plug her ears to prevent her eyeballs from blowing out of their sockets and her eardrums from bursting. She and her classmates practiced using bamboo poles, sharpened at the end, to stab invaders in the stomach. "Inhumane became the norm," Setsuko recalled.[26]

No one mentioned the possibility that Japan might be defeated—not teachers, friends, family members, or news reports. Setsuko knew Japan was losing many ships and planes, yet the word "surrender" was not in their vocabulary. "I was brainwashed," she later said. One evening, however, she found her father reading an English grammar book. He told her he was refreshing his English; he would need it. Only later did his word choice register: he had said "would," not "might."[27]

On July 16, 1945, Robert Oppenheimer's group successfully tested a plutonium bomb in the desert of Alamogordo, New Mexico. A uranium bomb was never tested before its use. The simplicity of its design was such that the scientists were certain it would work. Besides, purification of uranium-235 proved so difficult that Oak Ridge scientists could produce enough for only one bomb. Ten days after he learned of the success in New Mexico, President Truman joined British prime minister Clement Attlee and Chinese president Chiang Kai-Shek in issuing the Potsdam Declaration. It called for Japan's unconditional surrender. Japanese prime minister Suzuki Kantaro's response to the ultimatum was "*mokusatsu*," which literally means "kill with silence"—in other words, "no comment."[28] Interpreting the response as a rejection, President Truman scribbled a message to Secretary of War Stimson on July 31: "Release when ready."[29]

The evening of August 5 was hot and humid in Hiroshima, making it difficult to sleep. Setsuko's father was planning to go fishing at dawn on the Seto Inland Sea. Her mother was enjoying a visit from Ayako and her four-year-old grandson, Eiji. Ayako had a doctor's appointment in town the next morning for a sty in her eye. And Setsuko was reviewing military codes. She would start her official decoding duties at the Second Army Headquarters the next morning—the sixth of August, 1945.

4 August 6, 1945

the boy smiles
bites into a tomato
becomes a corpse
–Shibata Moriyo, *Haiku*

While Setsuko slept, 1,566 miles away on Tinian Island, a detachment of U.S. Army and Air Force specialists, the 509th Composite Group, was preparing for Mission No. 13—the bombing of Hiroshima. On May 10, three days after Germany's surrender, a select group of U.S. military personnel and scientists, known as the Target Committee, had met to determine on which Japanese city to test the power of their new weapon—the atomic bomb.

Several physical aspects made Hiroshima the best choice: built on the Ota River delta, where it emptied into the Seto Inland Sea, the city fanned out from Ujina Harbor, bordered on three sides by pine-covered mountains. This topography, the committee calculated, could cause a focusing effect to enhance the bomb's destruction. Hiroshima had two good navigational landmarks: Hijiyama Hill, which rose above the otherwise flat landscape; and the T-shaped Aioi Bridge, which spanned the Honkawa and Motoyasu Rivers near the city center, making a large *T* visible from the air. The copper dome of the four-story Prefectural Industrial Promotion Hall and the five-story Hiroshima Castle dominated the cityscape. Within and surrounding the city center lay dense residential areas. Homes constructed of wooden lathwork and clay with tile roofs housed three-quarters of Hiroshima's estimated 340,000 population. The Target Committee concluded that annihilation of this large, pristine urban center would best demonstrate the bomb's catastrophic capabilities. "When the meeting ended," a historian wrote, "the committee had no doubt about where the first atomic bomb would fall: on the heads of hundreds of thousands of civilians."[1]

In late May the 509th Composite Group, led by thirty-year-old Colonel Paul Tibbets Jr., had moved to Tinian Island, from whence Mission No.13 would be launched. The USS *Indianapolis* delivered component parts of the bomb and uranium-235 to the island on July 26. Four days later, on the cruiser's way back from Tinian to Leyte in the Philippine Sea, a Japanese submarine torpedoed it, along with its crew of 1,195. It sank in twelve minutes, resulting in the largest death toll in U.S. naval history. Of the 880 who did not go down with the ship, only 316 survived exposure, dehydration, ten-foot swells, and a horrifying bloodbath in which hundreds of their shipmates fell prey to an oceanic whitetip shark feeding frenzy.[2]

On August 1 Colonel Tibbets, pilot of the B-29 *Enola Gay*, named for his mother, picked eleven crew members—among the U.S. military's best pilots, navigators, and flight engineers—to man the strike plane. The bombardier, Major Thomas Ferebee, selected the T-shaped Aioi Bridge as their target. Tibbets concurred, "It's the most perfect aiming AP [aim point] I've seen in this whole damn war."[3] At a special briefing, the crew learned they would be carrying the deadliest weapon ever made, its destructive power calculated to be equivalent to about thirteen thousand tons of TNT. Capable of demolishing everything within a three-mile radius, this bomb might even crack the earth's crust. The explosion would be ten times brighter than the sun; looking at the flash could blind anyone without special goggles.

On Sunday, August 5, at 3:30 p.m., the five-ton uranium bomb, nicknamed "Little Boy," was lowered into the *Enola Gay*'s bomb pit. Scrawled on its casing was a message from its crew: "A present for the souls of the Indianapolis crew."[4] At midnight the group gathered for their preflight meal. Chaplain William Downey invited them to bow their heads. "We pray Thee to be with those who brave the heights of Thy heaven," he entreated, "and armed with Thy strength may they bring this war to a rapid end." After the weather scout departed, the twelve boarded the *Enola Gay*, and at 2:45 a.m. Colonel Tibbets directed his co-pilot, Captain Robert Lewis, "Let's go." Almost four hours into the flight, at 6:30 a.m., Captain William "Deak" Parsons, the weaponeer, notified Tibbets that the explosive's final connection had been made. The bomb was loaded and ready. Only then did Tibbets inform the rest of the crew: "We are carrying the world's first atomic bomb."[5]

On Monday morning, August 6, the sun rose at 5:24 a.m. over Hiroshima, revealing a cloudless, blue sky. The temperature approached eighty degrees as the workday began; it promised to be another sweltering day. Thousands of people squeezed onto streetcars en route to the city center. Bicycles, carts, cars, and pedestrians congested the streets along Shintenchi, the shopping district; Teramachi, the Street of Temples; and the Aioi Bridge. Boats with their graceful white sails dotted the Ota River and its tributaries. On the streets young women hurried to work in their *mompe*, while men from the neighborhood association gathered in their khaki-colored tunics to discuss fire drills. Shopkeepers were setting out their meager wares; soldiers marched in formation on the East Drill Ground; government clerks filed into the Hiroshima Prefectural Industrial Promotion Hall; and doctors were starting rounds at Shima Hospital, two blocks from the Aioi Bridge. Families watched as students mobilized by the Volunteer Army Corps razed their homes to create firebreaks in anticipation of a firebombing. Pedestrians had to sidestep the debris yet to be removed. Buses and military trucks rumbled by, evacuating third- to sixth-grade students who were too young to work yet old enough to be separated from their families. Younger children gathered on elementary school playgrounds, waiting for classes to start.

Setsuko woke up early that day. With a thrill of anticipation, she buttoned her short-sleeved white blouse with its red trim, pulled on her *mompe*, and rushed through breakfast. That morning, after weeks of rigorous instruction, she would begin working as a full-fledged decoding assistant. When she said goodbye, her mother was washing the breakfast dishes. Her sister and four-year-old nephew, Eiji, had left for a doctor's appointment; her father was fishing off the coast of Miyajima Island.

At 7:09 an air-raid alert sounded. Few rushed to take shelter; a U.S. weather plane flew over Hiroshima every morning at that time. Unbeknownst to those below, this was a weather reconnaissance plane for Mission 13. At 7:25 the pilot radioed Colonel Tibbets, "Cloud cover less than three-tenths at all altitudes. Advice: bomb primary."[6] Major Ferebee, the bombardier, took over. At 7:31 an all-clear sounded as the weather-observation plane flew away.

At about that time, Setsuko met her decoding group in front of the railway station. "We start," she commanded, assuming her role as their leader. "March. Right, left, right, left." The teens fell in line and followed her past the East Drill Ground and over to the Second General Army Headquarters, a large two-story wooden building located a mile from the Aioi Bridge. When they reached the entrance, she saluted on behalf of the group, and they marched in formation up to the second floor. At 8:00 Major Kenji Yanai entered the General Assembly room, and the thirty new decoders stood at attention. "You girls have been fortunate," he began his inspirational talk. "You have had many weeks of intensive training and learned a special skill."[7]

Shortly after 8:00, air defense spotters observed three B-29s proceeding toward Hiroshima. No air-raid siren rang. Mistakenly assumed to be a reconnaissance mission assessing the terrain, the strike plane and its two observation aircraft met no resistance. Major Ferebee maneuvered the *Enola Gay* to line up with the *T* of the Aioi Bridge with the crosshairs of the bombsight. At 8:15 he said, "I've got it."[8] And the bomb-bay doors opened.

"Now is the time you prove your patriotism, your loyalty to the emperor by using what you have learned," Major Yanai told the decoding group. "This is the day you start repaying the emperor for his grace and blessing. So do your very best."

"Yes sir," the girls replied. "We'll do our best for the emperor's sake."[9] At that moment Setsuko saw a blinding flash in the window.

After releasing Little Boy, the *Enola Gay* made a sharp right-hand turn. It was eleven and a half miles from Hiroshima when the bomb detonated. Looking back at the destruction below, Captain Lewis scribbled in his logbook, "My God, what have we done."[10]

Setsuko awoke in total darkness, total silence. She didn't know what had happened or how long she had been unconscious. It slowly came back to her—a bluish-white flash, like a magnesium flare outside the window, the sensation of floating, then falling. She felt no pain, but she couldn't move. The walls, beams, and roof had collapsed, thrusting her down onto the first floor, pinning her beneath tiles and timber. She could hear nothing, see nothing. Perhaps she had failed to plug her ears and cover her eyes in the event of a bomb as she had been trained. Had she been blinded by the flash, her eardrums blown out by the blast? Buried in a grave of rubble, she sensed death was imminent, yet she did not feel scared. A blanket of serenity seemed to cover her as she faced death unflinchingly.

Faint cries disturbed her reverie. "Mother, help me," someone pleaded. "God, help me," prayed another. A chorus of desperate voices resounded in the dark. Setsuko recognized that of a friend nearby. She wasn't alone; she was surrounded by classmates. Then someone pushed her left shoulder, and she heard a man's voice say, "Don't give up. I'm trying to free you. Keep moving, keep pushing, keep kicking." He struggled to loosen the timbers that immobilized her. "See the ray of light? Crawl toward it and try to get out. Crawl, crawl." A distant glimmer heartened her; she had not been blinded. She began to drag herself on her belly over splintered wood and shards of glass. The beacon became less distinct. Dust? No. Smoke. She dug her fingers into the dirt and crept over broken tiles and twisted pieces of metal. Faster, faster, she struggled to reach the fading light.

When she squeezed through the opening, it appeared to be twilight outside. The air was heavy with dust, smoke, and heat. Frantic screams erupted. She turned back to see if she could help her classmates, but the remains of the Second General Army Headquarters were ablaze. Setsuko spotted classmates Hideko and Keiko emerging from the wreckage. The inferno spread closer; she had to step back from the flames. Within minutes the collapsed building was reduced to ashes.

That bright August morning, Setsuko had met twenty-nine classmates, full of hope, beaming with pride. She had led them into the Army Headquarters, where they had pledged to serve the emperor. Twenty-seven had just been burned alive while she watched helplessly. Setsuko was thirteen years old.[11]

At 8:15 Little Boy had detonated above the Shima Hospital, just 551 feet from its intended target—the Aioi Bridge. The temperature on the ground reached seven thousand degrees Fahrenheit. Almost every human being, animal, and tree within a five-hundred-yard radius was incinerated in an instant: doctors, nurses, and patients at Shima Hospital; three thousand troops on the East Parade Ground; 150 army horses; all but three cherry trees; 400 children at Honkawa Elementary School; and 1,800 teens mobilized to create firebreaks from eleven schools, among them the Second Hiroshima Prefectural Junior High School and the First Municipal Girls' High School. Those not obliterated had been mangled and seared to the extent that their bodies were unrecognizable. An enormous fireball, over three hundred yards in diameter, devastated five square miles around the bomb's hypocenter. Flash burns scorched exposed skin of those within a mile, including 6,200 students from the Hiroshima Municipal School, First Hiroshima Prefectural School, and Sotoku Junior High School. Few survived. The firebreaks the students had been clearing proved futile.

A thunderous, violent shock followed the flash, shooting bullets of glass, wood splinters, and tile fragments through the air in all directions, slashing and impaling anyone in their paths. The blast hurled people into the air, blew them through glass windows, bashed them against walls, trapped them under falling buildings. The sudden drop in air pressure ruptured eardrums, stomachs, bladders, and spleens. As the Target Committee had predicted, the blast wave rebounded off the mountains surrounding the city, demolishing 90 percent of the buildings and spreading fire in all directions. Incinerated, lacerated, crushed, eviscerated, beheaded, eighty thousand perished in an instant. Most were women and children.[12]

Although just a mile from the hypocenter, Setsuko suffered only minor cuts and bruises. She stood dazed, staring at the smoldering remains of the Army Headquarters, when a soldier directed her and her two classmates to retreat toward Mount Futaba, lest they be engulfed in flames. Through the smoke she saw a procession of ghostly figures, streaked with blood, dirt, and ash, their hair like wires standing on end, shuffling away from the city center. Some had tattered clothes draping from their shoulders, fragments of *mompe* embedded in their legs. Others were naked, their clothes blown off by the blast. Strips of skin and flesh hung like ribbons from their bones. Many held their arms up in front of their bodies, palms down to ease the pain from the raw flesh of their arms rubbing against their chests. Setsuko thought they looked like sleepwalkers. Those with eyes swollen shut were pushed forward by the crowd. Some held their eyeballs, blown from their sockets, in their hands. Every few steps someone silently collapsed.

The three girls joined the throng, trying to avoid the downed wires and utility poles as they trudged toward the hills, just to the north of Hiroshima Station. Setsuko's shoe caught on something, and she almost tripped. She looked down to see a charred body at her feet. The street was strewn with the dead and dying—men, women, children—once human beings, now indistinguishable forms. She tried to step over them, but the increasing number of fallen left few places to set her feet. No one was pushing or crying or screaming. No one. The slow, noiseless movement made Setsuko feel like she was in a silent movie.[13]

In other parts of the city, people reported a brilliant burst of light, *pika,* followed by a loud boom, *don.* An expansive cloud loomed above them. It seemed in constant motion, billowing out to the east, then to the west. Some described it as a mushroom, others as a jellyfish with fire shooting up through its core—a writhing demon breathing death and destruction. After that a murky pall descended, throwing the city into darkness, perhaps a blessing so that those still alive could not immediately perceive they had been thrust into hell.

Thousands rushed to the waterways to cool their scorched skin and escape the spreading inferno. Scores of middle school girls jumped into the Koi tributary, their flaming gaiters scorching their legs. Most could not swim. An overwhelming thirst from heat-inflicted dehydration drove others to the riverbanks, many crawling on all fours. While they drank from what was now a black cesspool, a dead horse or severed limb or headless corpse floated by. Crowds trying to reach the water pressed those on the edges into the rivers; many, swept away by the currents, drowned. Bloated, charred bodies clogged the Ota, Motoyasu, and Honkawa.

Several hours after the explosion, black clouds hovered over the northwest part of the city. Thunder rolled; a strong whirlwind sucked trees and debris and bodies up into the air, then dropped them precipitously on the ground below. A sudden downpour drenched people with large, sticky black raindrops, which left an indelible film on skin and clothing. For several hours rain beat down on the naked, burned backs like thousands of needles. The air turned cold. Those who minutes before sweltered now shivered. In attempts to allay their unquenchable thirst, people cupped their hands to catch and drink the muddy water falling from the sky.[14]

At the base of Mount Futaba, Setsuko and her two classmates came upon an army training ground, approximately two acres in size. Thousands of injured people lay before them. Burned, blackened, and swollen, many were covered with blood; parts of their bodies were missing—an arm, a hand, an eyeball. Among them lay an equal number of bodies. The smell of vomit, feces, charred flesh, and death filled the air. Yet no one was wailing or shouting for help. A deadly hush prevailed, except for a chorus of piteous supplication: "*Mizu. Mizu o kudasai.*" (Water. Water. Please give me water.) The three girls located a stream, where they washed the blood and dirt from their faces. Since they had no containers, they tore off parts of their blouses, soaked them in the cold water, then rushed back to place the wet cloths over the lips of the injured, who sucked in the moisture.[15]

Setsuko looked for a doctor or nurse or even a soldier to help. Finding none, the three girls continued to run back and forth to the stream. That was all they could do. In a sense it was like the ritual known as giving the last earthly water: when death is imminent, family members wet the lips with a brush dipped in water in an effort to keep the soul from departing through the mouth.[16] Setsuko would never forget how, despite their agony, those to whom she provided a few drops of water whispered "thank you" through their swollen lips.

After the sun set, Setsuko, Hideko, and Keiko climbed farther up the mountain, from where they watched a ball of fire sweep over the city. The three sat in stunned silence, unable to share their grief. Appeals for water, like the call of cicadas, continued throughout the night. Setsuko tried not to think about her family; it would overwhelm her. Likewise, she didn't brood over the flames consuming their beautiful garden or the *kura* with the family treasures. Instead, she fixated on a plastic pencil holder. She didn't remember who gave it to her. She liked its pretty red trim. Now it was gone.

Part 2

AFTER

5 Necropolis

I wonder
if there is an operation
that removes memories.
Where is a cure
for my pain-filled heart?
–Shoda Shinoe, "Tanka"

When the sun came up on August 7, the first thing Setsuko saw were the islands in the Seto Inland Sea. Miles away, they normally weren't visible. Now they seemed right in front of her. Besides that she saw nothing. Hiroshima seemed to have disappeared. The young teen climbed back down to the military drill ground, where she faced thousands of people, many now still; a blank stare marked their passing. Just as she was preparing to start her rounds, providing sips of water, someone called her name: "Setsuko Nakamura. Is there a Setsuko Nakamura?"

"Here I am. Here I am," she cried out.

A soldier holding a megaphone came across the field. "Your parents are looking for you," he said. Just then she spotted her mother and father maneuvering through the human obstacle course. As they got closer, she spotted no visible injuries. "They are alive," she thought. "Good." Later she wondered at her muted reaction. Her father asked if she was all right; her mother said she was relieved. They seemed emotionally numbed by the carnage around them, as was she. Setsuko asked the soldier for permission to leave and followed her parents toward a friend's summer house, located in another part of Mount Futaba. Along the way Benkichi told his daughter what he knew about the rest of the family.[1]

At dawn he had left home to spend the day fishing. He took a train to a marina on the Seto Inland Sea, where he rented a boat and directed the fisherman to take him to Miyajima Island. About an hour and a half from the city, he found a peaceful spot to fish. He was casting his line when he heard a deafening boom and saw an enormous cloud, shaped like a mushroom, rising above Hiroshima. He ordered the fisherman to return to the marina at once and took the next train headed for the city. On the western outskirts of Hiroshima, the train stopped abruptly. Everything beyond had collapsed as if a giant scythe had leveled the city. He pressed on toward their home on foot, following streetcar tracks and dodging fires springing up around him. At the first bridge he crossed, he encountered a mass of half-naked, bleeding, blackened people streaming out of the city.

With the help of a few remaining landmarks, Benkichi located the area where their home had stood, now flattened. Fires had not yet erupted in the area. He dug through the remains with his bare hands but could not find Shigeno. Without stopping to gather up any of their belongings, he started to leave; he needed to locate his family, who had disappeared among over three hundred thousand. Just then a neighbor approached and told him that his wife had been pulled from the wreckage unhurt; she did not know where Shigeno had gone. Benkichi assumed she had tried to reach her brother's home in Fuchu, east of Hiroshima, as they had agreed on in the case of an emergency.

After she left, the neighbor added, Ayako appeared. She was carrying her young son. Both were badly burned. She started searching through the rubble, looking for a bottle of cooking oil to apply to their burns. The neighbor helped her unearth it. Ayako told her she was headed for a summer house that belonged to family friends on Mount Futaba, above the army drill ground. Struggling to hold onto her injured child and the bottle of cooking oil, she barely could crawl. The neighbor offered to take her there in a cart.

Setsuko's mother, Benkichi said as he continued his narrative, had been washing the breakfast dishes when the second story of their home crashed down on her. She managed to dig herself out and, unscathed, had walked almost four miles to the home of her brother, Shuichi Namba, in Fuchu, as planned in case Hiroshima was bombed. Once reunited, Benkichi and Shigeno began searching for Ayako. When they reached the summer house, they found their daughter and grandson still alive but burned beyond recognition. Shigeno could identify her daughter only by a unique hair clasp; Benkichi recognized her voice. Ayako told them she and Eiji had been crossing the Yanagi Bridge on foot when a bomb exploded, and the bridge caught on fire. She just managed to reach the other side before it collapsed.

Having completed his account, Setsuko's father fell silent. No words could prepare Setsuko for what she was about to see. Inside the partially damaged house lay her beloved sister, Ayako, blackened and swollen, her skin covered with weeping blisters. Her beautiful face was ravaged—almond-shaped eyes reduced to white slits, no trace of her lush hair and arched eyebrows. Lips once painted cherry red had melted into a fleshy mass. Next to her lay Eiji. Setsuko would never forget that image: "My four-year-old nephew had been transformed into a chunk of burnt flesh," she later said.[2]

With no available medicines, nurses, or doctors, Shigeno treated their burns with the cooking oil. Both remained conscious and in great pain; their low moans punctuated the stillness. A soldier in charge of distributing the meager food supply stopped at the house. When he saw the situation, he brought some frozen tangerines. Setsuko and her mother spooned tangerine juice into the mouths of her sister and nephew; most of it dribbled down their cheeks.

Even in his critical state, Eiji never complained. His body may have been destroyed, but his sweet personality remained. He kept asking for water, his thirst seemingly never quenched. Instead of whining, he said, "Grandpa, tell Grandma to give Eiji water," showing respect for his grandfather's place in the family. Ayako apologized every time she requested water. And she lamented her failure to protect her precious child. When her husband came home from the war, she said, she would have no face to show to him because of her guilt: she had not kept the promise she had made to him. "That broke my heart," Setsuko later said.[3] Among all the tragic things she heard that day, her sister's regret was the most touching.

The next morning Benkichi saw no flames rising from the area where Hiroshima had stood. "Maybe it's possible for us to walk into the city," he told Setsuko.[4] He wanted to find Michie, the wife of his deceased son, Isamu. She had been directing a student work group near the city center on August 6. Setsuko's third sister, Yukiko, who lived with Michie and her two children, joined them.

Overnight, fire had swept through their neighborhood, making it almost impossible to locate their home. On the day of the bombing, the dark sky and smoke had obscured the devastation. Now Setsuko could see it all. Except for an occasional concrete structure, almost every house, store, school, hospital, and shrine had vanished, replaced by ashes. She said nothing. Her father led them in the direction of their home. Along the way Setsuko saw roof tiles fused together and wooden telephone poles tilted at strange angles, like sticks of charcoal. Army trucks had started to pick up the dead; human corpses and body parts along with carcasses of army horses littered what was left of the streets.

Even though Benkichi had been to their house the day before, it was difficult to find it again. "Ah, there is the gate of the dentist," he said at last, as he pointed out a distorted iron shape. "In that case, we must be about ten meters away from our street."[5] At last they reached what he thought was the site. A metal ornamental clock Setsuko found in the debris confirmed it to be their home. Benkichi thought the *kura*, with its thick, earthen walls, would be impermeable to typhoons and fires. Not a vestige of it and the family heirlooms remained except a few shattered rice bowls and several tea cups, twisted and melded into one mass. He said nothing. Setsuko could imagine the anguish he felt over the loss. The samurai swords, lacquerware, jewelry, family photos—everything connected with the past—had vanished, except the clock. Setsuko asked if she could keep it. He nodded. How could he refuse? There was nothing left.

As they made their way toward the city center, the skeleton of the Hiroshima Prefectural Industrial Promotion Hall stood as a stark image among the ruins. All that remained of the majestic Hiroshima Castle was a heap of wreckage. Its gracious eucalyptus trees had been reduced to stumps, except for one giant tree at the main gate. On Hijiyama Hill the beloved cherry trees had been torched; a few scorched stalks remained.

The closer they got to the city center, the more bodies they saw. The stench of decomposing corpses, fusing with the sharp smell of cremated flesh, assaulted Setsuko's sense of smell, creating an olfactory memory that would remain with her forever. Hiroshima had become a massive graveyard, a necropolis. She, her father, and Yukiko turned over one body after another, trying to identify Michie—relieved not to find her among the dead but disheartened that they couldn't find her. Of the eight thousand middle school students she had been supervising, most had been decimated in a flash. A student, however, told them she had seen Mrs. Nakamura, her teacher, for a moment. Although badly injured, she was still alive. Perhaps they might find her at the Red Cross Hospital or an aid station.

The Red Cross Hospital looked like a mortuary. Outside the entrance corpses were stacked one on top of another. Inside, a confused mass of moribund men, women, and children sprawled in the waiting rooms, hallways, and stairwells. Of the city's 200 doctors, only about 20 had survived and remained healthy enough to work. Less than 10 percent of the 1,700 nurses were alive and capable of tending the sick.[6]

Most of the injured, in particular those within two and a half miles of the hypocenter, sustained flash burns from the direct action of the bomb's thermal rays. When the skin sloughed off, it left raw wounds exposed to the heat and filth. Many had sustained blast injuries—broken bones, lacerations, an arm or leg severed, bellies split open. Before long, unattended wounds became infected, leading to gangrene. Rank, squalid smells of the wounded and unwashed tainted the hospital air. Maggots propagated in the pus, even of those still breathing. Swarms of flies harassed doctors and nurses trying to work and patients trying to recover or die in peace. One elderly woman called them *nimbai* (human flies). "Human beings are hatching them," she said.[7] The once-sanitized hospital wards with beds in orderly rows and spotless white sheets now overflowed with the afflicted. Many lay on the floor in blood, vomit, urine, and feces as if the plague had descended on the city. Michie was not among them.

Benkichi, Setsuko, and Yukiko continued to search around the city center. Thousands of people had entered the area looking for loved ones, hoping to discover them alive or, if not, to find their bodies so they could perform prompt and respectful cremation. According to Buddhist philosophy, the cleansing fire of cremation is transformative, enabling the soul of the departed to move into the ancestral realm. "Even corpses have the right to be treated respectfully," wrote poet Itsuko Ishikawa.[8] Yet clean-up crews shoveled remains into dump trucks and hauled them away; bulldozers ground under piles of carcasses, mixing those of humans, cats, dogs, and horses. In desperation families searched along the riverbanks, in the few remaining hospitals, outside aid stations, and along the remnants of streets, trying to locate a son or daughter, mother or father. Because the faceless corpses were unrecognizable, they looked for an identifiable headband or necklace or pocket watch. At the very least, they wanted to recover the bones so they could honor the deceased. "None of those who had left that morning ever came home again," wrote one survivor, "not my five children, my grandfather, my sister or my cousin. Not a bone remained for me to find and treasure."[9]

Benkichi and Setsuko spent several more days hunting for Michie. They never located her, not even her bones. She left behind two young children as orphans.

Meanwhile, Setsuko and her parents took turns providing Ayako and Eiji with sips of water and trying to soothe their burns with cooking oil. Setsuko wanted to give her sister words of comfort. She had none to give; death alone could relieve their agony. Ayako and Eiji lingered for four days and nights. Eiji didn't notice when his mother died; he passed away soon thereafter.

Setsuko, Benkichi, and Shigeno watched as soldiers threw Ayako and Eiji into a ditch, poured on gasoline, and lit a match. They turned the bodies with bamboo poles to quicken the cremation. "The back is done, but the stomach is only half-burned," Setsuko heard one soldier comment. "The brain hasn't even started to burn," said another. They were talking about her sister Ayako, "child of elegance," who had shown her fashion magazines and introduced her to Western movies, whom she admired for her independence. In a flippant tone, they spoke about Eiji, her beloved nephew, an innocent child. Setsuko stood watching without weeping, the embers of her sorrow extinguished. That memory troubled her for years. "What kind of human being am I," she asked herself again and again, "when loved ones are treated like roast pigs, and all I could do was stand there and watch, stunned?"[10] At thirteen Setsuko had witnessed a grotesque violation of human dignity with no tears. She felt nothing. And that was the worst feeling of all.

A few days after Little Boy detonated over Hiroshima, the Japanese government wired a document to the U.S. government via neutral Switzerland, protesting the new bomb's "uncontrollable and cruel effect," concluding that it constituted "a new crime against humanity." It demanded that further use of such a weapon be renounced immediately.[11] No response was forthcoming. On August 9, at 11:02 a.m., the United States dropped a plutonium bomb, nicknamed Fat Man, on Nagasaki, unleashing a force equivalent to twenty-one thousand tons of TNT—one and a half times that of Little Boy. Fat Man slaughtered 40,000, mostly civilians. The tally included 23 American prisoners of war and 3,200 nisei, sons and daughters of Japanese immigrants who held American citizenship and had been sent to Japan before World War II to be educated. With their new weapon, the U.S. military could turn all of Japan into a graveyard. Still, most Japanese citizens were surprised by what followed.

Five days later a soldier came by the summer house and announced that Emperor Hirohito was to deliver a special news broadcast at noon the next day. He planned to speak directly to his almost eighty million subjects. Gathering places had been set up for the public to listen to His Imperial Highness. For the first time in the country's three-thousand-year history, the Japanese people would hear their emperor's voice.

By the time Setsuko and her father arrived at a specified spot, a large crowd had gathered around a radio, set up on a tree branch. When the broadcast began, they rose to their feet. At first, static made the announcer almost inaudible. Then they heard the high-pitched voice of their forty-four-year-old emperor. With gravitas he read his prepared comments: "To our good and loyal subjects: After pondering deeply the general trends of the world and the actual conditions obtaining in our empire today, we have decided to effect a settlement of the present situation by resorting to an extraordinary measure. We have ordered our Government to communicate to the Governments of the United States, Great Britain, China and the Soviet Union that our empire accepts the provisions of their joint declaration." He used long words and courtly language, Setsuko noted, not easily understood by commoners, more appropriate for the well-educated. "The hardships and sufferings to which our nation is to be subjected hereafter will be certainly great. . . . However, it is according to the dictates of time and fate that we have resolved to pave the way for a grand peace for all the generations to come by enduring the unendurable and suffering what is insufferable. . . . Cultivate the ways of rectitude, nobility of spirit, and work with resolution so that you may enhance the innate glory of the Imperial State."[12]

Although he did not use the word "surrender," Setsuko knew he was saying the war had ended—an unexpected, shocking message. The people around her stood dumbfounded; no one spoke. Some shed tears, their cries muffled. A few young soldiers threw themselves onto the ground sobbing. This was an unacceptable, dishonorable fate. Setsuko later heard that in Tokyo, in front of the Imperial Household with tens of thousands of people present, a group of soldiers committed hara-kiri. In the subsequent weeks, nine high-ranking military leaders also committed suicide. On the way back to the summer house, her father said nothing. Setsuko sensed he had thought defeat inevitable; after all, he had started relearning English.

The formal surrender would take place on September 2, on board the USS *Missouri.* All Japanese military and naval forces were disbanded. Japan was placed under Allied control, and Emperor Hirohito relinquished his divine status. After news of the surrender sunk in, many Japanese expressed relief that the war had ended. Nationwide over 2.5 million had died, including an estimated eight hundred thousand civilians; fifteen million had been left homeless. "If only the war had ended a little sooner" became a common refrain.[13]

The day after Emperor Hirohito's broadcast, Setsuko and her parents walked to the home of Shuichi Namba, her mother's elder brother. They found him grieving. His wife and two daughters had been in central Hiroshima at the time of the bombing. Tokiko, Setsuko's dearest friend throughout childhood, had been demolishing houses and never returned. Shuichi's older daughter had married recently, and, after a week's honeymoon, her husband had been shipped out, she knew not where. She and her mother had prepared some sweets for his family and had gone to deliver them. Uncle Shuichi found their skeletons sitting in a circle around a table.

Soon thereafter Benkichi got news that his younger brother, Hiroshi, and sister-in-law, Sadayo, had become ill. He and Shigeno set out to their home near Mount Futaba, leaving Setsuko with Uncle Shuichi. Setsuko had rejoiced when she first learned her dearest aunt and uncle had escaped injury. If they had been in their city home, within three thousand feet of the detonation point, they would have been incinerated. In the eastern end of the city, they had survived unharmed. Several days after the bombing, however, both developed lethargy and nausea.

Sadayo and Hiroshi appeared to be improving when they began to lose their hair and develop purple blotches on their arms and legs. Profuse vomiting and diarrhea followed. Benkichi and Shigeno found their chic sister-in-law bald and pale, with blood oozing from her gums. The once-dashing Hiroshi looked emaciated. Racked with fever, he had become bedridden. Benkichi and Shigeno tried to keep them hydrated, but the two continued to deteriorate. Their internal organs seemed to be rotting and coming out as a thick, black liquid. Shigeno used bolts of fabric intended for kimonos and old newspapers announcing Japan's glorious victories as diapers. Sadayo died on August 30; Hiroshi lasted six days longer. Setsuko never saw her beloved aunt and uncle again. They were cremated, along with thousands of others slain by this bewildering sickness. "The whole city turned into a crematorium," Setsuko recalled.[14]

In the first few weeks after the bombing of Hiroshima, survivors began to develop a mysterious ailment in alarming numbers. The rapidity and ugliness of the disease generated fear among those who considered themselves lucky enough to have survived. A rumor spread: if purple spots appear on your body, it is a sure sign you will die. Setsuko had been spared. Then one morning, when she combed her hair, dark strands fell out.

6 Life among the Ruins

It is a very pleasant way to die.

–General Leslie Groves

Every morning before she dressed, Setsuko examined herself for purple spots. She felt relieved when she found none. She did notice dark strands of hair on her pillow. And when she bathed, clumps of hair floated on the water. At first she had only patches of baldness; before long she had only patches of hair. Now she understood why so many young women wore their padded cotton air-raid bonnets or covered their heads with scarves. Several of her friends had become bald, and they hadn't died, she consoled herself. What concerned her more was the bleeding that followed: a trickle from her nose, oozing from her gums, red stains on her bedding. She dreaded going to the bathroom; her urine looked like berry juice. Chewing hurt, and the food she didn't throw up surged through her bowels. Then purple spots erupted on her legs.[1]

Dr. Michihiko Hachiya, director of the severely damaged Hiroshima Communications Hospital, located a mile from the hypocenter, recognized this perplexing malady early on. Despite his own painful lacerations, he, along with the few surviving staff, tried to deliver care to a never-ending crowd of patients—five thousand in the first month. While doing so, he observed something unusual: many patients who were recuperating from burns and wounds suddenly developed vomiting and diarrhea, sometimes up to forty stools per day. Others, uninjured by the blast, began to experience similar symptoms, filling the beds vacated by the dead. Hachiya assumed this was an outbreak of dysentery and isolated the stricken. Before long, however, he detected a constellation of symptoms not related to dysentery: hair loss, bruising, painful ulcerations in the mouth and throat, bloody urine, and excessive menstrual bleeding. Some patients spontaneously recovered; others, tormented by high fevers and shaking chills, died days later.

On postmortem examinations Dr. Hachiya found massive internal bleeding in the abdominal cavity, lungs, wall of the heart, and brain. Once he could obtain a microscope and examine blood smears, he discovered a profound reduction in platelet and white-blood-cell counts. This explained the spontaneous hemorrhages and inability to fend off infections. The bone marrow, the body's factory for blood-cell production, had been severely damaged. The closer to ground zero, the more likely patients were to be afflicted, suggesting that radiation exposure from the atomic blast was the cause of what he called "radiation sickness."[2]

At the end of August, doctors at Hiroshima's Teishin Hospital issued a warning about what they called "atomic-bomb disease." Hachiya's findings corroborated their hypothesis. He gave his manuscript, titled "Atom Bomb and A-Bomb Disease," to a reporter from *Sangyo Keizai*, the national newspaper headquartered in Tokyo.[3] He anticipated rapid publication. To his dismay the report was never circulated. U.S. occupation authorities had started prohibiting Japanese physicians from publishing scientific articles on the medical consequences of the atomic bomb. They proceeded to confiscate physicians' case notes, biopsy specimens, autopsy material, and photographs. So neither health-care workers nor the public could fathom what had befallen them.

One journalist did slip through the barrier. Australian war correspondent Wilfred Burchett had gained permission to travel to Tokyo aboard the USS *Missouri* to cover Japan's surrender. Then, without approval, he boarded a train to Hiroshima. With just a typewriter, an umbrella, and rations for seven meals, Burchett arrived in a wasteland and proceeded to write the first news account of radiation sickness. On September 5 his article, titled "The Atomic Plague," made front-page news in London's *Daily Express*. "In Hiroshima, 30 days after the first atomic bomb," he wrote, "people are still dying mysteriously, horribly—people who were uninjured by the cataclysm—from an unknown something which I can only describe as 'atomic plague.'" He reported hair loss and bleeding from the mouth, nose, and ears and how the doctors, thinking this was caused by general debility, had given vitamin shots. "The results were horrible," Burchett continued. "The flesh started rotting away from the hole caused by the injection of the needle." Death followed in every case. Japanese physicians who had entered the burned-out city concluded that the symptoms stemmed from exposure to radioactivity released by the bomb. Of those who had come to aid the suffering, he wrote, "Now they themselves have become sufferers."[4]

Concerned that Burchett's article and the handful of medical reports that had slipped through the ban might stir up sympathy for the Japanese, Lieutenant General Leslie Groves, director of the Manhattan Project, dismissed these accounts of delayed deaths from radiation as Japanese propaganda.[5] He ordered the formation of a survey team, the Manhattan Project Atomic Bomb Investigation Group, composed of military surgeons and engineers, to investigate the radiation effects from the bomb. Led by his second-in-command, Major General Thomas Farrell, their explicit mission was "to observe and to document but not to intervene."[6] Their implicit mission was to counter any horror stories propagated by the press.

The team arrived in Hiroshima on September 9, and soon thereafter Farrell held a press conference, at which he reported they had found no residual radiation. Thus, there was no danger to those living in or entering the area. His medical team concluded that most casualties had resulted from the blast and fires and that injuries from radiation occurred only in the first second of the explosion.[7] These statements proved to be incorrect. Hours after the explosion, many people had been drenched with sticky, black raindrops contaminated by lethal ash that contained radioactive particles, later termed "fallout." Those who had come into Hiroshima during the first few days after the bombing to search for family members had been exposed to radioactive ash as well. The number of deaths was rising. General Groves could no longer label these reports as propaganda. When called to testify at a Senate committee hearing, he used a new strategy. Compared with other ways of dying in times of war, he said, "[As] I understand from the doctors, it is a very pleasant way to die."[8] He did not want the atomic bombs to be considered in the same category as chemical warfare because of radiation poisoning.

Scientists involved in the Manhattan Project had not anticipated the extent to which Japanese civilians would be exposed to radiation. Horrified by that revelation, some of the team at Los Alamos vomited when they heard the news. They deplored the gruesome deaths from acute radiation toxicity. Added to that, they anticipated that with time even more would suffer from another consequence of radiation exposure—cancer.

Setsuko Nakamura received no medical care. No one knew how to treat radiation sickness; the meager supply of medications was dwindling, and the number of moribund patients overwhelmed the small number of doctors and nurses who had survived the bomb. Many health-care workers became incapacitated by the same illness. Weak and dizzy if she stood up too quickly, Setsuko determined not to take to her bed as had her Uncle Hiroshi. Although she felt anxious, she did not want to bother her parents while they were tending to her aunt and uncle. With frequent sips of water to diminish the dizziness and rice gruel to enhance her strength, Setsuko gradually recovered over several weeks.

Each day the citizens of Hiroshima faced a sea of rubble. Just surviving became an ordeal. In a state of bewilderment and mourning, people seemed unable to act. An infant whimpering from an empty stomach or a child shivering in the rain roused parents from their wretchedness. They had to seek food, water, and shelter or else watch their family perish. Already near starvation from severe wartime rations, people became desperate; they spent much of the day searching for food. Hunger pains drove many to eat rotting fish floating on the rivers. Vegetable gardens and stores of rice had been incinerated. A rumor spread that nothing could grow in the barren, irradiated ground for the next seventy-five years.[9] The central Japanese government seemed to have abandoned Hiroshima. There was talk of rebuilding the city elsewhere.

In the midst of despair, an unlikely hero emerged—thirty-eight-year-old Shinzo Hamai, an unassuming, midlevel municipal worker. As chief of municipal distribution, he had supervised rationing of food and supplies during the war. When the bomb fell, he was at home, several miles from the hypocenter. He rushed to city hall, which he found in shambles, most of the city officials dead. With enormous energy, ingenuity, and leadership skills he didn't know he had, he set to work. Food was the first priority. He arranged for volunteers from Eba and other suburbs to prepare and distribute rice balls. Adulterated with railroad grass—weeds that grew along the railroad tracks—rice balls served more to curb hunger than to provide nourishment. He set up emergency cook houses in Kure, Hatsukaichi, and other nearby towns and commandeered trucks from the Armored Car Training Center to collect and deliver the food. When he discovered a tanker in Ujina Port filled with cooking oil, he pumped out the precious fluid and dispensed it to as many households as possible. When he heard that an army warehouse refrigerator contained a large quantity of beef but had no electricity, he persuaded the supervisor to donate the meat. Still, thousands were starving. A week passed before the Japanese military set up food-distribution centers. Bribes and favors corrupted equitable allocation. As a result, black markets and price gouging flourished, forcing people to sell their few belongings to feed their families.

Clean water was scarce as well. Hiroshima's rivers remained fetid, clogged with sewage and corpses. Many believed that the bomb had poisoned the city's reservoirs and cisterns. Driven by thirst, however, they took their chances and drank whatever they could find. Some resorted to tapping into underground water pipes. Hundreds of leaks from these punctures lowered the water pressure; faucets ran dry even in intact homes. Hamai authorized an army engineer to plug seventy thousand holes in the pipes.

Most people had just the clothes they were wearing on August 6 or remnants thereof. With the August rains and cool autumn weather approaching, Hamai needed to find clothing for over a hundred thousand survivors. He coaxed an army official to divulge the out-of-town location of a large warehouse full of new army uniforms and negotiated the release of ten thousand sets of military clothing. He secured a substantial store of cotton cloth held by the navy to make dresses for women and clothing for children.[10]

The large population of homeless lived in half-destroyed buildings, air-raid shelters, and huts made from salvaged bits of wreckage. They slept on rags or dirt. Pieces of tin sheeting provided some protection from the sun and rain. No longer did people offer food to the dead at their family shrines. In most cases they didn't know where their family's ashes lay. Before long wooden shacks sprang up along the Ota River numbering into the hundreds, dubbed the "A-bomb slum." Although they provided some protection, they posed a major fire hazard. Barefoot, half-naked children wandered among the ruins.

Although the Nakamura home had been destroyed, Setsuko's proud father, the head of his family, did not want to continue living in his brother-in-law's home as a guest. Uncle Shuichi understood and offered Benkichi a cottage he owned in Fuchu, apologetic that it had just a partial roof and damaged walls. Benkichi thought it good enough.

Loss prevailed. As had so many others, Setsuko lost family, neighbors, friends, and her home. She'd lost photographs of her deceased brother, Isamu; the copy of *Grimm's Fairy Tales* he had given her; the velvet dresses she had modeled for Aunt Sadayo; and her pretty plastic pencil holder. As fall approached, few trees remained to display their gold, orange, and red colors. And Hijiyama Hill stood naked. Where would the remaining family celebrate the Cherry Blossom Festival in the spring?

No longer could the community count on the public utilities they had taken for granted: electricity, gas, sewage disposal, and telephones. The Japanese military lacked the wherewithal to help restore them. All public means of communication and transportation had ceased: postal and telegraph services; newspapers and radio; streetcars and railroads. Gone were most police and fire stations, shrines, hospitals, and schools, as well as department stores, restaurants, and markets. Most centers of business and commerce—banks, courts, and municipal offices—had been leveled or stood as concrete skeletons against the barren landscape. A full 68 percent of all buildings had been demolished, another 24 percent severely damaged. It wasn't just the structures that had been decimated. Lost was their community. Hiroshima's society had crumbled.

Worse yet was disruption of the family structure, so central to Japanese culture. Between the war and the atomic bomb, almost no family in Hiroshima remained untouched. In many the husband had perished, leaving a wife, untrained for work outside the home, to provide for her children and elderly parents. In others death of the mother left the father in the unconventional position of caregiver. If both parents died, it was unclear who would raise their sons and daughters. No one knew the number of "A-bomb orphans," as they were called; estimates now reached over six thousand.[11] Many of the youngest did not even know their names. If left alone, they, along with countless infants, would die within days.

Temporary orphanages were set up in seven school buildings, where the cries for food, milk, and mother resounded day and night. Thousands of elementary school children had been evacuated to the countryside prior to the bombing. Now truckloads of these children were brought back to Hiroshima and dropped off in a desolate place they didn't recognize to find no family, no home, no food. The lucky ones were retrieved by an older sibling or aged grandparent. Some found shelter at an orphanage. The remainder became street urchins. Unsuccessful begging gave way to theft or starvation. Some became subservient to *yakusa* (gangsters), submitting to their directives in exchange for food.

As bewilderment and numbness began to fade, anger filled the void for many. Survivors talked of taking the Americans to international court or demanding compensation from the United States until they learned that the Japanese government, in signing the peace treaty, had agreed that Japan would not ask for such measures. The indiscriminate killing of women and children and the annihilation of their community should have been enough to leave a lifelong scar of hatred. Surprisingly, however, resentment toward Americans did not prevail. Besides, since the U.S. military would soon be occupying Japan, many suppressed their feelings. Setsuko never heard her parents or relatives or friends or teachers condemn Americans. She had to subdue the indignation welling up inside of her: "Why did this happen to Ayako, to Eiji, my classmates? Who can stay calm and pacified? How dare America call itself a Christian nation? How could God allow such inhumanity?"[12] Some directed their bitterness at their own military. The leaders of the Imperial Japanese Army received the brunt of censure for having betrayed the emperor's trust and deluded the Japanese people, generating shame and ruination. Dr. Hachiya heard one of his patients yell from his hospital bed, "General Tōjō, you great thick-headed fool, cut your stomach and die."[13]

More powerful than anger, however, was overwhelming demoralization (*kyodatsu*), hopelessness in the face of so much loss and suffering. Haunted by nightmares, debilitated by wounds, and disfigured by burns, former breadwinners became ineffective. People who were once driven and dedicated walked around in an aimless daze. It was hard to find purpose in this godforsaken place. Yet, as Japanese author Kenzaburo Oe pointed out, the citizens of Hiroshima were "people who did not commit suicide in spite of everything."[14]

In late August, when the rains washed away the ash, railroad grass began to sprout in the fallow ground. If it could germinate, survivors speculated, why not other plants? The assertion that nothing would grow in Hiroshima for seventy-five years appeared to be incorrect. This observation had a remarkable effect: it began to revive the city's lost vitality. And with that arose the resolve to rebuild Hiroshima.[15] The rapid resumption of streetcar service generated a burst of pride. Families started to search for and reclaim plots of land where their homes had once stood. There they built temporary dwellings, even imagined a future home similar to their prior one. Limited train service resumed; mail delivery restarted where addresses could be found. Several remaining banks began making transactions, even without verification from account holders. The Chugoku News Company began to print a newspaper in the remnants of its building, with a fraction of its staff. On August 21 elementary school principals announced that school would resume on September 1, although many had no building to which they could return. They held classes outside, calling them "blue sky" classrooms.[16] On September 13 the city administration, at Hamai's prompting, announced that it would provide building materials at no charge for those whose homes had been demolished. Restoration plans were underway, with a focus on the rapid repair of public buildings. Hope had sprouted along with the grass.

On the afternoon of September 17, a typhoon made landfall near Makurazaki, at the southern tip of Japan. No one was expecting it.[17] During the July to October typhoon season, numerous storms threatened the Japanese archipelago, bringing torrential rains. The Makurazaki typhoon would be among the most violent and destructive storms in Japan's history, with wind gusts reaching 140 miles per hour. No one was prepared for its fury. Hiroshima's Ebayama Meteorological Observatory had lost most of its staff and instruments from the atomic bomb. The weather map on September 17 was later found to be blank.[18] Even if someone at the observatory had noted the rapidly falling barometric pressure and wanted to alert the public, their communication devices had been damaged beyond use. And even if the public had been warned to evacuate, where would they go—to higher ground to avoid the storm surge, only to be buried by landslides hurtling down the denuded hillsides?

The typhoon advanced in a northeast path and reached Hatsukaichi, nine miles west of Hiroshima, by evening. There Ono Army Hospital, built on a terraced slope above the city, housed one hundred patients, mostly atomic-bomb casualties and soldiers. Forty members of the Kyoto Imperial University A-Bomb Disaster Survey Team, which included prominent professors of medicine and physics, had set up headquarters at the hospital to study the effects of radiation. At 10:20 most had settled down for the night. Those awake might have thought the rumble to be thunder. By the time they realized the sound was that of trees snapping and rocks crashing, it was too late. A massive mudslide, intensified by the roiling Maruishi River, cascaded down the mountain, carrying boulders up to six feet high, pushing the hospital, patients, staff, and researchers into the sea: 156 perished.[19]

In the middle of the night, the typhoon hit Hiroshima in full force. Lashing winds and rain battered the area, ripping apart rickety shacks, blowing newly rebuilt homes sideways. Those living in air-raid shelters, driven out by rushing water, watched helplessly as their few remaining possessions floated away. Others awoke to shattering glass, as a wall of mud broke through their bedroom windows. Debris dammed the upper branches of the Ota River, intensifying the flooding. Bridges that had withstood the atomic bomb collapsed as their embankments washed away. Recently hung telephone wires dangled in the breeze; railroad ties were uprooted; acres of ash were replaced with sludge. Ujina Harbor became a tangled mass of wooden planks, fishing nets, shredded sails, splintered masts, and battered bodies.[20] By midmorning, the storm had already moved on toward northwestern Japan, leaving a trail of destruction in its wake.

In the late afternoon, before the typhoon hit Hiroshima with full force, Setsuko Nakamura was visiting a friend some distance away from Fuchu. On her way home, she got caught in a sudden downpour, drenched by the pelting rain. Water splashed over her shoes, soaking them. Her feet sunk deeper into the mud with each step. The Ota River, calm and clear the day before, became a churning swill. Its murky water rose above its banks and spilled onto her path. It filled her shoes, then ran up her legs to her knees. She tried to move forward against the wind and rushing water, striving to maintain her balance lest she stumble and be swept away. She dodged pieces of splintered wood and tiles, pushed aside clothing and bedding. Several times she lost her way; landmarks had been obfuscated, rivers turned into lakes. Still she trudged on, amid garbage, dead animals, and human waste carried by the current. A bloated body floated by.

Setsuko remained composed. As she struggled on, however, almost blinded by the wind, all the ugliness and sorrow from the past six weeks intensified until feelings of despair engulfed her. She had been nearly buried alive under Army Headquarters, watched her city burn, witnessed the agonizing deaths of her family and friends, and suffered radiation sickness. Now she faced being entombed in mud, blown into a wall, or drowned, her bloated body seen floating along by some other innocent girl.

When she reached her uncle's cottage, soaked and exhausted, she threw herself onto the floor, sobbing—the first time she had shed tears since before August 6. "Why did this happen to me?" she cried. She had plummeted from a comfortable life to this wretched state. Anticipating solace from her parents, she was surprised at her father's response: "What right do you have to say that?" he scolded. "You have us; you have a roof over you. You have your life. What more do you expect?" Up to that point Setsuko had eaten, slept, and moved with almost no emotion. Her father's words jolted her. She stopped crying. "I am alive," she whispered.[21]

The Makurazaki typhoon left over 2,000 dead in the Hiroshima Prefecture, almost 1,000 missing, and 135,000 homeless. Just as the city had begun to rebuild, it was flattened. Many who had lost almost everything now lost everything. Shinzo Hamai surveyed Hiroshima from the top of the remains of city hall. "The city looked like a huge lake," he said. "Beneath its waves it was possible to detect tiled roofs. . . . I felt as though this were the final burial."[22]

The following day, the storm passed, and the sun came out. Only then did Setsuko see the immense damage wrought by the typhoon. Yet an uncanny peace overlaid the city—and her. She had passed from a state of numbness and bewilderment to anger to demoralization and now to a reawakening. "Yes, I am *alive*," she exclaimed. "I *am* alive."[23]

7 Occupied

> We have resolved to pave the way for a grand peace for all the generations to come by enduring the unendurable and suffering what is insufferable.
>
> –Emperor Hirohito

"The 41st Infantry Division and the X Corps have landed in the Kure Hiroshima area," reported the *Nippon Times* on October 10, 1945.[1] General Douglas MacArthur, Supreme Commander of the Allied Powers (SCAP), had arrived in Tokyo six weeks earlier to supervise Japan's occupation by the United States with help from Australia, the United Kingdom, India, and New Zealand. Subjected to foreign military control for the first time in its history, the Japanese people did not know what to expect—pillage, forced labor, rape? With the destruction of most major cities, they knew the occupation forces would find few possessions to plunder. What families feared most was rape, especially of their marriageable daughters. Such fear was not unfounded: soon after Japan's surrender, reports of widespread rape appeared at several naval ports. A Japanese official circulated the following notice: "Subject, *female attire*: Thin, one-piece garments, such as we wear out of doors, will normally be regarded by the foreigners as night attire. This could lead to impulsive treatment with severe detrimental consequences. You are therefore instructed to wear . . . *mompe*. . . . Women left alone at home must take especial precautions and must ensure at all times that all doors remain effectively locked."[2]

As Hiroshima's occupation date approached, people seemed to disappear. "When we first arrived, there was almost no one to be seen," wrote Dr. Averill

Liebow, one of the first American scientists sent to investigate the medical consequences of the atomic bomb. He attributed it to "dread of the imminent arrival of the unknown conqueror."[3] MacArthur was more blunt: "When American troops landed in Japan," he wrote in his memoir, "the image of the sadistic commander and his rapacious soldiery was in every Japanese mind." In attempts to allay their fear, he issued a public statement a few days after his arrival: "SCAP is not concerned with how to keep Japan down, but how to get her on her feet again."[4] Although Japan's military forces were disbanded, Emperor Hirohito was allowed to remain on his throne as a figurehead. Respectful treatment of Japanese citizens, MacArthur reasoned, would build trust and serve the long-term goal of creating a strong ally in the Asia-Pacific region.

President Harry S. Truman had approved a document titled "US Initial Post-Surrender Policy for Japan," which stated the goals of the occupation: demilitarize the country and convert it into a Western-style democracy.[5] The mission did not encompass decontamination of Hiroshima and Nagasaki, delivery of medical care, or assistance in rebuilding the cities. Not much remained to demilitarize in Hiroshima; the bomb had annihilated most of its military installations and more than twenty thousand Japanese soldiers. Still, forty thousand U.S. troops were stationed near Hiroshima over a five-month period.

With the pending arrival of U.S. soldiers, Setsuko heard that many mothers cut their daughters' hair short and dressed them like boys or sent them into the countryside to hide. She didn't fret. "The war had ended," Setsuko said. "That was the number-one issue."[6] In the evening the family didn't have to sit in the dark with blankets covering the windows. She didn't have to sleep in her blouse and *mompe*, ready to dash into a shelter whenever a siren sounded. Now she could wear her pajamas at night and turn on the light to read. And nothing could dissuade her from resuming her studies once she received news that Jogakuin High School was to reopen.

Setsuko knew Jogakuin wouldn't be the same; nevertheless, she hadn't anticipated just how much had been lost. Of the attractive two-story white clapboard building, designed in the colonial revival style, a few concrete blocks remained. Jogakuin owned land at the foot of Mount Ushita, and the school principal, Dr. Takuo Matsumoto, persuaded army personnel to give him leftover lumber and cement to build a temporary school there. One of the first things Setsuko noticed about the makeshift structure was that the windows had no glass panes. In the coming months, she would find herself shivering as gusts of wind and sleet rushed through the open frames. Although the corrugated tin roof would keep the students dry, the clatter of rain on its surface would drown out their teacher's voice. Setsuko's two-hour walk along a busy road from Fuchu to the new location didn't faze her until the cool, wet autumn weather arrived.

Setsuko looked forward to reuniting with friends and teachers. Still, on the first day, her excitement was tempered when she realized how many students and teachers were missing. Twenty-seven had been incinerated when the collapsed Army Headquarters had burst into flames. Most of Jogakuin's seventh and eighth graders, along with their teachers, had been mobilized to help demolish buildings in Zakoba-cho, six-tenths of a mile from the hypocenter; there 20 teachers and 352 students had perished.[7]

Nevertheless, Setsuko tried to focus on her studies. She appreciated the changes the occupation authorities required of the Japanese educational system: rote memorization, characteristic of much of their prior schooling, would be replaced by a curriculum that encouraged initiative and self-reliance. English was reintroduced, academic freedom guaranteed, and coeducation allowed, although Jogakuin remained a private girls' school. "It was a tremendous liberation," she said. Moral training as a means of indoctrination would be abolished, supplanted with instruction in democratic ideas. "Democratic ideas" resonated with Setsuko.[8] In time, however, she would perceive the hypocrisy of General MacArthur's emphasizing democracy and academic freedom while at the same time inhibiting freedom of expression by imposing strict censorship.

A week after the Japanese surrendered, MacArthur had issued a press code that outlawed any publication seen as detrimental to the objectives of the occupation. The authorities tried to control all information about the atomic bomb's aftereffects by censoring newspaper articles and confiscating films and photographs of the devastation shot by Japanese cameramen. They forbade Japanese physicians to divulge their medical findings without strict oversight. As a result, not only did the public learn few details about the "atomic plague," but also the total death count from the atomic bombs in both Hiroshima and

Nagasaki remained contested. The artistic community had to comply as well. Creative images of the bombs' effects were prohibited. Fourteen poems from *Kuoroi Tamago* (*Black Eggs*), a book of poetry by Sadako Kurihara, who would be lauded as an atomic-bomb poet, were deleted prior to its release.[9] These constraints left much of the world ignorant of the ravages wreaked by the two atomic bombs. Nonetheless, most of the Japanese public admired General MacArthur and appreciated his magnanimous approach to governing their defeated nation: the relief shipments of food, the protection of women and children from assault, and the expedited repatriation of millions of soldiers. They dubbed him "Shogun MacArthur."[10]

Setsuko focused on the positive side of democratization, starting with the new constitution, which she heard referred to as the "MacArthur Constitution," given his central role in its creation.[11] Although it was promoted as an amendment to the 1889 Meiji Constitution to make it more palatable to the Japanese public, it barely resembled the old document. They could keep their beloved emperor as a symbol of Japanese unity and culture, but he had no political authority. Japan's parliament, the Diet—composed of a House of Representatives and a House of Councillors—became the supreme political institution, consistent with a democratic state. Women achieved equal rights, among them the right to vote. Because the constitution guaranteed all citizens basic civil liberties, it generated wide public acceptance. In social studies class, Setsuko and her classmates discussed political reform and applauded how it might change a woman's place in society. "Could women really run for office?" Setsuko asked. "What impact would it have on the Diet?" (In an election seven months later, voter turnout was 79 percent among men, 67 percent for women.) In private the students debated Emperor Hirohito's status. "Millions of young lives were dedicated to him," Setsuko argued, "and he got off scot-free? Is that right?"[12]

One aspect of the new constitution posed a threat to Benkichi Nakamura—its stance on family hierarchy. The head of a Japanese household had always maintained control over his relatives. In large part he determined their education, arranged their marriages, and selected their vocations. Under the new democratic constitution, family members held equal rights, including shared inheritance. This challenged Benkichi's status. Setsuko didn't hear her parents disparage the mandate; they had lived long enough in the United States to understand the democratic viewpoint. She did notice that her father set to work to reinstate his position.

Even though Uncle Shuichi welcomed Benkichi to stay in Fuchu, Benkichi suddenly announced he had purchased a house in Ozu-cho, on the periphery of Hiroshima. Setsuko thought an important consideration in her father's decision was its location near a bus stop, which allowed her to commute to school instead of spending a third of her day walking—a particularly welcome change when the weather turned colder and the hours of daylight shortened. There may have been a more compelling reason: as head of the Nakamura family, it likely vexed him to receive charity from his wife's brother. Besides, he wanted to reestablish their own home where the remaining family could gather.

Although Setsuko wanted to like their new house out of respect for her parents, she did not like its location. "In those days, we didn't have the luxury to choose," she later said, "but my sense of ego, my pride was disturbed." She had grown up in a peaceful residential neighborhood—homes with courtyards, ornate gates, and manicured shrubbery as well as neighbors with professions. Their home in Kojinmachi had a spacious living room, decorated with exquisite scrolls and chests inlaid with ivory, and a modern bathroom. Their house in Ozu-cho had no courtyard, no gatepost with a plaque to identify them as *shizoku*, members of the former samurai class. Setsuko considered the backyard utilitarian, with its small vegetable garden and a few straggly fruit trees. "I wouldn't call it a garden," she said. "To me a garden should be a thing of beauty."[13]

Beauty—that was missing in Ozu-cho. Located in a crowded working-class neighborhood, their new house stood among modest homes, many of them partially destroyed. Some doubled as small-scale businesses. A lumber yard nearby contributed to the constant noise and congestion. Setsuko's mother seemed comfortable in the community, with always a kind word for neighbors. Although Setsuko admired her mother's adaptability and social ease, she found it difficult to follow her example.

Besides Benkichi, Shigeno, Yukiko, and Setsuko, two grandchildren lived in the house. Six-year-old Masataka and his younger sister, Kyoko, had been left orphans by the deaths of Benkichi's first son, Isamu, and his wife, Michie. Concerned that the Allies would target Hiroshima, Michie had moved with her children to a cottage in the suburbs, from where she commuted into the city to teach. On August 6 she was supervising her students in housing demolition near the city center. At 3:00 p.m. Masataka waited as usual for his mother at the train station, not far from their cottage. When the train arrived from Hiroshima, he saw a young man hobble off, his clothes tattered. Then four men carried out a wounded young mother and her child. Passengers looked stunned, mumbling about how the city had turned into hell. He kept searching for his mother. The train pulled away. For weeks thereafter he returned to the station every day. His mother never came home. Now he and his sister were being raised by their grandparents.[14]

Slowly family began to gather around Benkichi and Shigeno. It had been reduced in number, however. Among the known deceased were Isamu; the second daughter, Ayako, and her son, Eiji; Benkichi's brother, Hiroshi, and his wife, Sadayo; several nephews who had perished in battle or as POWs; and a number of other family members, including Michie, who simply disappeared on "that day," as people began to refer to August 6. At no time did Setsuko hear her parents lament their plight. Her mother continued to chant daily prayers to Buddha. The number of souls to which she now had to attend seemed countless.

Before long those serving in the Imperial Japanese Army were released, among them Aunt Sadayo and Uncle Hiroshi's son Henry. Setsuko adored her cousin; she thought him the most handsome man she knew. An early photo shows him dressed in a three-piece worsted suit. In another he is modeling a Western-style swimsuit, hands on his hips, his long, muscular legs displayed in a playful pose, a broad smile showing his perfect teeth. Setsuko didn't know where Henry had been stationed; she could not imagine such a genial young man crawling in the mud, blowing off the head of another young man. Even though he had survived the war, Setsuko never saw him again. He had been wounded, she learned, and a leg had to be amputated to save him. He never returned home. One day Henry shot himself.

Benkichi and Shigeno's third daughter, Yukiko, continued to wait for news of her husband, Takamasa Tamura. He had been captured in Soviet-occupied Manchuria and imprisoned in Siberia. Approximately 580,000 Japanese were incarcerated in POW camps; 60,000 died from the harsh winters, exhausting labor, starvation, disease, and brutality of the guards. Repatriation of the remainder took years. The delay afforded the Russians free labor and a prolonged time for communist indoctrination. Three years after the Japanese surrender, the Soviet Union still held over 200,000 POWs. Many never returned home. Decades later the Russian government could not account for most of them.[15]

Months passed and Yukiko heard nothing about her husband. Correspondence with family continued to be restricted. Almost resigned to Takamasa's fate, she received a letter: her husband was alive. When he reunited with Yukiko, they seemed like strangers. They had spent just a week together before he left for the front. They built a shack on the land where they had started their married life and tried to piece together the fragments of their existence. Setsuko remembered her brother-in-law as a gentle, distinguished man, a labor consultant for the prefectural government. She never understood his duties, yet, when he died years later, the emperor honored him for his contributions.

When Benkichi and Shigeno's second son, Susumu, returned to Hiroshima, he built a temporary dwelling for his wife, Hideko, and daughter Suzue where the original Nakamura home had stood. There were few jobs in Hiroshima, and prior commissioned officers in the armed services were purged from public positions. Eventually, Susumu was hired by an American company in Tokyo, as his English proved advantageous in the chaotic postwar period. Setsuko wondered about her brother's wartime experiences: Where was he stationed? What did he do? How did he survive? He did not talk much about the war, although he seemed the most unscathed of all the Nakamura men. This did not surprise her; Susumu personified his name, which meant "to advance." Her first clue as to her brother's importance was a large box of chocolates sent to the family from Manila. Susumu told his parents that "somebody" wanted his family to have this token of appreciation. Family members later talked about how he had served as an interpreter for Lieutenant General Masaharu

Homma when General Jonathan M. Wainwright, the commander of Allied troops in the Philippines, tried to surrender.[16] They did not know Susumu's role until General Wainwright included him in his memoir. And they did not know that his assignment with General Homma almost cost Susumu his life.

A month after Wainwright had succeeded General MacArthur as commander of Allied forces in the Philippines, Bataan fell, and Wainwright retreated to the island fortress of Corregidor at the entrance to Manila Harbor. There his troops of almost eleven thousand were suffering from injuries and starvation. And they were trapped. On May 6, 1942, Wainwright determined that he had to surrender Corregidor.[17] That day he and several staff members were waiting on the veranda of a wood-frame, ramshackle house on Cabcaben, Bataan, for General Homma to arrive. In a flurry of dust, a Cadillac pulled up, and out stepped a short, stocky man, the commander of the Imperial Japanese Fourteenth Army. His uniform displayed numerous medals and service ribbons; a long sword hung at his side. Wainwright wore wrinkled khakis with no decorations; he leaned on a cane, looking emaciated and defeated.

Homma strutted onto the veranda and motioned Wainwright to sit across from him at an oblong table. Beside him sat his interpreter, Lieutenant Susumu Nakamura. With no preliminaries Wainwright passed his signed surrender document across to Homma, who passed it to Nakamura. He read the document aloud in Japanese, after which he translated Homma's response: "General Homma replies that no surrender will be considered unless it includes all United States and Philippine troops in the Philippine Islands." His perfect English marked him as highborn. Wainwright replied that he commanded only the harbor defense troops and the island of Luzon. Major General William F. Sharp now commanded all other forces (a transfer Wainwright had just made in anticipation of Homma's demands). Nakamura said General Homma did not believe him: "He says it has been reported many times by the United States radio that you command all troops in the Philippines. He will not accept any surrender unless it includes all forces."[18]

When Wainwright again tried to bluff, by stating he had no control over Sharp, Homma pounded his fist on the table and yelled, "I wish only to negotiate with my equal. Since you are not in supreme command, I see no further necessity for my presence here."[19] As he stood up to leave, Wainwright tried to stop him. He said that, to prevent further bloodshed, he would assume command of all forces in the Philippines at the risk of reprimand from his government. Nakamura translated General Homma's response: he wasn't convinced. Homma got back into the Cadillac and left. Wainwright despaired: earlier that day they had lowered the Stars and Stripes and raised a white flag at Corregidor. Thousands of his men had already laid down their arms. If he couldn't broker a peaceful surrender, his troops would be massacred.

The next morning, May 7, after a fitful sleep, Wainwright was dressing when Colonel Haba entered his room. He was from Homma's headquarters and had come to discuss Wainwright's petition to terminate combat. With him was Lieutenant Susumu Nakamura, who would be translating. With his excellent comprehension of English, Nakamura was able to clarify the current situation and help orchestrate the formal surrender of all American and Philippine army troops in the Philippine Islands. Wainwright was relieved, although, to his chagrin, it included a radio broadcast of his instructions to his senior officers. (Decades later Setsuko saw a photo of the making of that broadcast, with a Japanese soldier she thought to be her brother sitting adjacent to Wainwright. His expression was not one of jubilation but almost one of compassion for this great warrior.) At 12:30 a.m. on May 8, 1942, Wainwright formally surrendered all American and Filipino troops. On June 9 he became a prisoner of war, eventually incarcerated in Manchuria, until Emperor Hirohito announced Japan's surrender on August 15, 1945.

Three months later the U.S. secretary of war announced plans to form an international tribunal to try Japanese war criminals. While awaiting trial, they were held at Sugamo Prison in Tokyo. Two thousand Japanese war criminals were incarcerated there during its operation. Wartime prime minister Hideki Tōjō, who had ordered the attack on Pearl Harbor, was one of the first to be convicted and hanged. General Homma was not far behind. He had perpetrated the Bataan Death March, in which sixty thousand Allied prisoners trudged sixty-two miles to a prisoner-of-war camp. More than five thousand had died along the way from starvation or illness. The "Beast of Bataan," as soldiers referred to Homma, was convicted of war crimes and executed by a firing squad on April 3, 1946.[20]

Susumu Nakamura had served under General Homma, so it was just a matter of time before he was summoned to Sugamo Prison. Although Susumu had been under Homma's direct command, he maintained that he had acted merely as his interpreter at the time the Allied forces surrendered the Philippines. Susumu was no war criminal, and he knew the best person to vouch for him—General Jonathan M. Wainwright. He likely had not forgotten that, in expediting acceptance of his surrender, Nakamura had helped prevent a massive slaughter of U.S. troops who had already laid down their arms. Wainwright contacted General MacArthur. The summons was revoked; lists of those reporting to the prison for judgment never included the name Susumu Nakamura.

Meanwhile, Benkichi and Shigeno had no word from their eldest daughter, Fumiko Takei, since before August 6. Then, unexpectedly, a large package arrived from the United States. Fumiko had located them. Fumiko, Norman, and their three children had been interned at Tule Lake Segregation Center in northern California since 1943. One morning, in early August 1945, Fumiko saw people running, shouting, and crying. They had just heard on contraband radios that Hiroshima had been destroyed by a powerful new bomb. On August 7 President Truman announced the over the airways, "Sixteen hours ago an American airplane dropped one bomb on Hiroshima. . . . That bomb had more power than 20,000 tons of T.N.T." The Japanese had started the war at Pearl Harbor, he continued, and had now been "repaid manyfold." He called it an "atomic bomb," which harnessed the basic power of the universe. "The force from which the sun draws its power," he concluded, "has been loosed against those who brought war to the Far East."[21]

Rumors circulated in the camp: tens of thousands had been killed by the blast or consumed by the fire that followed. Macabre reports of something called atomic-bomb plague, in which bodies seemed to disintegrate, made Fumiko shudder. She could obtain no information about her mother, father, brother, sisters, or cousins. Had any survived or had the Nakamura family been wiped out? If still alive, were they buried under rubble or suffering from ghastly burns with no one to relieve them? Had they succumbed to starvation or to the atomic-bomb plague? The uncertainty of her family's fate tormented her. Watching his anguished wife, Norman told her, "You've got to give yourself some peace. For your sake, for your own well-being, let's consider your parents at rest."[22]

Shortly thereafter they learned the emperor had surrendered, and the camp at Tule Lake was closing. With no money and few possessions, where would they go? That question was answered with a jolt. Because Fumiko had renounced her U.S. citizenship, she would be deported. Booked on a November 15 passage to Japan, she would be separated from her husband and children—perhaps forever. Just in time she heard about Wayne Collins, a San Francisco lawyer who took up the plight of Japanese Americans. He obtained a mitigation hearing for Fumiko, which suspended her deportation; his fight to restore her U.S. citizenship took years. On March 20, 1946, Fumiko and her three children left the wooden barracks and barbed-wire fences of Tule Lake Segregation Center behind and boarded a train for Los Angeles. Norman had preceded them. Even though strong anti-Japanese sentiment lingered in the city, they felt secure in a Mexican neighborhood in East Los Angeles, where they restarted their dry-cleaning business.

Once Fumiko learned that her parents, two sisters, and brother had survived, she began shipping care packages. Her son George, who later became a well-known actor on the television series *Star Trek*, recalled how he carried heavy parcels almost every week to the post office to ship to the grandparents, aunts, and uncles he had never met. These unexpected gifts—canned Spam, white rice, and Campbell's chicken noodle soup—delighted Setsuko. "You just had to add water to make a beautiful soup," she said. "My goodness, we were lucky to have that feast."[23]

Life in Hiroshima remained unbearable for most. Before long Benkichi was facing financial disaster. Everything had changed—the banks, savings, investments—in the face of rapid inflation. He called Susumu and several uncles to a family gathering to determine what to do about their financial situation. They had just one real asset—their land. Everything else had been destroyed. Their investments proved useless; they needed money. Benkichi had decided to sell their property in the city. Susumu opposed the idea: the land was their legacy; it had been in the family for four hundred years. He offered to help with their floundering finances. The relatives could not agree. Although according to the new constitution, all family members, including women, had equal rights, Benkichi still led the Nakamura family. "We are going to sell it," he decided. So that's what happened.[24] Benkichi and Shigeno's home had always been the center for family gatherings. Uncles, aunts, and cousins congregated there for birthdays, graduations, and weddings, all celebrated with lavish banquets. After "that day" it was never the same. "In a single moment," Setsuko said, "the blast of one atomic bomb completely tore to pieces the dynamic lives and the human dignity of my family."[25]

During the occupation Setsuko tried to remain optimistic. From time to time, however, a memory abruptly surfaced, exposing the great loss and pain. Rather than dwell on it, she tried to redirect her reflections: "I was happy that the war had ended," she said. "Peacetime came. The school opened, and at least some of us survived." One image did make her tear up, even decades later—the day she saw her father coming home in a surplus military uniform. Cold weather had set in, and he had no warm clothes; he had few clothes at all. The deputy mayor had contacted a former official in charge of an army warehouse and negotiated for the remainder of the military clothing to be released to citizens. When Setsuko saw her father, it stunned her. She had to catch her breath. The head of their family, he had been reduced to wearing a leftover military uniform. "I hated the very sight of it," she said. She looked again. His back was not bent; his head was not bowed; he did not shuffle. She saw a man with a strong, steely sense of himself. After all, "my father was of samurai blood," Setsuko said.[26]

8 Where Was God on August 6?

I believe in God,
even when he is silent.

–Unknown, from concentration camp after World War II

"Somebody's blood had splashed on my breast," recalled Keiko Hatta in her testimony to Jogakuin students. On August 6 the eighth grader had just started decoding in a barracks at the Second Army Headquarters when she saw a sharp flash and was hurled across the room. The first thing she spotted through the darkness was a classmate, Miss Nakayama, her mouth open in a silent scream, her front teeth shattered. Keiko's new schoolbag her mother had made lay near the front door, the shoulder strap ripped off. As she moved to retrieve it, a soldier called her to help with two other girls. Miss Kawamoto, crushed under the collapsed roof, was vomiting blood. Keiko dipped her handkerchief into a pool of water and placed it on her chest. She continued to retch. The second teen, Miss Yamaoka, did not seem to be in pain, Keiko noted, yet "her eyes, which used to be bright and charming, were vacant." Both died before sunset. The next day, Keiko said, she stepped over bodies and dodged smoldering fires, as she tried to reach her home in Hatsukaichi, ten miles away. "I caught my breath," she said, "at the sight of a baby crying 'Mommy! Mommy!' and shaking its mother who was burned black and already dead."[1]

Almost every student at Jogakuin had such searing memories. Upon return to the school, Setsuko and her classmates tried to bolster their spirits by reaffirming, "We are fortunate that we are here together again." Yet Keiko could not erase the memory of the child trying to awaken its dead mother. Setsuko could not expunge the stench of rotting flesh, which invaded her sense of smell at unanticipated moments. And she strived to check the recurring images of the bloodbath she had witnessed on the army training ground. "You can't be thinking of these things all the time," she told herself. She had always been optimistic, future oriented. The war had ended, and school had started. Yet in moments of reflection, flashbacks besieged her. As did her classmates, Setsuko desperately needed a balm for her troubled spirit. When Jogakuin's daily chapel services resumed, the teachers shared their experiences and how the scriptures influenced their thoughts and emotions. They used Bible studies to help students deal with their losses. A period of meditation after the service compelled Setsuko to contemplate a number of questions: "Why did this happen to me? What kind of future will I have? Will I have a future?" Looking inward, she found no answers.[2]

Some aspects of the occupation had improved their lives, in particular educational reform and the introduction of women's rights; others impeded their psychological recovery. That was the case with the press code. *Nippon News* and *Asahi Shimbun* had been censored, and the distribution of any unfavorable publications was restricted. General Douglas MacArthur denied that John Hersey's 1946 book, *Hiroshima,* a harrowing account of six people who had lived through the atomic bombing, had been banned in Japan; however, the Japanese translation wasn't published until forty months after that fateful day, and the number of copies was limited.[3] By suppressing public discussion of the atomic bombs and collective expressions of bereavement, the occupation authorities hampered the public's efforts to come to terms with their traumatic ordeal. Setsuko heard that authorities had confiscated survivors' diaries, photographs of injured family members, and haikus written, she said, "to ease the pain in their hearts."[4] Years later she charged that survivors had been deprived of the normal grieving process, so crucial for recovery. They had to repress their anguish in silence and isolation. Although some survivors expressed hatred toward Americans, it did not dominate public sentiment.

The Atomic Bomb Casualty Commission (ABCC), established in Hiroshima per President Harry Truman's directive, inadvertently added another impediment to survivors' psychological healing. Scientists did not know the immediate and long-term effects of massive radiation doses on the human body or on the offspring of those exposed. Now they had the chance to find out. Three weeks after the bombing of Hiroshima, a colonel in the U.S. Medical Corps sent a memorandum to Brigadier General Guy Denit, chief surgeon of the Pacific. "A study of the effects of the two atomic bombs used in Japan is of vital importance to our country," he wrote. "This unique opportunity may not again be offered until another world war."[5] With thousands of radiation-exposed individuals at their disposal, the ABCC team proposed to study visual disturbances, developmental disorders, alterations in life span, and incidences of cancer, sterility, and genetic abnormalities in their progeny.

Hiroshima residents reacted with measured enthusiasm when the ABCC team first arrived. Medical assistance had been inadequate due to a severe shortage of Japanese doctors, nurses, hospitals, and medications. Finally, they thought, the occupation authorities had heard their plea. When the ABCC initiated its activities in March 1947, survivors soon realized that it had not been established to provide health care. "You had the strange spectacle," wrote Norman Cousins, editor in chief of *Saturday Review of Literature*, after a visit to Hiroshima, "of a man suffering from radioactive sickness getting thousands of dollars' worth of analysis but not one cent of treatment from the Commission."[6] Disappointment turned to bitterness. Nonetheless, because of occupation policies, the public had to repress their outrage at being treated as guinea pigs twice—first as a target of the bomb and second as subjects for research.

Although Setsuko had not been selected as a human subject by the ABCC, she knew many who had. The medical team sent a car to schools to round up subjects for their appointments. Setsuko heard that at one boys' school a student lookout announced when the ABCC station wagon was approaching. Students on the research list disappeared, hiding until given the all clear. The girls were not as courageous or mischievous. No one talked about what happened at those visits. So Setsuko didn't learn until much later what Koko Tanimoto, the daughter of her minister, Reverend Kiyoshi Tanimoto, had faced as a teen: "The doctor told me to go up the stage, but the spotlight was so strong I could not see how many people inside," she said. "I could hear all the different languages so I could guess, 'Oh, this must be the doctors' meeting.' Then the doctor said, 'Please take off your gown.' Puberty age. Your body changes from childhood to adult woman. I was so furious. . . . I didn't start that war. Why do I have to show almost naked body to the people." Koko obeyed and stood in the glaring light. Tears ran down her cheeks. She felt such humiliation that she could not tell her parents or her friends. "It's something deep inside for a long time," she later revealed.[7] Her story infuriated Setsuko: How could people recover from their emotional trauma while being subjected to such demeaning behavior?

Initially the ABCC carried out its studies in a few rooms at the Hiroshima Red Cross Hospital. Before long a medical officer met with Mayor Shinzo Hamai to discuss relocating the project. When the mayor offered a suitable central site, the officer declined; typhoons could flood the area, he said. Besides, he informed Hamai, they had already chosen a site atop Hijiyama Hill. The mayor told him that it was considered a sacred site: it contained a military cemetery and an emperor's memorial. The official was not asking for a recommendation or seeking approval; he was delivering a notification. Before long the people of Hiroshima found their favorite place to celebrate the Cherry Blossom Festival fenced off and the Japanese military cemetery covered with Quonset huts. "Located at the top of the tallest hill in the middle of the city," a historian wrote, the facility "was a constant, conspicuous reminder of Japan's defeat."[8] Poet Sadako Kurihara, a later mentor and friend to Setsuko Nakamura, expressed the sentiment of many:

Hijiyama, filled
with all our many dreams!
American ABCC atomic research station
towering there!
American scientists
beside the cool and gleaming instruments inside,
stripping us, taking pictures of our keloids,
compiling our case histories!
As you measure
with care
the scars of the atomic bomb
your country dropped

> and record the number of white corpuscles it destroyed,
> you feel no pain at all.[9]

In the end the ABCC studied 120,000 subjects over almost three decades. Although the commission made valuable scientific observations, it conducted no substantial research on the psychological state of survivors.

The authorities may have suppressed survivors' recollections of their ordeal, yet they were reminded of it every day. One of Setsuko's best friends, Setsuko Muramoto, continued to wear an air-raid bonnet to cover her baldness. She had been assigned to demolition in the city center on August 6. After the explosion a water pipe burst, and she and her workgroup found themselves stuck in a large pool of mud. An unquenchable thirst drove them to drink the muddy water. Their math teacher, Miss Yonehara, tried to organize them. "Come," she called out. "Let's be together." Those able to move inched through the sludge. Miss Yonehara formed a circle and led them in singing, "Nearer, My God, to Thee." Their faint voices became dimmer and dimmer. One by one they ceased. "Those of you who can walk, let's go to the Red Cross Hospital and see what help we can get," Miss Yonehara said. "If you have trouble balancing, hold onto my shoulder."[10] So Muramoto reached out and touched her teacher's shoulder. To her dismay the flesh slid off, revealing bare bone beneath. When the dwindling group reached the hospital, they found no available space. Miss Yonehara lay down on the ground and died.

Suffering from the acute effects of radiation, Setsuko Muramoto missed a day of school, then another. Before long A-bomb poisoning took her life. Even though the authorities denied that horrendous consequence of radiation exposure initially, the girls at Jogakuin knew. Many not only suffered from it themselves, as had Setsuko Nakamura, but also watched family members and classmates succumb to the illness.

Jogakuin's chaplain recognized the need for the girls to share their grief with others, and what followed provided among the most restorative actions conceived of by the school. After chapel, the girls could participate in small support groups. At first tentative, the girls began to relate their experiences and disclose their nightmares. One story particularly touched Setsuko—that of Fumiko Sasaki. She had been working in a different part of the Army Headquarters complex on August 6. "A sea of flames" and "the smell of blood": those were her first recollections when she regained consciousness. She told how she watched two friends die from internal bleeding in what she called "a terrible hell-like scene beyond description." The next day she set out to find her home, located near the Fukuya Department Store, not far from the Aioi Bridge. She lost her bearings until she spotted remains of the store. As she stood in a pile of ash which once had been her home, she could barely grasp what she saw: "Four dead bodies were lying there like baked potatoes," she recalled. Everyone in her family had died. "My tears dried out at that actual sight," Fumiko said. She had no idea how to live without them. "If my parents were alive and saw me not shedding tears for their deaths, they might be grieved at having a cold-hearted daughter."[11]

Numbness—that was what Setsuko had experienced as well. As she watched her dear sister and four-year-old nephew's cremations, she admitted, "I didn't even shed tears. What kind of human being am I?" Once she heard classmates tell similar stories, she stopped berating herself. "If we had responded normally," she later reasoned, "we would not have survived." At last she could forgive herself. "I wasn't such a horrible human being after all," she concluded.[12] She had lost nine family members and never cried. Relating that to others helped unburden her. Increasingly, she viewed herself as a survivor, not a victim.

Those conversations also dispelled the notion that she or they had been saved for a reason. Some people asserted, "Setsuko, you are alive. God saved you because you have a big job to do." Having discussed this onus in the inviolable sanctity of Jogakuin's chapel, she could reply, "No. God did not save me. If you say that, then God chose not to help the other people who were killed. That is blasphemy. I just happened to live. A few centimeters away from me, another person died."[13] For the girls at Jogakuin, sharing their grief generated a solidarity with those who had endured similar anguish and in doing so helped mend the bruises in their hearts and the lacerations of their souls.

In the summer of 1947, construction began on a new Hiroshima Jogakuin High School at its original downtown site. Its building may have been destroyed, but Jogakuin's essence remained unchanged. Founded by Reverend Sadakichi Sunamoto after his travels to the United States and led by Methodist missionary Nannie Gaines as its first principal, Jogakuin never wavered from its original goal of educating young women while instilling concern for the community. The development of individual independence and compassion underlay the curriculum.[14] The former was already embedded in Setsuko's character; the latter took longer to blossom.

"I felt like I was breathing fresh post-war air deep into my lungs," Setsuko recalled thinking when she entered high school.[15] She learned to read and speak English and excelled in all her studies. She initiated the publication of the school's first newspaper, *Hiroshima Jogakuin Koko Shimbun*. And, as president of the school's Young Women's Christian Association (YWCA) chapter, the largest student organization at Jogakuin, Setsuko helped provide community support such as aiding orphans and collecting money for those overwhelmed by another typhoon. She worked with YWCA national leaders from Tokyo to organize the first western Japan YWCA conference, where representatives from other Christian schools gathered in Hiroshima to debate their obligations: As Christians, what special responsibilities do we have? As atomic bomb survivors, what unique duties should we perform?

Although Setsuko considered her high school years the best of her life, she still struggled with her spirituality. During her childhood, her mother, a devout Buddhist, had a significant moral influence. Together they knelt at the Buddhist alcove every morning and offered food to the dead souls of relatives. She attended the Buddhist temple, recited sutras, and learned about the Four Noble Truths, the basis of Buddhism. The First Truth is that suffering, pain, and misery exist in life. Her parents' acceptance of that principle likely helped them endure their tremendous losses with grace. At Jogakuin the virtues nurtured by her mother gained an additional spiritual perspective, a Christian perspective. Still, Setsuko grappled with a number of questions: How could a God of love let Hiroshima be destroyed? How could America as a Christian country commit such an inhumane act?[16] She wasn't challenging God's existence, as did many, subsequent to the horrors of World War II; nevertheless, she sought answers. She needed to know. Then she met Reverend Kiyoshi Tanimoto.

Born into a Buddhist family in 1909, Kiyoshi Tanimoto was the seventh of eight children. When he joined the Methodist Church at age seventeen, his father disowned him. Tanimoto studied Christianity at Kwansei Gakuin University, after which he received a scholarship to attend Emory University in Atlanta, Georgia, earning a master of divinity degree. He returned to Japan, and in 1943 he was appointed minister of the Nagarekawa Methodist Church of Christ in Hiroshima. There the Japanese military police checked the substance of his every sermon.

On August 6, 1945, Tanimoto had been helping a friend move some belongings to the outskirts of Hiroshima in anticipation of firebombing by U.S. forces when he heard a deafening blast. He rushed back into the city to find his wife, Chisa, and infant daughter, Koko, unharmed; his wife had dug them out from under the parsonage's wreckage. All that remained of his stately Gothic church were slabs of reinforced concrete. Tanimoto spent the next five days trying to rescue people trapped under debris and ministering to the dying. For weeks he helped set up aid centers for the wounded and shelters for orphans; he pushed a cart through the devastated city, handing out food, until radiation sickness confined him to bed for two months. He later became a central character in John Hersey's *Hiroshima*.[17]

Reverend Tanimoto often spoke at Jogakuin. He was easy to recognize: youthful in appearance, he wore his hair longer than most men, parted in the middle. His ready smile made him approachable. Setsuko became enthralled by this humble, caring minister in his midthirties, a superb teacher and orator with boundless energy. She began to attend the partially restored Nagarekawa church, regarding him as her spiritual leader.

In the chaos that followed August 6, Setsuko felt she desperately needed to find God. Under Reverend Tanimoto's tutelage, she realized that God had already found her. Through prayer she could ask for the strength to persevere and for the courage to move forward with hope. On December 19, 1948, Setsuko Nakamura, along with thirty other girls, was baptized at the Nagarekawa church. She needed more than faith alone, however. Reverend Tanimoto preached that faith must be demonstrated through love and action. Setsuko had received a balm for her wounded soul. Now she committed herself to using that strength to help others—a journey that would continue for the rest of her life.

9 Born to Serve

> As Hiroshima became more and more just another large city, so the gulf that separated the survivors of the bomb . . . from the world in which they lived grew wider and wider. The houses and streets might be rebuilt, but they remained ruins, human ruins.
>
> –Robert Jungk, *Children of the Ashes: Story of a Rebirth*

"Alive" and "vital": that's how Norman Cousins, editor in chief of the *Saturday Review of Literature,* described Hiroshima on his September 1949 visit. Four years after its near total destruction, a revived Hiroshima was emerging from the rubble. He applauded plans already underway to reconstruct it as one of the world's most beautiful cities. The population had doubled after the bomb, from 136,000 to 278,600. Cousins wondered what beckoned back those who had fled the devastation. When he observed young baseball players singing on their way to a game, children laughing in a schoolyard, or the lively step of young adults, he concluded that the determination not just to survive but also to thrive had revitalized them.[1]

Not everyone sang or laughed or stepped lively, however—not those living under a sheet of canvas propped up by a piece of wood; not orphans scrambling like seagulls for a scrap of stale bread; not those deformed beyond recognition by the bomb, hiding in the shadows; and not the thousands of survivors who faced prolonged, unanticipated inequity. "The flash burned out the city, blew away buildings, filled seven rivers with corpses, scorched the very soul of those who survived," wrote poet Sadako Kurihara. "But it didn't destroy discrimination."[2]

The number of A-bomb orphans in Hiroshima now exceeded six thousand. The War Orphans Home had been filled to capacity the moment it opened. Despite efforts from priests and teachers, thousands of teenagers, even young children, lived on the streets near Hiroshima Station, begging or pickpocketing, forgotten by society. Also visible were youngsters with noticeably small heads—microcephaly—a sad consequence of radiation exposure while still in the womb. Pregnancies among women within a mile of the hypocenter often terminated in miscarriages or stillbirths. Of those fetuses who did survive, almost a quarter had microcephaly, with resultant mental and physical disabilities. Their appearance gave rise to the public opinion that those exposed to the bomb might carry genetic defects that could be passed on to their offspring. Marriage bureaus considered them unacceptable as prospective brides or grooms. "It was feared that they might father, or give birth to, deformed children," historian and peace activist Robert Jungk pointed out.[3]

Setsuko Nakamura became increasingly aware of this social alienation and discrimination. She heard people from outside affected areas of the city say, "Those survivors are a lazy bunch. They are always tired and sick. We should avoid hiring them."[4] Some referred to them as "atomic cripples"; others thought radiation effects were contagious.[5] Setsuko found it disturbing that the national government not only failed to provide assistance but also neglected to counter these misconceptions. Atomic-bomb survivors felt abandoned.

For the most part, public reaction ranged from ambivalence to antipathy. It wasn't until 1950 that these survivors were categorized as *hibakusha*, meaning "explosion-affected individuals."[6] Hibakusha tried to hide their identity; they no longer admitted exposure to radiation, no longer talked about their harrowing experiences, and thus no longer received consolation from others. Nevertheless, hiding was almost impossible for those marred by keloids. Several months following flash and thermal burns, unsightly pink, rubbery, heaped-up scars replaced scorched skin. When a scar contracted, it created disfigurement: a chin attached to the chest wall, hands transformed into claws. After attempted surgical resection, keloids often recurred, even worsened. Those so afflicted were barred from public baths. People recoiled as they passed these disfigured hibakusha in the street; children shrieked. At medical clinics, patients sat across the waiting area from those marked by keloids, worried they might be transmitted by bodily contact. "Keloids had the segregating power of leprosy," observed one historian.[7]

"I hated for people to stare at me," fourteen-year-old Shiro Nakayama wrote. "I secluded myself at home and spent hours before the mirror looking at my own face. What I saw was ugly hunks of flesh, like lava oozing from a crater wall, covering the left half of my face, with the eyebrow burned off and my eye and lips pulled out of shape."[8] Hibakusha afflicted by keloids shied away from attending school and church activities and visiting family. They sought night jobs to avoid humiliation. Treated like untouchables, they disappeared from society, which resulted in more isolation and overwhelming loneliness. Neighbors whispered about suicides.

Just as hibakusha were starting to recover from or adjust to their injuries, a new specter arose. A twenty-seven-year-old soldier who had survived burns over most of his exposed skin developed leukemia. Before long, more young people, including one of Setsuko's classmates, were dying from this previously rare form of cancer. Those exposed to as little as one hundred rads of radiation appeared susceptible to this malignant transformation of bone marrow cells. No effective treatment was available, and in a brief period victims succumbed to infection or bleeding. Although the peak number of deaths from leukemia would pass after the mid-1950s, the chance of developing another type of cancer—breast, thyroid, or lung—began to rise, creating a threat that hung over hibakusha for life.[9] Setsuko considered herself fortunate to have been spared—at least for now.

In the fall of 1950, Setsuko entered the college of Hiroshima Jogakuin, the first private women's college in the Hiroshima Prefecture. Destroyed on August 6, it was rebuilt in the hills of Ushita, north of the city center. The college's stated mission, similar to that of the Hiroshima Jogakuin high school, emphasized what Setsuko would gain from her education: mastery of knowledge and skills for her chosen career and a fostering of her desire to serve others. Its president, Dr. Hamako Hirose, born in rural Japan, had been selected to study at Hiroshima High School at the turn of the century. She went on to receive bachelor's and master's degrees in America. After the war she studied at Columbia University in New York. When asked to lead Hiroshima Jogakuin, she persuaded an outstanding educator and missionary, Katharine Johnson, whom she had met at Columbia, to join her as vice president. Soon after Johnson arrived in Hiroshima, she wrote to friends, "Can you imagine a school with 1,700 students that has grown up from scratch in six years?"[10] Johnson taught American and English literature, with an emphasis on the portrayal of historical events. Setsuko thought her brilliant and found her course transformative. The influence of European immigration, transcendentalism, the restoration movement, spiritualism, and other social movements fascinated her. She called school a "sheer joy."[11]

As Setsuko began her second academic year, the Japanese delegation signed the Treaty of San Francisco, and Japan regained its sovereignty. On April 28, 1952, she and her classmates rejoiced when the Allied occupation ended. They felt emboldened. Setsuko continued to participate in the YWCA, collaborating with the Young Men's Christian Association (YMCA) at the University of Hiroshima, an all-men's college. As she evolved from a tomboy to an attractive young woman dressed in Western fashion, male students began to notice her. Whether she was collecting donations for flood victims or circulating disarmament petitions, they couldn't help recognizing how resourceful and outspoken she was.

Through the YMCA Setsuko met Ichiro Moritaki, a philosophy professor at Hiroshima University, who had lost his left eye on August 6. He wasn't an armchair philosopher, she was quick to appreciate; he spoke about the nuclear age at public events, emphasizing that they should not consider the suffering as limited to Hiroshima and Nagasaki. This was a global issue, related to all of humanity, and it would continue into the future. As she worked with Professor Moritaki, Setsuko got drawn into Hiroshima's fledgling antinuclear movement.

On July 1, 1946, the United States conducted its first postwar nuclear test, followed by four more over the next couple of years. Then, on August 29, 1949, the Soviet Union tested its first atomic bomb. President Truman ordered the production of an even deadlier weapon—a hydrogen bomb. A race appeared to have commenced. In response the World Peace Council issued the Stockholm Appeal in March 1950, which read, "We demand the outlawing of atomic weapons as instruments of intimidation and mass murder of peoples. We demand strict international control to enforce this measure. We believe that any government which first uses atomic weapons against any other country whatsoever will be committing a crime against humanity and should be dealt with as a war criminal."[12] The U.S. secretary of state, Dean Acheson, dismissed the Stockholm Appeal; he called it a piece of Soviet propaganda. Three months later war broke out in Korea.

Initially part of the Japanese Empire, Korea had been divided in half along the thirty-eighth parallel between the Soviet Union and the United States at the end of World War II. On June 25, 1950, the Soviet-backed North Korean People's Army invaded the pro-Western Republic of Korea. "If we let Korea down," President Truman stated as he deployed troops, "the Soviet[s] will keep right on going and swallow up one [place] after another."[13] Throughout the Korean War, many Japanese feared that the U.S. president might once again employ nuclear weapons. Meanwhile, on October 3, 1952, the United Kingdom became the third nuclear power, when it tested a plutonium bomb in the Montebello Islands off the coast of western Australia. That November the United States detonated the first hydrogen bomb in the Marshall Islands. The Korean War ended in a stalemate on July 27, 1953, leaving almost five million dead, even without nuclear weapons.

Just as Setsuko began her final year of college at Hiroshima Jogakuin, the Soviet Union tested its first hydrogen bomb. Seven months later, on March 2, 1954, a front-page headline in *Mainichi Shimbun* read, "US Experiment of Atomic Explosion at Bikini Atoll."[14] The head of the Atomic Energy Commission (AEC) reported that the United States had detonated the largest hydrogen bomb to date on Bikini Atoll in the Marshall Islands, the first in a series of nuclear-weapon tests under the code name Castle Bravo. Over the next two weeks, the Japanese press reported more details: "Radioactive Dust Hits 264 at Test," read the *Nippon Times*.[15] Relocated at what was thought a safe distance from the blast, 28 U.S. observers and 236 island natives were showered with radioactive particles. According to the *New York Times*, the AEC stated that none of the natives had been harmed, yet Pacific Islanders sustained burns and experienced hair loss, headaches, vomiting, and diarrhea. The natives on Bikini had been asked to leave their home temporarily "for the good of mankind," but their island would remain uninhabitable in perpetuity.[16]

Scientists calculated the bomb's power to be a thousand times that dropped on Hiroshima. A mushroom cloud shot up ninety thousand feet into the stratosphere, with a fireball at least four miles in diameter. Fallout, as radioactive particles were now called, covered seven thousand square miles. In a news conference, President Dwight D. Eisenhower said the blast force surprised the atomic scientists, leading the AEC to reclassify the test as a "misfire."[17] What shocked Japanese citizens even more was the report that twenty-three Japanese fisherman had suffered radiation burns from the blast. "Why must Japanese fishermen operating on the high seas suffer from the U.S. atomic testing?" many asked. The story of *Daigo Fukuryū Maru* (*Lucky Dragon No. 5*) slowly unfolded.[18]

The tuna trawler with its crew, composed mostly of men in their teens and twenties, had left the port of Yaizu, 125 miles southwest of Tokyo, on January 22, 1954, headed for Midway Island. They found the catch poor and proceeded to the Marshall Islands, reaching the area at the end of February. There they found a large school of tuna. They let out their trawls and retired for the night. At dawn on March 1, a flash of light just above the horizon startled them; the sky glowed an orange color. Several minutes later a thunderous explosion shook the *Lucky Dragon*. No one suffered injuries. Anxious to leave, they began hauling in their catch. Several hours later a white dust showered down on them, covering their heads, arms, and chests, as well as the tuna. They finished the job and headed back to port, still oblivious as to what had befallen them.

Upon their return crew members reported feeling nauseated. Four days later their skin darkened, and blisters broke out on their scalps and ears and under their fingernails. When the shipowner welcomed them back on March 14, he told the men what had happened and suggested that they might have the atomic-bomb illness. Nine required hospitalization. Three days later, when nuclear experts set out to examine the 156-ton trawler, Geiger counters started buzzing within twenty yards of the ship. They found the entire catch contaminated with radioactivity. "The scientists said there was enough radioactive substance in each fish to cause death if a person stood within one foot of the fish longer than an hour," reported the *Nippon Times*.[19]

Authorities ordered tuna from the *Lucky Dragon* buried. The directive came too late; much of the cargo had already been shipped to markets in Tokyo and other cities. And this wasn't the only tainted fish. Several boats tested positive for radioactive tuna and shark. "Another JAP Boat Hit by H-Bomb Ash," reported the *Chicago Daily Tribune*.[20] When Japanese citizens learned of the radioactive contamination, panic ensued. Fish was a mainstay of their diet. At Tokyo's Waseda University, thirty professors and staff had eaten what was now called "atomic tuna" before the news broke.[21] A businessman said he was alarmed to learn his wife had fed him tuna for breakfast. It had been marked down to a special bargain price, she told him.[22] As far away as Fukui on the west coast, at least six hundred people were thought to have eaten radioactive fish. Authorities posted warnings about the dangers of consuming sushi or sashimi throughout Japan. Overnight the sales of tuna declined by 40 percent, with an estimated loss of two hundred million yen.[23] Anger erupted. Members of the Diet urged the Japanese government to bring the case before the International Court of Justice at The Hague.[24] U.S. officials tried to shift blame: the *Lucky Dragon* must have wandered inside the designated danger zone. Atomic Energy Commission chair Lewis Strauss alleged that the crew had been spying for Russia.[25] Both had received inaccurate information. The fishing boat had been at least ten miles outside the restricted area.

The director of the Atomic Bomb Casualty Commission (ABCC) offered to treat the twenty-three fisherman from the *Lucky Dragon* at the facility on Hijiyama Hill, provoking further outrage. Since hibakusha had been told that the ABCC did not have the facilities to provide health care, they concluded that the commission must be planning to use these fishermen as guinea pigs, just as they had been used. For far too long, the rest of the country had remained uninformed about the impact of radioactivity on the health of the public. Now that the fish supply had been contaminated, affecting their daily lives, Japan's antinuclear movement seemed to erupt overnight, started by housewives in Tokyo who circulated a petition protesting U.S. nuclear-weapons tests.

In the summer of 1954, Setsuko would graduate from Hiroshima Jogakuin. Then what? Most of her classmates planned to wed eventually. Having eschewed an arranged marriage, Setsuko set out to determine her lifework. She enjoyed writing and found journalism fascinating. Her father suggested she study law; her mother thought education a noble profession. Setsuko appreciated how they encouraged her to become more than just a good wife and mother—quite progressive for the times. She resolved to pursue a career, to make a difference. The caption under her picture in the high school yearbook had read, "Nakamura, Setsuko. Ambition is her middle name."[26]

"What do you want to do in life?" Dr. Hirose, the college president, asked her.[27] Setsuko didn't know. As she pondered her future, she was drawn to the kind of selfless public service she had witnessed during the rebuilding of Hiroshima. The American Friends Service Committee had been among the first to help, by sending relief supplies called peace boxes. Setsuko remembered how the Quakers asked the people of Hiroshima to forgive them for their government's grave mistake. Floyd Schmoe, a botanist at the University of Washington in Seattle, while in charge of an internment camp for Japanese Americans, had developed great respect for them. When he learned that many hibakusha lived in air-raid shelters or shanties made from bits of rubble, this white-haired professor collected donations and traveled with a group of Quakers to Hiroshima, where they constructed forty Japanese-style single and multifamily homes.

Likewise, Setsuko admired Shinzo Hamai, the enterprising midlevel municipal worker who had secured food, water, and clothing for survivors in the days and weeks following August 6. He became the first popularly elected mayor of Hiroshima and set out to rebuild the city. His Hiroshima Declaration of Peace, read on the third anniversary of the bombing, inspired many and resonated with Setsuko. "The new Japan, to which we now belong, declares in its constitution, the renunciation of war," he said. "Aspiring sincerely to an international peace based on justice and order, the Japanese people . . . pledge our national honor to reach these high ideals."[28] Furthermore, he led the effort to have Hiroshima designated a "city of peace." A five-year reconstruction plan included the iconic Memorial Peace Park. Near its center was erected a cenotaph, an ancient arch-shaped house to protect the souls of those who had died from the atomic bomb. A stone chest beneath the arch held a registry of their names, regardless of nationality. "Let all the souls here rest in peace," read the inscription on the cenotaph, "for we [meaning all humanity] shall not repeat the evil."[29]

Reverend Kiyoshi Tanimoto had been a guiding light for Setsuko since she began to attend the Nagarekawa church. Noting her English fluency, Reverend Tanimoto asked Setsuko to serve as an interpreter for foreign visitors, among them Norman Cousins, editor in chief of the *Saturday Review of Literature*. Cousins had toured the four available orphanages on his first visit to Hiroshima. Impressed with the level of care, he was troubled that so few children could be accommodated. He thought many concerned Americans would be willing to adopt an atomic-bomb orphan, but the Immigration Act of 1924 prohibited legal adoption of Japanese children. Not dissuaded, he conceived of "moral adoptions," a program whereby Americans would become unofficial foster parents and send $2.25 each month to support the child. Cousins wrote an article in the *Saturday Review of Literature* titled "Hiroshima: Four Years Later," in which he encouraged readers to adopt orphans.[30] When asked about the rapid, favorable response, he said, "The campaign might be called an act of atonement by citizens for the mistake their government committed."[31] Helen Keller further inspired the public when she became a foster parent. To coordinate adoptions Cousins established the U.S. Hiroshima Peace Center Association, whose esteemed directors included Pearl Buck, prior winner of a Nobel Prize in Literature; and John Hersey, author of *Hiroshima*.

Adoptive parents received a photograph and profile of the child. Letters, birthday cards, and holiday gifts followed. Clothes, shoes, baseballs, dolls, and candy delighted the adoptees. For those orphans who had no American parent, however, the gifts and letters received by others made them feel rejected and underscored their own loneliness. Although four hundred moral adoptions ensued, they reached just a fraction of the total number who had lost their families. A 1954 survey found an estimated 1,800 orphans in Hiroshima primary or middle schools and another 1,300 living outside the city. The fate of the other 3,000 remained unknown.[32] "The orphans who starved to death," recalled one who had survived, "were merely registered as 'missing.'"[33]

Setsuko also watched Reverend Tanimoto reach out to the most neglected hibakusha—young women disfigured by keloids. Shunned by society, with no hope of marriage and no means to support themselves financially, they remained out of the public's view. Reverend Tanimoto started a Bible class for these women called the Society of Keloid Girls. He bought sewing machines, opened a dressmaking workshop, and encouraged Setsuko and other girls from the church to invite them to social events. Although he offered them camaraderie and purpose, above all they needed reconstruction of their deformed faces and limbs. When the ABCC and the city government rejected his requests to fund plastic surgery, he appealed to Norman Cousins for help. In 1951, when Cousins and his wife came to Hiroshima to deliver some moral-adoption funds, Tanimoto introduced them to members of the Society of Keloid Girls. Touched by their plight, Cousins enlisted the help of plastic surgeons at Mount Sinai and Beth Israel Hospitals, and Tanimoto accompanied twenty-five young women, the "Hiroshima maidens," to New York City, where their lives were transformed by the reconstructive surgery.[34]

Setsuko revered these individuals: Floyd Schmoe, Mayor Hamai, Reverend Tanimoto, and Norman Cousins. She aspired to make a difference in her community as had they. Her mother stressed her duty to help those in need; Hiroshima Jogakuin's mission included preparing young women for serving others. And thanks to Reverend Tanimoto, Setsuko could quote James 2 by heart: "What good is it, my brothers, if someone says he has faith but does not have works?"[35]

"What do you want to do in life?" Dr. Hirose asked Setsuko again as she neared graduation. Now Setsuko could answer: "I want to be a helping person." She felt she had been born to serve. President Hirose suggested Setsuko pursue a career in social work. Furthermore, she should consider studying in the United States, with its advanced professional preparation. Just such an opportunity had presented itself in the fall of 1952, when the World Federalist Conference was held in Hiroshima. Setsuko, having volunteered as an interpreter, assisted Dr. Joseph Hunter, a professor of religious studies at Lynchburg College in Virginia. As they talked about the aftermath of the atomic bombing and the growing antinuclear movement, Dr. Hunter was impressed with Setsuko's passion and clarity of expression. He suggested that, after graduating from Hiroshima Jogakuin, she should come to Lynchburg College for further studies. Anticipating that she could open the minds of students and educators with regard to nuclear weapons, he arranged a scholarship for her. President Hirose encouraged her to accept it. "You know, the times have changed," she said. "Women can do important things; we need to help women in this city. Go learn about group work. Then come back and provide leadership for women in Hiroshima."[36] Setsuko faced a difficult decision, however. She had fallen in love.

10 Falling in Love in Bibai

> What greater thing is there for two human souls, than to feel they are joined for life—to strengthen each other in all labor, to rest on each other in all sorrow.
>
> –George Eliot, *Adam Bede*

In the summer before her senior year of college, Setsuko and two friends had planned to combine travel and volunteer services. They applied to work at a Christian camp on Hokkaido, the northernmost of Japan's main islands, known for its *onsen* (natural hot springs) and cooler summer weather. Every year the National Council of Churches sponsored International Christian Work Camps, in which university students and teachers from around the world came together for two months to help communities with specific needs. Separated from her friends, Setsuko was assigned to a camp in Bibai, a coal-mining town located northeast of Sapporo. The National Council of Churches had assessed the unmet social needs in Bibai and determined that, although the new constitution encouraged labor unions, the coal miners still felt exploited by capitalists. They requested a community center for labor-union members to gather, as well as a place for children's after-school activities. That's what the volunteer group would build. At the same time, they would learn how to work with a community of miners and farmers.

Bibai was a somewhat desolate town, its name derived from a word for swamp. Half of the summer days were overcast, making everything look gray. Thirty men and women volunteers shared space in a Shinto shrine, where they slept on foam rubber mats. The schedule proved hard: they worked at the building site during the day, in addition to performing other tasks such as bussing tables, cleaning bathrooms, and doing laundry. In the evenings they met with townspeople, after which they had lengthy discussions on their own searches for meaningful, productive lives.

When Setsuko entered the camp's dining area a couple of days after most of the volunteers had arrived, heads turned to see a petite, pretty, young woman, in a sleek, checkered sheath. Curls peeked from under her red cap, which matched her lipstick. She smiled broadly. "Well, a new arrival," thought Canadian teacher James Thurlow. "Camp is looking more interesting."[1] Jim was delighted to learn he had been assigned to kitchen duty with this captivating newcomer. As he and Setsuko cooked and washed dishes together, Jim appreciated her near-constant conversation, her fluency in English, and her good humor and spirit.

Setsuko had never met a Canadian and asked numerous questions about his life. She learned Jim was born on December 20, 1928, in Edmonton, Alberta, after which his family moved to Saint Thomas, near Toronto. His father was a railroad engineer. His mother, a missionary's daughter, had grown up on the prairies and taught Blackfoot children in a one-room schoolhouse. She now taught at Alma College in Saint Thomas. His younger brother, Jack, completed this close-knit family. Jim had studied at the University of Western Ontario and at the University of Toronto. In 1952 he had responded to a call from the United Church of Canada to go to Nishinomiya, Japan, to teach English to junior high students, followed by a commitment to teach history at Kwansei Gakuin University. This experience changed his perspective from a traditional, Western-focused view to a broader, deeper world view. When Jim learned that Setsuko was a hibakusha from Hiroshima, he gently asked about her story, amazed at her seeming lack of anger or self-pity.

A coal-mining town did not offer an idyllic setting for a courtship. "At first, I didn't see him as a love object," Setsuko recalled.[2] He was nice-enough looking, slender and taller than most Japanese men; she just reached up to his shoulders. He was gentle and somewhat reserved, a grown man with a career; she was still a college student. Before long, however, a romance blossomed over a hot stove and dirty dishes. Setsuko had never met a man like Jim, and he discovered Setsuko to be quite different from the traditional Japanese female. Jim found himself drawn out by this perceptive, committed young woman, who seemed to sparkle with energy when she talked. Setsuko found herself drawn in by this passionate man who held strong convictions about unfair labor practices, racial discrimination, denial of human rights, and the status of women, yet maintained a calm temperament.

They had grown up almost seven thousand miles apart. Canada had played a central role in developing the atomic bomb, having refined and supplied uranium for the Manhattan Project; Setsuko's world had been blown apart by that bomb. Nevertheless, they shared Christian beliefs, a strong work ethic, and an intense determination to remedy social injustice. And they had a similar sense of humor, laughing over their good fortune at being assigned to KP (kitchen police) duty, which both preferred to cleaning toilets. Setsuko noticed how Jim undertook cooking and scrubbing dishes with ease. That's how she learned more about his mother: Jean Thurlow was working toward a PhD in psychology as she raised two sons. After dinner, while she studied, her sons cleared the table and washed the dishes—quite different from the Japanese custom. Jim had grown up respecting his mother, her career, and, as an extension, women's role in society.

Jim and Setsuko had almost no private time together. During the day Setsuko carried lumber and bags of cement; Jim pounded nails and mixed the cement. Years later she still blushed when she remembered how he stripped off his shirt when he started to perspire. He likely had trouble concentrating on his work as Setsuko stood by in her shorts and sleeveless blouse. They did manage to eat most meals together. In that coal-mining town in northern Japan, what may have started as a flirtation was evolving into an attachment.

Setsuko had met several interesting young Japanese men, none of whom she could imagine marrying. Her primary introduction to romance came from watching *Gone with the Wind* several times in high school. Public displays of affection between members of the opposite sex—hand-holding, hugging, and kissing—were considered rude in Japan. Yet a photo from the time showed Setsuko and Jim with fingers entwined. Jim later told her, "I was infatuated the moment I saw you."[3]

Setsuko's mother had never discussed prospective husbands. As a *nakōdo* (matchmaker), Shigeno often talked about the marriages she was arranging. She did ask her daughter to don a kimono one day for a professional photograph. Setsuko suspected her mother wanted to show it around. Harking back to the Meiji period, when samurai marriages followed an arranged introduction by a *nakōdo*, dating was uncommon, as boys and girls remained separated at school and most social events. Even though the Constitution of 1947 established mutual consent of both sexes before wedlock, arranged marriages prevailed as more respectable. And Setsuko was approaching the age at which Japanese women were expected to marry—between twenty-three and twenty-five. Those who remained single after that were referred to as "Christmas cakes," those stale pastries in which no one is interested after December 25.[4]

Up to that point, Setsuko had not thought about the kind of man she might marry, let alone whether she would consider a Caucasian. An interracial romance posed nearly insurmountable difficulties. Many Japanese girls did date white men during the occupation, but Setsuko knew her parents could never accept such a union, so she avoided mentioning Jim. Before long, however, it became clear that he was the man with whom she wanted to spend the rest of her life. As their conversations centered on the state of the world, Jim began to understand Setsuko's aspirations and tenacity, providing an inkling of what kind of woman she was and what she doubtless would become. He didn't shrink away. He believed in her and felt increasingly committed to her. When he wrote to his parents about his intentions, they replied, "If our son has chosen somebody, she must be a fine person."[5] Setsuko did not write to her parents. She warned Jim that it would not be easy for them to accept him. In the 1950s almost 70 percent of Japanese marriages were still arranged. And Setsuko knew they expected her to marry a Japanese man.

That fall Jim returned to Kwansei Gakuin and Setsuko to her senior year of college, separated by almost two hundred miles. When Jim asked permission to visit her in Hiroshima, Setsuko confided her concerns to Reverend Tanimoto. He knew Setsuko's parents would feel uncomfortable having a white man as a possible suitor visit them. So he hosted Jim in his home, treating him like a younger brother. Setsuko arranged to spend some time with Jim, whom she described to her parents as "an acquaintance from Bibai." She never introduced him to them, however. Although her parents likely suspected he represented more than a casual "acquaintance," they ignored the situation, likely hoping it would fade.[6]

In the summer of 1954, Setsuko received her bachelor of arts degree in English literature and education from Hiroshima Jogakuin. The time had come to determine her next step. She decided to accept the scholarship at Lynchburg College, giving Jim three reasons beyond the academic: First, she and Jim needed to be honest with themselves. Was theirs a summer romance or a binding of kindred souls? Second, she wanted to see if she could survive in North American society. Third, she wanted to respect her parents' position. They had grown up in the Meiji period, when marriage to a non-Japanese person was taboo. She thought they should have time to adjust to this idea. Unhappy about a year's separation, Jim felt this would give her time to resolve her concerns. He would wait.

On August 28 Setsuko stood at the dock in Nagoya Harbor. Her mother, sister, and sister-in-law had traveled there to bid her farewell. While they were occupied elsewhere, Jim suddenly appeared. Without a word he took a small box from his pocket and opened it to reveal a diamond ring. Setsuko remained speechless. Just after he slipped the ring on her finger, her family joined them. She concealed her hand. An awkward moment ensued with no kissing, no hugging. This was not how she had envisioned an engagement. Setsuko introduced him as a missionary friend. When the time came to board, she stood on the deck waving until Jim and her family disappeared from sight.

Setsuko Nakamura had lived through one of the most grievous episodes in history and, as a young teen, experienced sorrow and adversity. For the past nine years, she had faced an emotional, spiritual struggle. Supported by her parents, her ministers, her teachers, and Jim, she had emerged with a remarkably positive vital spark. Now she anticipated the excitement of a new adventure, as had her father five decades earlier. As the ship pulled out of Nagoya Port, Setsuko looked forward. The sea spray mixed with her tears.

Fig. 1. Benkichi Nakamura in California. Courtesy of the Thurlow family.

Fig. 2. Shigeno, Setsuko, Ayako, Yukiko, Isamu, and Fumiko Nakamura in Hiroshima. Courtesy of the Thurlow family.

Fig. 3. Shigeno, Setsuko, Yukiko, and Benkichi Nakamura. Courtesy of the Thurlow family.

Fig. 4. Setsuko's sister Ayako and nephew Eiji prior to the atomic bombing. Courtesy of the Thurlow family.

Fig. 5. Hiroshima after the detonation of the atomic bomb. Wikimedia Commons, https://commons.wikimedia.org/wiki/File:AtomicEffects-Hiroshima.jpg.

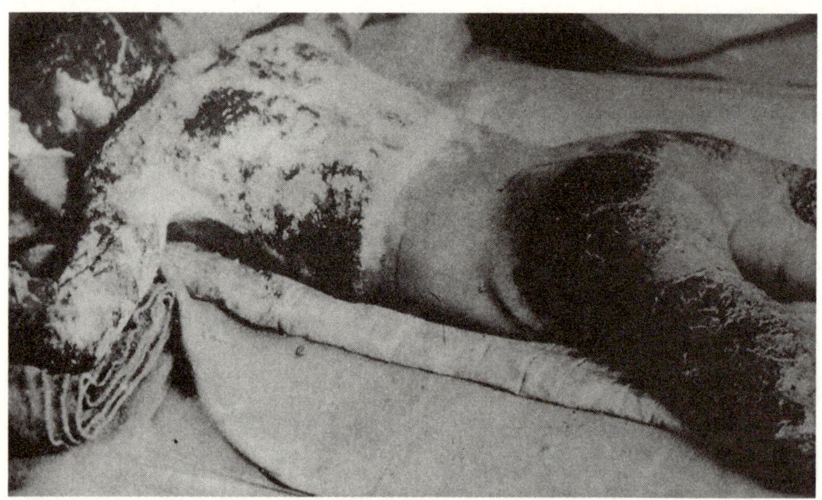

Fig 6. Victim of the atomic bomb with extensive burns. Wikimedia Commons, https://commons.wikimedia.org/wiki/File:Victim_of_Atomic_Bomb_002.jpg.

Fig. 7. Boy carrying his injured brother. The number of A-bomb orphans exceeded six thousand. Wikimedia Commons, https://commons.wikimedia.org/wiki/File:A_boy_carrying_his_injured_younger_brother_on_his_back.png.

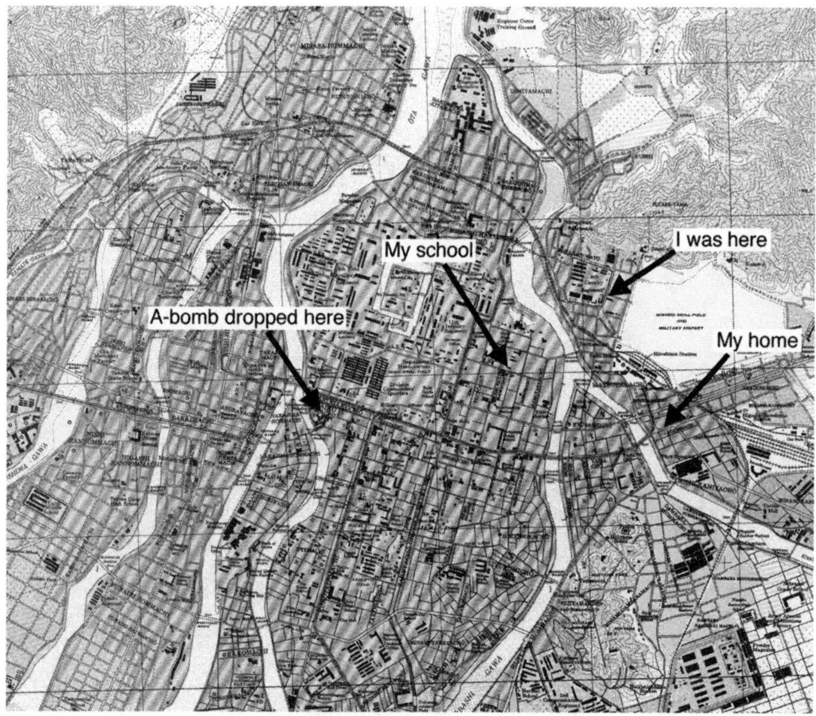

Fig. 8. Setsuko's location on August 6, 1945. Courtesy of the Thurlow family and Stanford University Libraries, Map Collections.

Fig. 9. Setsuko, circa 1950. Courtesy of the Thurlow family.

Fig. 10. Setsuko Nakamura and James Thurlow's wedding, July 2, 1955. Courtesy of the Thurlow family.

Fig. 11. Setsuko teaching in New York with Hibakusha Stories. Courtesy of Hibakusha Stories and Robert Croonquist.

Fig. 12. Setsuko on the Little White House lawn, with Kathleen Sullivan, Yasuaki Yamashita, and Clifton Daniel (Truman's grandson), May 16, 2014. Courtesy of Hibakusha Stories and Robert Croonquist.

Fig. 13. Setsuko confronting Toshio Sano, the Japanese ambassador, at the Third Conference on the Humanitarian Impact of Nuclear Weapons, Vienna, December 8, 2014. Courtesy of Hibakusha Stories and Robert Croonquist.

Fig. 14. Elayne Whyte Gómez and Setsuko at the adoption of the UN Treaty on the Prohibition of Nuclear Weapons, July 7, 2017. Courtesy of the International Campaign to Abolish Nuclear Weapons and Kathleen Sullivan.

Fig. 15. Kathleen Sullivan and Setsuko (*seated*), with Ray Acheson of Women's International League for Peace and Freedom and Akira Kawasaki of Peace Boat (*standing*) at the Paris Symposium, February 2020. Courtesy of Hibakusha Stories and Kathleen Sullivan.

Fig. 16. Setsuko relaxing prior to the Nobel Peace Prize ceremony, December 10, 2017. Courtesy of Hibakusha Stories and Ari Beser.

Fig. 17. Berit Reiss-Andersen, chair of the Norwegian Nobel Committee; Setsuko; and Beatrice Fihn (*left to right*), during the Nobel Peace Prize presentation, December 10, 2017. Courtesy of the International Campaign to Abolish Nuclear Weapons and Berit Roald.

Fig. 18. Traditional torchlight parade following the Nobel Peace Prize ceremony. Courtesy of Hibakusha Stories and Kathleen Sullivan.

Fig. 19. Setsuko meeting Pope Francis at the Vatican, March 20, 2019. Courtesy of the International Campaign to Abolish Nuclear Weapons.

Fig. 20. Treaty on the Prohibition of Nuclear Weapons going into force, United Nations Headquarters, New York, January 22, 2021. Courtesy of the International Campaign to Abolish Nuclear Weapons and Seth Shelden.

Part 3

THE QUEST

11 Crossing Borders

I ate waves and tasted wind
for more than twenty days
–Ronald Takaki, *Strangers from a Different Shore*

In late August 1954, the SS *Cotton State #1*, an American cargo ship, left Nagoya, headed for Seattle. As the ship entered open waters, Setsuko felt the thrill of her new adventure. She explored what would be her home for the next several weeks: modest accommodations and three small decks, with a length of only 440 feet on which to stroll. The passenger list included two other female Japanese students who had received transportation scholarships as had she, two American businessmen, and the American crew. She planned to spend her time reading, studying English vocabulary, and writing to Jim. Dinner at the captain's table each night would allow her to practice her English. The cloudless sky bode well for the crossing.

After her first meal, Setsuko began to feel queasy—perhaps from anticipation of the trip ahead, she thought. Before long she realized she was suffering from seasickness. Proud of her good health and stamina, she thought it would pass soon. It didn't. As Jim later explained, the cargo ship had likely not been ballasted properly to provide stability. The vessel rocked back and forth almost all the way across the Pacific Ocean. Setsuko couldn't read, write, walk on deck, or eat without nausea. As a result, she lost so much weight that she had to belt her skirt tightly to keep it from slipping down.

For a young woman used to an active life, the idleness and monotony of miles and miles of ocean with limited social interaction tried her patience. She began to wonder if she would ever see land again. When later asked about her crossing, Setsuko replied, "I spent several weeks on the Pacific, meaning 'peaceful in character,' but it's not a pacific ocean; it's a cruel ocean."[1] It wasn't clear if she was referring to her constant seasickness or to the recent U.S. hydrogen bomb test. Just as she began to get her sea legs, the weather worsened. The SS *Cotton State* was to dock in Seattle, where Dr. Floyd Schmoe, the Quaker peace activist who spearheaded a project to build housing for A-bomb survivors, planned to meet her and arrange travel to her sister's home in Los Angeles. The destination of the SS *Cotton State* had to be changed to a southern California port. Setsuko had no way to let Dr. Schmoe know her whereabouts. Still, she didn't despair. She had reached America, and she wanted to make the most of her experience.

Not sure where they had docked, Setsuko was relieved when told they were near Laguna Beach. She knew someone who lived there—a Mrs. Robinson, with whom she had been corresponding ever since the woman had visited Reverend Tanimoto's church in Hiroshima. She told Setsuko that if she ever came to the United States, she must visit her. Setsuko had her address, and a sailor volunteered to drive her there. After Setsuko had a delightful visit with Mrs. Robinson over afternoon tea, she asked the young man to drop her off at the medical office of her cousin, Dr. John Kashiwabara, in Long Beach.

When she arrived, her cousin looked shocked and, instead of welcoming her, dashed back into his office and called the police. Her sister, Fumiko, had reported Setsuko missing, last seen getting into a car with a sailor. Had she been kidnapped? The family was frantic, and the police were searching for her. Her cousin delivered Setsuko to her sister's home in Los Angeles, where she met the American family who had provided food and clothing in the aftermath of the bomb: her sister Fumiko, brother-in-law Takekuma Norman Takei, teenage nephews George and Henry, and niece, Nancy Reiko.

Even though Setsuko had seen photos of her older sister, she did not anticipate how traditional Fumiko would be. Perhaps she thought Fumiko would be more like her sister Ayako, who had returned to Hiroshima westernized and introduced her to fashion and makeup. Fumiko had been born in 1912 in Florin, California, where she attended Florin Elementary East School, learned English, and wore American dresses. At the age of eight, her family moved back to Hiroshima to live with her father's parents. There she experienced an environment of extreme nationalism, which emphasized the preservation of traditional Japanese culture and values, along with rejection of Western influence. After high school graduation, she had immigrated to Los Angeles and married Norman Takei, with whom she built a successful dry-cleaning business, until they were forced from their home and interned at Tule Lake.

Fumiko had spent her formative years and most of her adult life in California and held American citizenship, yet she spoke English haltingly; most of her friends were Japanese immigrants. "My mother has all the outward behavior of a proper Japanese lady," her son George later wrote in his memoir. "She bows on meeting people and punctuates conversations with small, refined nods."[2] The twenty-year difference in their ages made Fumiko seem more like an aunt than a sister. Since Setsuko had only $200, the maximum allowable amount for students to bring into the country, Fumiko took her to Macy's in downtown Los Angeles to shop for winter clothing and bought her plane ticket to Lynchburg. Throughout the year Fumiko would send spending money to her young sister. From the beginning Setsuko felt comfortable with her brother-in-law Norman, now a successful realtor. He was intelligent, sensitive, and knowledgeable, with a particular interest in American history.

In mid-September Setsuko arrived in Lynchburg, where Dr. Joseph Hunter, the professor of religion for whom she had served as an interpreter in Japan, met her. With him were Iee Nee Yoon, a Korean student who spoke Japanese; several representatives from the student body; and a photographer. Setsuko felt special and welcome. As they approached the Lynchburg College campus, she gazed at the acres of green, rolling hills—an uncommon panorama in Japan—and the Blue Ridge Mountains in the distance. She had never seen a building like Hopwood Hall with its tall white columns, inspired by Greco-Roman architecture, or like Westover Hall, which resembled a French chateau with its turrets. When she arrived at this peaceful oasis in central Virginia to blue skies and temperatures in the mid-seventies, she never anticipated the uproar she would cause.

Setsuko registered on September 15, excited to begin classes. Not long thereafter she was invited to a press conference. She had no experience with reporters, and, when asked her opinion about the U.S. hydrogen-bomb testing at Bikini Atoll, this demure appearing coed raised her voice and said she was appalled, startling them. The new bomb was a thousand times more powerful than that dropped on Hiroshima, she said. Bikini islanders had suffered radiation sickness, and their island became uninhabitable. Furthermore, a Japanese fishing boat had been showered with radioactivity; one fisherman had just died. She condemned nuclear weapons and criticized the press for focusing on their power instead of the misery they inflict. "I feel angry," she told them. "The United States has to stop preparing for nuclear war. Enough is enough. No more suffering."[3]

"Coed Stirred by H-Bomb Test Tragedy," read a headline on page 3 of the *Washington Post and Times Herald*.[4] An accompanying photo showed a petite Japanese woman with a curly bob and bright lipstick, which accentuated her affable smile, wearing a flowered kimono—by no means the picture of a rabble-rouser. Lynchburg's *News* and the *Richmond Times Dispatch* published excerpts from the interview as well. Virginia had its share of World War II veterans, and a flurry of hate mail followed: "Who started Pearl Harbor?" "How dare you?" "Go back to Japan." "I will kill you."[5] This was a defining moment for Setsuko. Unprepared for such a reaction, she felt traumatized. She sheltered in Dr. Hunter's home, afraid to attend classes. Distressed by the harsh response, she had to make a choice: go home, hold her tongue and pursue her studies, or follow her convictions and speak out regardless of the consequences.

Over the next week, Setsuko did a lot of soul searching and praying. She did not have time to consult Jim; it would take too long for an exchange of letters. Besides, when she decided to spend a year in Lynchburg, one of the reasons she had given Jim was to see if she could survive in North America. She considered her alternatives. How could she return home? She had been granted a scholarship and just arrived. Should she stay and pretend she knew nothing about the episode—in other words, silence herself? That would be the easiest and safest approach. Or should she rise to the challenge and ignore those who threatened her?

In the end Setsuko chose the last option: she considered it her moral obligation to teach others about Hiroshima and its significance. She felt "deeply disturbed by the way many Americans uncritically and blindly followed the government line justifying the atomic bombings," she later said. "It was a chilling reminder . . . of the wartime behavior of Japanese in unthinkingly swallowing government propaganda and brainwashing."[6] Worse yet, she knew the first two atomic bombs were not just isolated events in Hiroshima and Nagasaki. That was clear from the hydrogen bomb detonated in the Marshall Islands. Nuclear weapons were now a global threat. Setsuko did recognize the need to moderate her rhetoric, however. She would have to improve her speeches and interviews by including more relevant facts to which Americans could relate instead of just recounting the Japanese experience. And when presenting her message, she should sound less judgmental. In the meantime she needed to start her coursework.

When the furor subsided and she returned to her classes, Setsuko realized the limitations of her English. She had to work much harder than other students. While they enjoyed leisurely dinner conversations, she rushed back to her room to prepare her lessons. Although it pleased her that American professors sought their students' opinions, whereas many of her Japanese professors lectured with no student participation, this approach required more preparation. She spent evenings bent over her textbooks, painstakingly trying to understand many of the words. Some of the southern phrases classmates used, such as "I declare" and "y'all" defied translation. Her three suitemates at Hundley Hall tried to be helpful and sympathetic, often saying, "Bless your heart," another phrase she didn't understand.[7]

The American lifestyle fascinated Setsuko. In Japan students wore the same clothes for the entire day and evening. The girls at Lynchburg College seemed to change throughout the day. In the morning they dressed for class, after which they switched into leisurewear to study, followed by dinner attire, then swing dresses for evening socials. Setsuko thought their fashion elegant and tried to copy some of their styles. Food proved a challenge as well. She found grits and collard greens distasteful and missed silver white rice. She did look forward to Sunday dinner, when the menu included her new favorite fare: fried chicken.

Setsuko appreciated the city of Lynchburg with its seven hills, located at the edge of the Blue Ridge Mountains. Compared with Hiroshima, this town of fifty thousand seemed slow-paced. Most of Hiroshima's buildings, with the exception of the Prefectural Industrial Promotion Hall, dated from 1945; commercial, manufacturing, and residential structures were intermingled. In contrast, downtown Lynchburg, built along the James River, displayed a number of historical churches and a Greek Revival–style courthouse dating back to the 1800s. Initially she didn't notice the "For Coloreds Only" warning posted on drinking fountains or the "We Serve Whites Only" signs in restaurant windows. She had been oblivious to segregation—a topic none of her classmates mentioned—until the day she first took a bus downtown. When she boarded, she took the first available seat. Only then did she notice that white people sat in the front half of the bus; black people sat in the back. She was sitting halfway in between.

Setsuko enjoyed shopping along Main Street. She found the clerks at Woolworth's and S. S. Kresge friendly and helpful. She frequented Miller Shoe Store, where the son of the college dean worked after class. They became friends, and she dropped in to talk on a regular basis. She thought him a good salesman, as he succeeded in selling her six pairs of shoes, including her first pair of saddle shoes. She also enjoyed browsing in the jewelry store, where she chatted with the owner, a Rotarian. He invited her to join his family for dinner on several occasions. And with her lifelong sweet tooth, she usually stopped at Dairy Queen for ice cream.

Before long Setsuko became a popular student. Her friend, Korean student Iee Nee Yoon, was a wonderful dancer, and although every girl wanted to partner with him at socials, he favored Setsuko. She was chosen as a member of the Varsity Court—one of four attendants for the crowning of the Varsity Dance queen.[8] Setsuko looked stunning in her layers of chiffon and sparkling headband. On the other hand, she did devote an increasing amount of time to more sobering activities: the Student Christian Association, Lynchburg Methodist Youth Fellowship, World Responsibility Committee, and the Religious Activities Committee, which collected textbooks for Asian libraries destroyed during the war.[9] She, Iee Nee Yoon, and Israeli student Fouad Abu

Fadil participated in programs around Lynchburg and the state that commemorated the Brotherhood Week Observance and the Week of Compassion.[10]

As Dr. Hunter had anticipated when he had sponsored her scholarship, Setsuko volunteered to address the dangers of atomic weapons at college and civic gatherings. "Japanese Girl to Tell Lions of Atom Blast," announced a Lynchburg newspaper, with a subsequent report under the headline, "Jap Girl in Plea against A-Bomb's Use."[11] The Business and Professional Women's Club invited her to speak about Japan's customs and the change in the position of women after the war. Setsuko soon realized that most of the audience wanted to hear about her ordeal on August 6—how she had escaped from a burning building, tripped over bodies, and witnessed the agonizing deaths of beloved family members. "It was hell on earth," she told them. "I didn't think I could go on living."[12]

In time Setsuko found that talking about her own experiences drew in the audience and got their attention so she could educate them not only about the aftermath of Hiroshima's atomic bombing but also about what took place during the occupation under General Douglas MacArthur. From there she moved on to the U.S. detonation of a hydrogen bomb at Bikini Atoll and how a Japanese fishing boat had been covered with radioactive ash. When Tokyo housewives learned fallout had contaminated their tuna supply, they stood outside markets and informed other housewives. She recounted how they collected thirty million petitions in what became Japan's biggest antinuclear movement.

Although Setsuko and her audience considered the same historical facts, they often viewed them from different perspectives. To have a meaningful discussion, she realized she needed to study history and political science in depth so her presentations could be more convincing. A picture in the local newspaper showed her conversing with two "atomic experts" on radiation effects from atomic explosions at the Institute on World Affairs meeting held on the Lynchburg College campus.[13] No matter whom she was addressing, she beseeched them that Hiroshima and Nagasaki should be the end, not the beginning, of nuclear weapons. And she concluded her speeches with an urgent plea: "Never, never again."[14] Now she received no hate mail; no one yelled, "Remember Pearl Harbor" or "Go home." As she delivered her message, Setsuko spoke to their common humanity. That's what she learned from the hostile response of her first press conference in Lynchburg. And that's how she would make the case for banning nuclear weapons decades later. In the end the initial unsettling experience had strengthened her resolve to work for disarmament and peace. Her life as an antinuclear activist began in Lynchburg.

When Setsuko decided to spend a year at Lynchburg College, she had given Jim three reasons besides the educational opportunity. First, she and Jim needed time to determine if theirs had been just a summer romance or a binding of kindred souls. During Jim's final year at Kwansei Gakuin University, they corresponded frequently, and before long neither had any misgivings. Second, she wanted to see if she could survive in North America. Early on threatening letters almost sent her packing. She had persevered, however, soon to become highly regarded on campus and in the community. One incident toward the end of the academic year touched her in particular. As was customary, the local Lynchburg newspaper announced her engagement. In response she received invitations from several downtown merchants to choose something from their stores as wedding gifts. She selected a sophisticated dress for her honeymoon from a high-end dress shop and was delighted when a package arrived from the store. Yes, she concluded, she could survive—and thrive—in North America.

Finally, a year in Lynchburg would give her parents time to adjust to her relationship with Jim. Unbeknownst to Setsuko, Reverend Tanimoto had visited her parents a number of times while she was in Virginia. He discussed James Thurlow's fine character and proceeded to accompany him on visits to her parents' home. Shigeno liked Jim, and she suspected that her willful daughter would never accept an arranged marriage. Benkichi did not live to see his daughter marry. He died of liver failure in February 1955. Setsuko's grief was tempered when she learned that before his death he bequeathed his daughter a special gift: his consent for her to marry James Thurlow.

On June 6, 1955, Setsuko graduated from Lynchburg College with a degree in sociology, and she and Jim began to plan their wedding. They wanted to be married in Canada; however, immigration law banned all Japanese immigrants from entry into the country except those closely related to a Canadian citizen. Fiancée did not meet that criteria. Next they chose Lynchburg. To their disappointment they learned that Virginia was one of seven states that outlawed marriage between white and "colored" people. Throughout her year in Lynchburg, Setsuko never had to drink from the "coloreds only" drinking fountain, and she could enter any restaurant. To her surprise, in this case, "colored" meant any color. When it came to marriage, she had been relegated to the back of the bus.

Washington DC had no such restrictions, and Setsuko had a relative on her mother's side, Mike Masaoka, living there. A lobbyist and leader in the Japanese American Citizens League, he had helped pass the Japanese American Evacuation Claims Act of 1948, which compensated Japanese Americans for their losses resulting from internment. He also played a major role in the Immigration and Nationality Act of 1952, which allowed Japanese immigrants to apply for U.S. citizenship.[15] Masaoka agreed to stand in for her deceased father.

Dr. Hunter suggested the National City Christian church for the ceremony. Neoclassical in design, this majestic church, with its ten columns, had been designed by the same architect who had created the Jefferson Memorial. It stood on a terrace overlooking Thomas Circle, less than a mile from the White House. Dr. Hunter would officiate. To her surprise her own minister, Reverend Tanimoto, happened to be in New York at the time with twenty-five female hibakusha who were undergoing surgical reconstruction. He offered to participate in the ceremony. Jim's parents and his younger brother attended, along with Setsuko's friends and professors from Lynchburg. Setsuko wanted a traditional American wedding with bridesmaids and groomsmen. She wore a long, white, satin gown, decorated with lace, and a tiara with an attached veil that flowed down her back. Jim's mother brought a homemade wedding cake from Canada. On July 2, 1955, Mike Masaoka walked Setsuko down the aisle. The couple vowed everlasting love and commitment, sealing their pledge with a kiss. Jim had married a woman who also had made a vow to her family and classmates slaughtered on August 6: never again. And Setsuko had married a man who would give her the courage and strength to pursue it.

After the reception Jim loaded his father's car with gifts, and they headed for the Canadian border, five hundred miles away. Jim wanted to enter into Canada as soon as possible because of Setsuko's uncertain legal status and possible changes in immigration policies. This might be her only time to explore America, she pointed out, and they would pass a lot of interesting places along the way. Above all, she wanted to visit New York City and see a Broadway show. It was just a half day's drive from Washington, she calculated. Although uneasy, Jim acquiesced.

Then she noted that they would be going right through Philadelphia, where one of her pen pals, Reverend Robert Walker, lived. During her high school years, the missionaries had encouraged them to acquire pen pals to learn more about America and to improve their English. Her correspondence with Reverend Walker had continued ever since. When he learned that she and Jim were driving to Canada, he insisted they stay at his home. Again Jim conceded, and they spent the first night of their honeymoon with Reverend Walker and his wife, sleeping in their daughter's bedroom. Doubtless Jim had other plans. For a wedding gift, the minister gave the couple a book on sex. At twenty-six years of age, Jim may have felt a bit embarrassed. Setsuko found it fascinating; her mother had never discussed the topic.

New York City was as spectacular as Setsuko had imagined, except for the heat wave, with temperatures reaching 100 degrees Fahrenheit. Jim obtained tickets for *The Pajama Game*, the Tony Award for Best Musical winner that year; and *The Tea House of the August Moon*, a satirical portrayal of Japan's occupation, which had won the Pulitzer Prize for Drama and five Tony Awards. Back on the road, Setsuko pressed Jim to stop at Niagara Falls. When he declined because of time, she extracted a promise to return. They crossed the border without incident and reached Jim's home in Saint Thomas, Ontario, 124 miles southwest of Toronto.

The approximate size of Lynchburg, Saint Thomas had no green rolling hills or picturesque river. The town could brag that twenty-six railways passed through, designating it the "Railway Capital of Canada." The mayor held a welcoming event for Setsuko at Alma College, where Jim's mother taught. Those attending included the college president, town dignitaries, several Japanese Canadian students whose families had been interned during the war, and Jim's friends and relatives. Having craved Japanese food for a year, Setsuko appreciated the traditional dishes prepared by the Japanese Canadian caretaker and his wife.

Jim and Setsuko moved in with his parents for the summer. Setsuko thought Jim's father, Hubert, handsome and funny. People didn't tell jokes in her family or in most of Japan. At first, she didn't understand them. Still, he made her laugh. Setsuko admired Jim's mother, Jean, whom she considered a saint. She openly expressed concern for others and a deep love for her husband. Setsuko took a summer position at a children's welfare agency, where she worked with unwed mothers, delivering babies to foster care.[16] Jim devoted his days to gathering information for his history thesis at the university library. They spent most weekends at the family's lake cottage north of Toronto, along with a continual group of guests. A home movie shows the newlyweds playing croquet—Setsuko in shorts and a halter top with her effervescent smile and Jim looking lovingly at her instead of the wicket as he hits the ball. Setsuko felt embraced by Jim's family, their friends, and the community.

In the fall Setsuko and Jim moved to Toronto, eager to begin their graduate studies. Although Setsuko considered herself adaptable, she had not anticipated that living on a limited student stipend meant a basement studio apartment with faulty heating. With the winter temperature dropping below freezing and an average snowfall of forty-four inches, Setsuko had to turn the oven on high to warm up the room. But for Jim's sake, she tried to hide her disappointment—and her tears.

The program to achieve a master's degree in social work at the University of Toronto posed further challenges. The oldest school of social work in Canada, it prided itself as being at the forefront of education, research, and practice in the field. During her two years of study, Setsuko would learn the fundamental concepts, values, and skills of social work, after which she would select a specialty in which to develop expertise through advanced study, research, and practical experience. The academic rigor at the University of Toronto far exceeded that which she had encountered as an undergraduate at Lynchburg College: extensive reading assignments, numerous papers, and expected class participation. The latter proved the hardest. She had to digest volumes of new material, frame arguments, and convey her point of view to the class. Although ready to help her, Jim was working to complete his thesis in the history department while obtaining elementary and high school teacher certificates. Setsuko felt overwhelmed.

In the fall of her second year, Setsuko began her fieldwork at the YWCA with groups of teenagers. This required integrating theoretical concepts learned in the classroom into practical skills with real people. It proved the most arduous part of the curriculum for her.[17] During the introductory course in social work, her professor had stressed the necessity of accepting others in a nonjudgmental way, no matter their origin or social standing. Setsuko had been born into a family of means with samurai ancestors. Her mother had stressed to her at a young age their duty to help the commoners. At the same time, she had emphasized, "We are different."[18] Setsuko began to perceive her problem: she was lacking in humility. How could she be a social worker if she did not have humility? Intellectually, she understood, but she couldn't seem to remove the film of superiority that clouded her vision. And so she struggled.

Setsuko's life as an activist may have begun in Lynchburg, but it stalled in Toronto. The press sought to interview her, it seemed, because they thought her experience in Hiroshima made a good human-interest story. Although she faced no hostility, she found Canadians surprisingly complacent about nuclear weapons, as if the bombing of Hiroshima and Nagasaki was not their country's problem. Several ministers asked her to speak about her ordeal; no one asked what she thought about nuclear weapons. The anniversaries of Hiroshima's and Nagasaki's destruction passed without notice. Each year, on August 6, she and Jim rowed a canoe onto the lake near their cottage. They bowed their heads in remembrance and prayed for the souls of those who had died. And Setsuko renewed her vow: never again. Still, she asked herself, what had she done recently? Her studies had preoccupied her. When at last she completed her courses and fieldwork for a master's degree, she contemplated addressing the Canadian attitude toward nuclear weapons. Time had come to take a stand; however, they were returning to Japan, "going home," as Setsuko wrote friends. Jim needed to fulfill his teaching commitment to the United Church of Canada.[19]

While they were making their travel plans, she faced another obstacle: the Canadian consulate informed Setsuko that she could not hold dual citizenship. She had to choose. Jim didn't know what discrimination she might face should Canadian immigration laws become stricter. So in 1957 Setsuko joined a group of immigrants and repeated the Oath of Citizenship, beginning, "I swear that I will be faithful and bear true allegiance to Her Majesty Queen Elizabeth the Second."[20] The ceremony ended with singing the Canadian national anthem. With that, this samurai descendant, this member of the Nakamura family, relinquished her Japanese citizenship. She never expressed regret, for she had made a more important vow to her beloved Jim: "to love and to cherish till death do us part."

12 Blood on Our Hands

There can be no reconciliation without remembrance.

–Richard von Weizsäcker, speech to German Parliament

Modern buildings covering the scars left by firebombs; store windows displaying American-style bathing suits; *Adventures of Superman* playing in the movie theaters; Elvis Presley topping the Hit Parade; crowds filling baseball stadiums; a three-story driving range, Hula-Hoops, and Coca-Cola: that was the Tokyo to which Setsuko and Jim returned in September 1957. The economy was booming: most households had electricity, a washing machine, a vacuum cleaner—conveniences unavailable to the general public just a few years earlier. Many owned television sets. New cars crowded the city streets; well-dressed, well-fed people rushed off to work. How much had changed in the three years since Setsuko had left for America.

Jim had committed to return to Kwansei Gakuin College after his doctorate studies in Toronto. To teach at the collegiate level, however, he needed a better command of the Japanese language. So the United Church arranged for him to spend a couple of years in Tokyo attending an intense language program. While there Setsuko put her social-work training into practice. Tokyo's Union Church asked her to counsel Japanese women married to non-Japanese men in so-called outmarriages—a not uncommon situation in postwar Japan. She formed support groups and helped them tackle a number of psychosocial issues: How do I get along with my husband? How do I raise our children? How do I communicate with the in-laws back home? At the same time, a judge asked her to lecture for the Training Institute of the Tokyo Family Court, an experience that improved her speaking skills and the ease with which she faced a diverse audience.

Partway through their first year in Tokyo, Setsuko became pregnant. Concerns had been raised early on about increased infertility rates among women exposed to atomic radiation. Even though she and Jim rejoiced over her pregnancy, Setsuko tried to veil her unease. At age thirteen she had been just a mile from the atomic bomb's hypocenter. She had spent days searching for her sister-in-law in the city center, after which she had suffered from radiation sickness. What did this exposure mean for her unborn child? One survey had revealed a higher rate of stillbirths in women who had been teenagers at the time of the bombing. Even if born alive, newborns exposed to radiation in the womb had a 20 percent chance of malformations. On trains and playgrounds, Setsuko had seen children with abnormally small heads. The possibility of such misfortune didn't apply to her baby, she consoled herself; those children had been contaminated by radiation before birth. Still, she did face a potentially graver concern: death from leukemia among hibakusha had been increasing since 1947—the closer to the hypocenter, the greater the risk. And physicians didn't know if that risk extended into the next generation. What other genetic mutations did she harbor that might be passed on to her child?[1]

In the first few years after the destruction of Hiroshima and Nagasaki, data on the health of survivors had been collected by the U.S. Army but not disclosed to the public or even to much of the medical community. This suppression of information about the consequences of fallout doubtless followed from the military's decision to maintain nuclear weapons in their arsenal. They had asserted that these weapons differed from conventional arms only in their power. The Atomic Bomb Casualty Commission (ABCC) found that not to be the case. It had initiated a clinical detection program, the Life Span Study, which involved 120,000 survivors and 77 of their offspring.[2] Researchers were starting to publish results from the study at the time of Setsuko's pregnancy. Most considered their conclusions tentative, saying it would be decades before more definite conclusions could be drawn. Besides, much of the Japanese public did not trust the ABCC. Given the paucity of decisive results in the late 1950s and the discrepancy between scientific data and public perception, Setsuko felt a bit apprehensive. When she expressed her concerns to Jim, he said, "If that happens, we'll deal with it at that time. This is a happy occasion. We'll just pray that the child will be a healthy one."[3]

Setsuko continued to work throughout her pregnancy, to her mother's dismay. Most employed Japanese women in her socioeconomic group gave up their jobs when they became pregnant. Why not work? Setsuko reasoned. She preferred to remain productive, and she felt fine. On October 27, 1958, Peter Thurlow was born. When Setsuko asked about the health of her son, the German missionary doctor who delivered Peter replied, "He's fine and dandy."[4]

According to the Japanese tradition of *satogaeri shussan*, the daughter returned to her parents' home for the first month after childbirth. There her mother, often with hired helpers, took care of her and the baby so she could rest and bond with the newborn. Most appreciated this luxury; others chafed at this period of confinement.[5] Setsuko did not follow this custom. When, soon after Peter's birth, her mother traveled to Tokyo, she was alarmed to find her daughter had gone to a beauty parlor to get her hair cut and curled. Setsuko enjoyed motherhood, and now she had more free time to work on her master's thesis, which she had started in Toronto.

After two years of Japanese-language training, Jim returned to Kwansei Gakuin University, located in Nishinomiya, halfway between Kobe and Osaka. One of the most reputable schools in western Japan, Kwansei Gakuin had been founded in 1889 to educate youth based on Christian principles. "Mastery for Service" was the school's motto.[6] Jim taught American history and English. Meanwhile, Setsuko took care of Peter and completed her thesis. In the fall of 1960, she received a master's degree in social work from the University of Toronto. Seven months later, on June 11, 1961, the Thurlows announced the birth of their second son, Andrew.

Setsuko was glad to be back in Japan, where she could eat traditional foods, celebrate the Cherry Blossom Festival, and communicate in her native tongue. She appreciated that her homeland was becoming a modern, forward-thinking country. Nevertheless, she detected a persistent victim consciousness, which had developed during the occupation. More than sixty cities had been destroyed by firebombs; Hiroshima and Nagasaki had become atomic wastelands.

At least three million had died nationwide, a quarter of whom were civilians. People continued to grieve the loss of family and friends at the hands of the Allied forces. Beyond that millions more were disfigured, maimed, and emotionally traumatized. Japan was not morally blameless, however. With time Setsuko and Jim began to learn the full measure of its atrocities.

Between May 1946 and November 1948, the International Military Tribunal for the Far East, known as the Tokyo War Crimes Trials, had taken place.[7] Initially twenty-five military and government officials were found guilty of war crimes and crimes against humanity; seven were executed within the month. In the course of these trials, some of Japan's notorious deeds came to light, even though U.S. authorities concealed many details with the intent of developing Japan as a democratic ally. Reports of Japan's barbarous behavior shocked the public. Many Japanese believed they had been deceived by the military, which had perpetrated the horrors. Even Emperor Hirohito had been kept ignorant of the most vicious acts. Thus, much of the civilian population felt absolved from responsibility.[8]

Setsuko's high school and college education did not cover the specifics of her country's infamous wartime behavior. The Ministry of Education had modified textbooks and muted descriptions of what might be considered war crimes, such as slave labor, death marches, and the indiscriminate slaughter of innocent women and children.[9] A specific national narrative, which focused on the Japanese public as victims, left educators and students, for the most part, ignorant about the military's brutality. "Victim identity has led to historical amnesia among the Japanese," two scholars later wrote, "which explains their reluctance to come to terms with the past."[10]

By the mid-1950s, military records had become more public. Unburdened from the restrictions of the occupation, writers and filmmakers began to express themselves freely, awakening civilians to the ugly truth. Movies were becoming popular in Japan, at first nostalgic films such as *Eagles of the Pacific*, which eulogized the armed forces. More controversial films soon replaced them. Three months after Setsuko and Jim returned to Tokyo, *The Bridge on the River Kwai* opened at Hibiya Theater on Christmas Day. The *Japan Times* called this British film "the best cinematic product to come out of World War

II and undoubtedly the most thought provoking."[11] Based to some extent on facts, the story takes place in 1943, when a fictional Japanese colonel is commanded to build a railway bridge between Thailand and Burma as part of the extensive Burma-Thailand railway. He forces a group of prisoners to work day and night under dire conditions to construct the bridge posthaste. The movie focuses on the relationship between the Japanese commander and a defiant U.S. colonel. It depicts not only the unlawful use of POWs for slave labor but also the pangs of conscience suffered by this decent Japanese colonel forced to follow orders. Several Japanese film critics included this popular film in their year's "Best 10 list."[12] Although the movie may have been "thought provoking," it did not expose the full human cost of the Burma-Thailand railway: thirteen thousand POWs buried along its course and one hundred thousand conscripted civilians dead from starvation, exhaustion, disease, and brutality.

In the meantime survivors began to publish memoirs confiscated during the occupation. Among the most popular was *Kike Wadatsumi no Koe* (*Listen to the Voices from the Sea*), a collection of letters, diary entries, and poems written by university students who had been forced to leave their studies to fight and die for their country. Edited by professors at Tokyo University, the book reveals the reflections and emotional turmoil of these student soldiers, many conscripted to be kamikaze pilots. The book sold 250,000 copies; an estimated ten million people saw the subsequent screen version.[13]

While Setsuko and Jim were living in Tokyo, *Ningen no joken* (*The Human Condition*) was released. Gomikawa Junpei's narrative, based on his own experiences, recounts the journey of Kaji, a fictional Japanese idealist who goes from an assignment as a labor-camp supervisor in Manchuria, where he tries to protect Chinese laborers, to conscription in the Imperial Army, ending up as a Soviet POW. The novel sold 2.4 million copies, and a film trilogy opened the next year. "It is intended, according to director Masaki Kobayashi, not merely to reveal the crimes committed during the war," wrote a movie reviewer for the *Japan Times*, "but to portray how extraordinary circumstances can change a human society into an inhuman organism."[14] *The Human Condition* received critical acclaim and won several international film awards.

Fiction, no matter how realistic, could not replace actual facts, figures, and photographs. And that's what Lord Russell of Liverpool, deputy judge advocate general for the British army, provided. "Japan War Crime Book Published," the *Japan Times* announced on April 10, 1958. The article stated that *The Knights of the Bushido* "is packed with reports of cannibalism, vivisection of war prisoners, use of Chinese prisoners as live targets for rifle and bayonet practice, death marches, burials of live prisoners, mass rapes, and extermination of civilian populations."[15] Japanese newspapers, movies, memoirs, novels, poetry, and historical nonfiction were compelling the Japanese public to grasp what their fathers and sons may have done in the name of imperialism.

Japan had signed but never ratified the 1929 Geneva Convention concerning the humane treatment of prisoners of war. Without legal restraints the Japanese army kept captives in appalling conditions with scant rations, no sanitation, and no medical care. Relocation of prisoners by foot for great distances, often in unbearable heat, without food or water, resulted in thousands of casualties, among the most notorious of which was the Bataan Death March. As punishment for air attacks, the Japanese chief of staff ordered the death penalty for all captured airmen, often by decapitation.

As unthinkable as these actions were, the unshrouded truth about Nanking stunned the public. "War Atrocity Book Becomes Legal Issue," read the *Japan Times* in the summer of 1958.[16] The byline referred to *Sanko* (*Three Lights*), a book written by members of the Japanese Liaison Council of Returnees from China about atrocities committed there by Japanese soldiers. Fifty thousand copies of *Sanko* were sold within two weeks of its release. This was not the first disclosure of the carnage in Nanking, however. "All Captives Slain: Civilians Also Killed as the Japanese Spread Terror in Nanking," read the *New York Times* on December 18, 1937.[17] When the Japanese troops stormed the walled city on December 13, most of the Chinese soldiers had already fled, leaving civilians helpless. The article described wholesale looting, rapes, and mass executions. The Japanese military immediately restricted access to the city by foreign correspondents and diplomats. Eyewitness testimonies at the Tokyo War Crimes Trials, confessions by members of the Japanese Liaison Council, and Lord

Russell's detailed descriptions in *The Knights of the Bushido* painted scenes from Dante's *Inferno*: gutters running with blood, the Yangtse River clogged with bodies, and hundreds of thousands of women and children massacred.

Why did it take such a long time for most of the Japanese public, including the Nakamuras, to learn of this egregious barbarity? Setsuko was five years old when the Imperial Army ravaged China. Although her father tried to keep up on international news, foreign newspapers and magazines were banned, and authorities suppressed news of the massacre until the Tokyo War Crimes Trials. Even then the Japanese media did not publicize the testimonies. Many politicians, reporters, and educators considered the atrocities and numbers dead in Nanking a fabrication, and, in 1955, accounts of the Nanking massacre vanished from Japanese textbooks.[18] "The full extent of these crimes will never be accurately known," Lord Russell concluded in *The Knights of Bushido*, "but in China they will never be forgotten."[19]

And just when one thought the atrocities perpetrated by the Imperial Army had reached the limits of comprehension, even more crimes came to light. What made Unit 731 stand out among the list of villainous deeds was human experimentation, conducted by physicians from top Japanese medical schools who practiced under a code of conduct titled the Seventeen Rules of Enjuin, similar to the Hippocratic Oath, by which doctors pledged to "abstain from whatever is deleterious and mischievous."[20] What also distinguished these war crimes was the extent to which U.S. authorities later tried to cover up their existence. That became more difficult after Shusaku Endo's popular and powerful novel, *Umi to dokuyaku* (*The Sea and Poison*) jolted the public in 1958.

Endo told the story of a young physician, Dr. Jiro Suguro, pressured by a senior physician to participate in the vivisection of an American airman. The purpose, Suguro was told, was to determine how much lung could be removed before a patient died—knowledge that would enhance the treatment of tuberculosis. Exploring the loss of a moral compass, how decent human beings could perpetrate such savagery, Endo followed the psychological disintegration of Dr. Suguro, haunted by guilt. "What is it that gets you?" a close colleague asked him, "killing that prisoner? The conscience of man, is that it?"[21]

Journalists and historians began to unearth details about Unit 731, revealing a story more unbelievable than Endo's fictional account. Established in 1936 by Lieutenant General Shiro Ishii, a Japanese army surgeon, under the official name of the Epidemic Prevention and Water Supply Department, Unit 731 was charged with turning diseases into weapons. To that end a large facility was constructed at a secret site in occupied Manchuria as the center of an extensive network. Unit 731 consisted of 150 buildings, which included a prison, an incinerator, laboratories, and operating rooms, where teams of medical researchers from universities and institutions conducted their experiments on Chinese and Russian prisoners, Allied POWs, and civilians. The facility bred rats and fleas and amassed an enormous stockpile of microbes.[22]

To determine the lethality of various biological weapons, Unit 731 scientists developed methods to spread disease to large populations. Low-flying planes dropped bubonic plague-infected fleas onto at least six Chinese cities, killing up to five hundred thousand. They dispersed cholera bacteria over battlefields, which caused tens of thousands of casualties, including 1,700 Japanese soldiers who entered a battlefield unaware of its contamination.

Even though the primary goal of the unit was to develop effective biological weapons, Japanese researchers spotted an opportunity to further medical knowledge through human experimentation. To determine the optimal treatment of frostbite in anticipation of a winter Russian invasion, they exposed subjects to extreme temperatures. After freezing an arm, a leg, or a foot, they amputated it to assess the effect of various therapies. Among the most heinous of acts was vivisection. Subjects were infected with microbes—anthrax, cholera, smallpox—to generate virulent infections. While victims were still alive, surgeons removed lungs, livers, and other organs without anesthesia, which was thought to obscure results, to determine the specific effects of these microbes.

Days before Japan's defeat, Ishii ordered the destruction of Unit 731, with the extermination of the prisoners and disposal of their remains. He told all members of the unit "to take the secret to their grave."[23] There was more to the story, however. During occupation, when the U.S. State-War-Navy Coordinating Committee learned of Unit 731's experiments in biological warfare, they proposed that data gleaned from the research could benefit their own secret program. Even though they knew American soldiers were among the subjects, U.S. authorities struck a bargain with Japanese physicians and scientists involved with the unit: in exchange for providing classified information to U.S. experts in biological warfare, they would receive immunity.[24] They agreed, and many went on to have distinguished medical careers. Never arrested or charged, Ishii lived quietly until his death from throat cancer. This collusion might have worked except for the 1950 publication in several languages of depositions taken at Russia's Khabarovsk War Crime Trials, where twelve members of Unit 731 were prosecuted for participation in human experimentation.

Testimonies from these Russian trials shocked and sickened those who attended them. "Only men devoid of honour, men who grovel before Japanese imperialism, morally corrupt haters of mankind could have committed these crimes so abhorrent to human nature," said the state prosecutor, in summing up the evidence. The final verdict of the military tribunal read, "The preliminaries and court investigations have established that the Japanese imperialists prepared to employ bacteriological weapons extensively in an aggressive war unleashed against the USSR and other states, and thereby plunge mankind into the abyss of new calamities."[25] U.S. and Japanese officials tried to dismiss the Khabarovsk War Crime Trials as communist propaganda, yet in a 1952 front-page article in *Sunday Mainichi*, titled "Bacteriological Warfare," extensive "flea nurseries" were described, where millions of fleas were bred and infected with the plague.[26] Testimonies by members of the Association of Returnees from China and Endo's novel, *The Sea and Poison*, further incensed the public.

Between the occupation's censorship, rescripted textbooks, and U.S. cover-ups, Setsuko and Jim didn't learn the extent of these atrocities until a decade or more after the war's end. Their reactions included a mixture of shock, distress, disgust, and anger. As a child, Setsuko recalled joining soldiers at the house next door as they sang and pledged loyalty to the emperor on their last night before deployment. She had worried how many might never return, not how many would slaughter innocent women and children. "At home they are good fathers, good brothers, good sons," wrote renowned poet Sadako Kurihara, "but in the hell of battle, they lose all humanity and rampage like wild beasts."[27] Setsuko couldn't help wondering about members of her own family—her brother, brothers-in-law, cousins. And what about her? Her parents hadn't stressed militarism, yet, as a product of an imperialistic culture, she had considered Emperor Hirohito sublime and Japan supreme. "I felt a part of the collective guilt," she later said.[28] What about individual perpetrators? Why didn't they ask forgiveness for their sins? Had they no remorse? "We believed that the orders from the top were absolute," a military surgeon said years later. "We erased any sense of culpability by doing so."[29] As the Cold War progressed, and the United States determined the importance of Japan as an East Asian ally, charges against thousands of war criminals were revoked.

Setsuko felt ashamed of her country. The emperor seemed to have been absolved, and military men returned to civilian life, many of whom prospered, even going on to hold high-ranking public offices. All this time she had focused on the victims of the atom bomb. Even though she had tried to forgive, the thought of her schoolmates burned alive, the agonizing deaths of her nephew and beautiful sister Ayako, the disfigured faces of the Hiroshima maidens, and the friends who died from leukemia, outraged her. Once she learned of Japan's wartime atrocities, her perception changed: she and her countrymen were victims, yes, but they were victimizers as well.

Sadako Kurihara's poem, "When We Say Hiroshima," best captured Setsuko's sentiments:

> When we say "Hiroshima,"
> do people answer, gently,
> "Ah, Hiroshima"?
> Say "Hiroshima," and hear "Pearl Harbor."
> Say "Hiroshima," and hear "Rape of Nanking."
> Say "Hiroshima," and hear of women and children in Manila
> thrown into trenches, doused with gasoline,
> and burned alive.
> Say "Hiroshima,"
> and hear echoes of blood and fire.

. . . .

That we may say "Hiroshima"
and hear in reply, gently,
"Ah, Hiroshima,"'
we first must
wash the blood
off our own hands.[30]

13 In the Interim

Every man, woman and child lives under a nuclear sword of Damocles, hanging by the slenderest of threads, capable of being cut at any moment by accident or miscalculation or by madness. The weapons of war must be abolished before they abolish us.

–President John F. Kennedy, address to United Nations General Assembly, September 25, 1961

In the fall of 1962, the Thurlows returned to Canada. Jim had been granted a leave to study international affairs at the University of Toronto. On October 22 they learned that the president of the United States was to deliver an urgent public address at 7:00 p.m.

"Good evening my fellow citizens," President John F. Kennedy said with gravitas, as he sat behind his desk in the Oval Office. His prepared remarks to the American public were being broadcast via international radio and television. "This Government, as promised, has maintained the closest surveillance of the Soviet military buildup on the island of Cuba," he began. "Within the past week, unmistakable evidence has established the fact that a series of offensive missile sites is now in preparation on the imprisoned island. The purpose of these bases can be none other than to provide a nuclear strike capability against the Western Hemisphere."[1] He had been notified of this six days earlier, on October 16, 1962, he said, and after extensive evaluation he now was reporting the crisis and his planned course of action to the nation.

Millions around the world were stunned, among them Setsuko and Jim Thurlow. They had just moved back to Toronto. Now they and their children sat in a possible line of fire.

Kennedy revealed that several sites held medium-range ballistic missiles, which could carry nuclear warheads for more than one thousand nautical miles—meaning that they could strike Washington DC, the Panama Canal, the southeast United States, and Central America. Additional sites appeared to be under construction for intermediate-range ballistic missiles, which could travel twice that distance and strike most of the Western Hemisphere. Added to that, jet bombers capable of delivering nuclear weapons were being assembled on the island. When he confronted Soviet premier Nikita Khrushchev with this discovery, Khrushchev contended that these weapons were for defensive, not offensive, purposes. Kennedy accused him of "deliberate deception."[2] Then came perhaps the most alarming of the president's statements: "We will not prematurely or unnecessarily risk the costs of worldwide nuclear war in which even the fruits of victory would be ashes in our mouth, but neither will we shrink from that risk at any time it must be faced."[3]

The president went on to disclose the immediate steps he had ordered. Among them were increased surveillance of Cuba and the quarantine of military equipment being sent to the island. Any ship carrying such cargo would be turned back. He requested an emergency meeting of the UN Security Council to call for the prompt dismantling and withdrawal of all offensive weapons from Cuba. Furthermore, he said he considered any nuclear missile launched from Cuba to be an attack by the Soviet Union, which would provoke a retaliatory response from the United States. Despite his harsh warnings, he hoped for a diplomatic resolution: "I call upon Chairman Khrushchev," he said, "to join in an historic effort to end the perilous arms race and . . . to move the world back from the abyss of destruction."[4]

What Kennedy didn't divulge in his eighteen-minute speech were the six days of agony he had spent considering how to respond to aerial photographs taken by a U-2 surveillance plane that had revealed a Soviet missile base under construction ninety miles off the coast of Florida. The Joint Chiefs of Staff urged the prompt bombing of all missile sites and a military invasion of Cuba, as did most of his ad hoc group of advisers. Instead, Kennedy had ordered a naval blockade, which he called a "quarantine," since a blockade was considered an act of war. He hoped to gain time to negotiate a settlement with the Soviet Union and avoid a nuclear confrontation. Were the quarantine to fail, they were prepared to invade. "If I make a mistake in this crisis," he confided to his press secretary, Pierre Salinger, "200 million people are going to get killed."[5]

Likely among the dead would be the Thurlows. They had rented a townhouse in a Toronto suburb, where they had befriended five families in their neighborhood who also had preschool or school-age children. From the wives Setsuko was learning about child rearing and home management. She helped at Peter's nursery school, attended PTA meetings, and shared homemaking problems such as how to make a shopping list, polish floors, and iron bed linens. Now the women spent most of the day gathered around a small television set in Setsuko's kitchen, watching the tense standoff unfold in Cuba.

On October 23, the day after Kennedy's startling address, the initial U.S. naval quarantine fleet of sixty-three ships—which included twenty destroyers, two cruisers, several submarines, and three aircraft carriers—surrounded Cuba. Soviet submarines moved into the Caribbean. A critical juncture arrived the next day, when the quarantine began, and Soviet ships bound for Cuba approached the line of U.S. vessels. Kennedy feared that any attempt by the Soviets to breach the blockade would spark a military confrontation, leading to a nuclear exchange, which he considered "the final FAILURE."[6] U.S. military forces were escalated to the highest level of alert in preparation for full-scale war.

Canadian prime minister John Diefenbaker condemned Kennedy as reckless. The Canadian government did not seem to have an emergency response plan in the event of a nuclear conflict. No one talked about bomb shelters or leaving Toronto for a safer spot. Almost frozen with foreboding, Setsuko and her neighbors watched the scene unfold. Then, to the surprise of most, Soviet ships stopped short of the blockade and began to turn back, with the exception of the oil tanker *Bucharest*. On October 25, the tenth day of the crisis, fear again gripped the public as two American warships, the USS *Essex* and the USS *Gearing*, prepared to intercept the tanker. Once it was determined that the tanker carried only petroleum, Kennedy allowed it to continue on to Cuba. Meanwhile, new surveillance photographs showed the rapid construction of missile sites on the island and unloading of Soviet IL-28 bombers capable of carrying nuclear weapons. Still maintaining a strong stance, Kennedy wrote to Khrushchev and urged him to change course.

On October 27 neighborhood children were attending Peter Thurlow's fourth birthday party. At the same time, newscasters announced that a U.S. pilot, Major Rudolph Anderson, had been killed when his U-2 surveillance plane was shot down over Cuba. "War appears imminent," reported the U.S. assistant secretary of defense, Paul Nitze. "They've fired the first shot."[7] The Thurlows felt certain that President Kennedy would order a retaliatory attack, pushing them closer yet toward nuclear confrontation. Setsuko couldn't help replaying the trauma of Hiroshima's destruction over and over in her mind. Peter was the same age at which her nephew Eiji was burned beyond recognition. Would their second son, Andrew, a sweet, innocent sixteen-month-old, survive to reach his second birthday? Tension was rising hourly.

On October 28, day thirteen of the Cuban missile crisis, citizens of the world awoke to learn that President Kennedy had deflected intense pressure from the U.S. military to attack Cuba and reached an agreement with Khrushchev by which the Soviets would remove their missiles in exchange for Kennedy's pledge not to invade the island. He released a public statement that morning saying he "welcomed Chairman Khrushchev's statesmanlike decision." He called it a "constructive contribution to peace."[8] He did not divulge that he had agreed to remove U.S. missiles located in Turkey at a future date. The Thurlows joined the rest of the world in breathing a collective sigh of relief.

The Cuban Missile Crisis did underscore how close the Soviet Union and United States had come to wreaking devastating destruction to the earth. It raised major concerns over nuclear-weapon proliferation and compelled leaders to pursue an arms-control agreement. The Limited Test Ban Treaty, signed by the United States, the Soviet Union, and Great Britain, went into effect on October 10, 1963. The treaty banned all nuclear-weapon tests in the atmosphere, underwater, and in outer space. It did allow underground nuclear tests but prohibited those that resulted in radioactive debris outside the territorial limits of the state under whose control they were conducted. It seemed as though the world might be entering a new era of peace and cooperation. Six weeks later, President Kennedy was assassinated.

“Mommy has her hands more than full looking after her family,” Jim Thurlow wrote in their 1963 Christmas letter.[9] Within a year it became clear that Setsuko was not content being a full-time homemaker, and he encouraged her to undertake more outside activities. Setsuko began translating for women leaders sent by Japan’s Ministry of Education to examine Canada’s adult learning and welfare programs; taught a Japanese-language course for Toronto’s Japanese Canadian Cultural Centre; prepared a Canadian Broadcasting Corporation team for a trip to Japan; and worked as an interpreter for Parliament, where she gained insight into international politics and diplomacy. Setsuko became restless preparing trips for others, however; she wanted to travel. And she grew tired of translating someone else’s speeches; she wanted to write her own.

Although Jim enjoyed his postgraduate studies at the University of Toronto, he missed his interactions with students. During his sabbatical he accepted a teaching assignment at Don Mills Collegiate Institute, a suburban high school. He enjoyed the way Canadian students engaged and challenged him—quite a contrast to his deferential Japanese students. Setsuko began to notice how Jim seemed more fulfilled in Canada. With a deep love for her husband, she encouraged him to accept a permanent faculty appointment at Don Mills.

For the next decade, Setsuko would waver between being a homemaker and pursuing her career in social work. She was seeking a balance between her personal and professional life—and her nascent activism. In 1965 Setsuko took a position at the Toronto YWCA. She was rapidly promoted to an associate, then executive director of the North York branch office. In particular she liked working with immigrants, who constituted a substantial portion of Toronto’s population. She found their social services inadequate and helped them integrate into their local communities. At the same time, she served as a field instructor for the University of Toronto’s School of Social Work. Jim’s positions as head of the history department at Don Mills Collegiate Institute and elder in the United Church of Canada kept him equally busy.

After an extended family camping trip in the summer of 1968, Setsuko concluded that she needed more time for her sons, her husband, and her own relaxation—oil painting, bridge games, sewing, cooking. She accepted a part-time job at the Ontario Crippled Children’s Centre, coordinating interdisciplinary parent education. This provided ample time for more family travel. As they traversed North America, she and Jim looked beyond the popular sights and became more aware of Canada's urban problems, unemployment, and pollution. They joined the fledgling, left-wing New Democratic Party, which pressed for social justice. Setsuko took a position at the Toronto Board of Education in 1972, where she stressed the importance of recognizing Canada's diverse population in planning educational programs. The Thurlows' 1972 Christmas letter didn't recount their camping trips or the boys' activities. Instead, it conveyed their Christmas wish "that somehow peace, freedom and justice may be reconciled; that the barriers of nation, ideology, race and class may be dissolved; and that all of us may have the guts to work persistently for these ancient dreams in spite of all disappointments and frustrations."[10]

Setsuko and Jim found the Canadian public indifferent and unenlightened with regard to nuclear weapons. This had not always been the case. In the early 1960s, the Canadian Campaign for Nuclear Disarmament and the Voice of Women had been quite active. After most nations signed the 1968 UN Treaty on the Non-Proliferation of Nuclear Weapons (NPT), reducing the movement's sense of urgency, Canada's antinuclear groups experienced a decline in membership or disappeared altogether. Few Canadians mentioned Hiroshima; its bombing was considered an issue between the United States and Japan. Yet their country had played a major role in the Manhattan Project. That history was neither taught in their schools nor reported by the media to any extent. It hadn't become a part of the country's collective memory.

Uranium had been discovered in 1930 near Great Bear Lake in Canada's Northwest Territories, and by the end of the decade Eldorado Mine was shipping large amounts of uranium ore from what was called Port Radium to American and British physicists. In 1944 the Canadian government took over control of the Eldorado Mine. Uranium ore from Port Radium was transported two thousand miles to Port Hope, Ontario. There it was enriched, increasing the percentage of uranium-235 to make weapon-grade material for use in the Manhattan Project.[11]

First Nations men living in the Deline community across the Great Bear Lake worked in those mines and carried sacks of uranium ore on their backs to barges for shipping. Added to that, almost two million tons of uranium waste from the mines were dumped into Great Bear Lake. Although the Canadian government had been warned of the health hazards of these radioactive materials, officials did not alert the ore carriers or miners.[12] Years later Deline became a village of widows as husbands, fathers, and grandfathers died of cancer.[13]

Individual Canadian scientists had participated in the development of both atomic bombs. In 1935 Toronto-born scientist Arthur Dempster had discovered the radioactive form of uranium—uranium-235—which later became the basic element of Little Boy, the bomb that had destroyed Hiroshima. Nuclear physicist Walter Zinn of Kitchener, Ontario, helped create the first nuclear reaction using uranium-235 with famed scientist Enrico Fermi. Chemical engineer Clarence Johnson, an Alberta native, designed a technique to purify uranium-235, which expedited completion of the new weapon. And physicist Louis Slotin from Winnipeg helped assemble the first plutonium bomb at Los Alamos National Laboratory.[14]

Shortly after the *Enola Gay* dropped the first atomic bomb on Hiroshima, Canada's minister of munitions and supply, Clarence D. Howe, released a press statement: "It is a distinct pleasure for me to announce that Canadian scientists have played an intimate part and have been associated in an effective way with this great scientific development."[15] That was the first time most Canadians had heard of their country's part in the Manhattan Project. Announcement of the war's end eclipsed this revelation, however. And on August 6, 1945, Canadian prime minister William Mackenzie King had written in his diary: "It is fortunate that use of the bomb should have been upon the Japanese rather than upon the white races of Europe."[16] (When Setsuko learned that bit of history long after she had become a Canadian citizen, the overt racism embittered her.)

Most of the Canadian public did not know that their government had continued to supply the United States with uranium and plutonium for two decades after the atomic bombing of Hiroshima and Nagasaki. And by providing their advanced methodology for extracting plutonium with the United Kingdom and France, Canada had helped initiate their nuclear-weapon programs. The

United Kingdom had detonated its first atomic bomb off the coast of Australia in 1952. Eight years later France had conducted its first nuclear test in the Sahara Desert.

After the Thurlows had relocated to Toronto, no one asked Setsuko to speak about Hiroshima; no one asked her opinion on nuclear weapons. If she brought up the topic of atomic bombs in conversation, she received an apathetic reaction: this is not a Canadian issue. In frustration she occasionally blurted out, "Look, the bomb which exploded above me carried the uranium from Canada that was dug up in Great Bear Lake in the Northwest Territories and was carried in sacks on the bare backs of native people, the First Nations. You can't say you aren't involved. Canada was deeply involved in the Manhattan Project."[17] Every August 6 she and Jim noted no newspaper articles, no television coverage, and no statements by public officials. "That's sad," she later said. "I just felt troubled."[18] Yet busy with her children and social-work career, she was not prepared to act. Besides, there appeared to be some positive movement in the control of nuclear arms.

On March 5, 1970, the UN Treaty on the Non-Proliferation of Nuclear Weapons, adopted by the UN General Assembly two years earlier, had entered into force. Under this landmark international agreement, countries without nuclear weapons agreed to never obtain them, although they could use atomic energy peacefully. The five countries that had nuclear weapons at the time—China, France, the Soviet Union, the United Kingdom, and the United States—all joined in signing the treaty, making a commitment to eventually disarm. Moreover, on May 26, 1972, the first of the Strategic Arms Limitation Talks (SALT I) had reached a successful conclusion when President Richard Nixon and Soviet general-secretary Leonid Brezhnev signed the Anti-Ballistic Missile Treaty and the Interim Agreement on strategic offensive arms. The world seemed to be moving in the right direction. The *Bulletin of the Atomic Scientists* set back its Doomsday Clock—crafted by Albert Einstein and other concerned scientists in 1947 to symbolize humankind's approach to a nuclear catastrophe—from 7 minutes to 12 minutes before midnight.[19] Then, in the spring of 1974, the Thurlows experienced a jolt that propelled them into action.

"India Becomes 6th Nation to Set Off Nuclear Device," read the headline in the *New York Times*. At 8:05 a.m. on May 18, 1974, a nuclear explosion, under the code name "Smiling Buddha," had been discharged in the Rajasthan Desert of northwest India. "It is nothing to get excited about," Prime Minister Indira Gandhi was quoted as saying. "We are firmly committed only to the peaceful uses of atomic energy."[20] The announcement may have boosted her popularity at home, but it sent repercussions across the world. Mahatma Gandhi pointed out that India had not signed the UN Treaty on the Non-Proliferation of Nuclear Weapons. Referring to their explosive as a "nuclear device," Indian officials stressed its design for nonmilitant purposes such as earth moving and mining. "There is no difference at all between a nuclear device and a bomb," one Western diplomat retorted. "You can take the 'device' exploded Saturday, put it an airplane, fly it over a city and drop it. That's a bomb."[21] The Doomsday Clock was moved forward—9 minutes to midnight.

Unbeknownst to most Canadians, their government had supported India's effort to a significant extent. In 1956 it had exported a research reactor called CIRUS to an eastern suburb of Bombay, counting over $10 million of the cost as foreign aid.[22] Seven years later it delivered a CANDU (Canada deuterium uranium) nuclear reactor, developed during World War II in Chalk River, Ontario, to the state of Rajasthan. Both reactors produced plutonium, the major component of Fat Man, the atomic bomb that had obliterated Nagasaki.

The Canadian public's reaction was muted; the Thurlows' was not. To begin they sought details of the secret verbal agreements and learned that Canada had provided technical expertise and significant funds to India for the production of nuclear energy. Although hundreds of thousands of Indians were starving, Prime Minister Pierre Trudeau had used much of Canadian aid to develop this nuclear device. And that money had come from Canadian taxpayers. Setsuko and Jim seethed. Although professors across the country expressed their disapproval, no one had taken action. So the Thurlows and their like-minded friends and colleagues did. They wrote a note—co-signed by seven professors, four ministers, and a rabbi—to members of the Canadian University Teachers Association:

Dear Colleague,

> On 26 Oct. 1974, a large advertisement in support of nuclear disarmament will appear in the Toronto *Globe and Mail*. Its theme is "Nagasaki must be the last place where a nuclear weapon was used." Please consider adding your signature and a financial contribution. Our call is urgent.[23]

Three hundred university teachers signed the advertisement and sent donations, enough for three full-page ads in Canadian newspapers, titled "An Appeal for the Total Abolition of Nuclear Weapons."[24] That bold statement from leading academics across the country drew the public's attention, sparking the initiation of study sections and peace groups in cities and at universities.

Jim and Setsuko invited professionals from different backgrounds into their home, where they proposed forming an antinuclear group. "It is time to break the silence," Setsuko told them at their first meeting.[25] Hiroshima-Nagasaki Relived, as the assemblage called itself, included a physics professor with expertise in nuclear weapons; professors of ethics, theology, and sociology; a city councilor; a science-fiction writer; several businesspeople; and friends. Since peace work raised suspicions of communist sympathies at the time, they needed to establish credibility. So they prepared stationery on which the letterhead listed the names of their patrons: the lieutenant governor of Ontario; the mayors of Toronto, Hiroshima, and Nagasaki; and leaders in academia, religion, labor, and business. The nascent antinuclear group became incorporated as a nonprofit with the stated purpose of awakening Canadians to the imminent and cataclysmic horrors of nuclear warfare.

Setsuko proposed that their first undertaking should emphasize lessons learned from Hiroshima and Nagasaki. She told the group about attending the August 6 memorial in Hiroshima on the twenty-ninth anniversary of the bomb. The people of Hiroshima—some scarred for life, some bearing flowers, some silently crying—had gathered in front of the Memorial Cenotaph in Hiroshima's Peace Memorial Park. At 8:15 a.m. the moment of the explosion, the park's Bell of Peace rang in unison with temple bells and factory sirens throughout the city. A collective prayer for those who had died as a result of the atom bomb followed. Moved by her description, members of Hiroshima-

Nagasaki Relived decided to plan activities to commemorate the upcoming thirtieth anniversary. On August 6, 1975, they held a service of remembrance for atomic-bomb victims in the council chamber of Toronto City Hall, presided over by Mayor David Crombie. He declared the sixth of August "Hiroshima-Nagasaki Relived Day."[26]

As Setsuko reflected on the people she knew in Lynchburg and Toronto who justified the use of atomic weapons from a political perspective, she felt a duty as a hibakusha to share her own story to help the public comprehend the horrific consequences for individuals, hoping to change their viewpoint and urge them to act. "I put that moral responsibility at the core of my very experience," she said.[27] To that end she obtained photographs from the mayors of Hiroshima and Nagasaki that demonstrated the bombs' devastation. Six weeks after Mayor Crombie had presided over their service of remembrance, Hiroshima-Nagasaki Relived held an exhibition at Toronto City Hall. Setsuko thought photographs would be more compelling than words. Dressed in one of her silk kimonos, she presented a tapestry depicting Hiroshima to an alderman at the opening. A multimedia public program followed a month later at the University of Toronto, highlighted by a panel discussion of a powerful film, *Hiroshima: A Documentary of Atomic Bombing*. Because of the positive response, members of Hiroshima-Nagasaki Relived concluded they had to do even more: the distribution of antinuclear educational materials to high schools; a multimedia presentation illustrating the thirty-year history of the atomic age; a Citizens' March to Ban the Bomb; and a petition urging the United Nations to hold a world disarmament conference that welcomed nongovernmental organizations.

"A-bomb relived," read a headline in Toronto's *Globe and Mail*. "You might wonder who wants to relive those ghastly mornings early in August, 1945 when the first atomic bombs were dropped by the U.S. Air Force on Japanese cities," the reporter observed. "The answer is that nobody wants to relive them—but a small group in Toronto has been stimulated by a Hiroshima survivor to do something special in this 30th anniversary year to remind the public of what happens to human beings when nuclear materials are misused."[28]

In a letter to the editor, Setsuko wrote that, although she appreciated the article's sensitivity, it had not completely captured the main emphasis of her message. Recalling the tragedies of Hiroshima and Nagasaki had a significant purpose: it attested to "a whole new dimension of horror that has been proliferating steadily ever since 1945," she wrote. These tragedies could happen again, she added, even in her adopted country. "I do not want the cities of Canada, which I have come to love, to be devastated as my home city was."[29] An informed, enlightened public could urge their leaders to make decisions that would eliminate the chance of a nuclear holocaust.

"Mommy has her hands more than full looking after her family," Jim had written in their 1963 Christmas letter. Now, twelve years later, with her husband's encouragement, Setsuko stood up and publicly declared, "I am Setsuko Thurlow. I am an activist for nuclear disarmament."[30] Propelled by her new consciousness of her adopted country's complicity in nuclear-weapon research and development and stimulated by conversations with Jim and the couple's professional colleagues and friends, she felt her unique moral authority and, with it, her obligation to speak out and keep speaking out. Even so, she hadn't anticipated stepping onto the world stage.

14 Witness

> I'm not interested in sympathy.
> I want your commitment. I want your action.
> –Setsuko Thurlow, qtd. in *The Vow from Hiroshima*

It was after midnight, and Setsuko continued to stare at a blank piece of paper. None of the scribbles on the crumpled sheets filling the wastepaper basket resembled a speech, let alone a major international address. Never could she have foreseen being thrust into the spotlight when she traveled to the University of York in northern England to attend the International Forum to End the Arms Race. She was there merely as one of the twenty-member Canadian delegation.

On March 28, 1976, hundreds of antinuclear activists from around the world convened at this conference, organized by the International Peace Bureau (IPB), one of the oldest global peace networks. United Nations secretary-general Kurt Waldheim commended its role in supporting the UN as it addressed nuclear arms control. Among the list of distinguished speakers were the secretary-general of the World Peace Council, secretary of the Anti-apartheid Movement, chair of the Trades Union Congress, and two Nobel Peace Prize laureates. Irish statesman and human rights defender Sean McBride, the current president of the IPB, had been a founding member of Amnesty International. British politician and peace advocate Philip Noel-Baker had participated in the formation of both the League of Nations and the United Nations.[1] Setsuko Thurlow was a forty-four-year-old Japanese Canadian social worker.

Setsuko had just arrived in York when a member of the Japanese delegation approached her. "I'm glad you're here," he said. The program listed "comments from atomic bomb survivors" for the next day. They didn't have a hibakusha in their group, and he asked her to speak for them. Setsuko had never addressed such a large audience or such an eminent group. "I didn't come prepared," she replied. "I can't do it."[2] He pleaded. She acquiesced. Setsuko would be speaking to leading antinuclear authorities without Jim at her side to edit her speech and encourage her. She couldn't sleep. She kept asking herself what she could contribute to these enlightened, veteran participants. Near dawn she found her answer: she could relate her own ordeal. No one else in the audience had witnessed firsthand the suffering unleashed by the atomic bomb.

Thurlow was identified in the program not by name but as an atomic-bomb survivor. The first time most of the audience had seen a hibakusha in person, they may not have expected an attractive young woman in a stylish suit, bearing no overt scars and fluent in English. "My name is Setsuko Thurlow," she began. Then, without hesitation, she told her story: She had been a high school student in Hiroshima when the United States detonated the first atomic bomb. Just a mile from the hypocenter, she had been "miraculously rescued from the inferno," she said. "I witnessed the whole city collapse and disintegrate into ashes, thousands and thousands of people dead, dying in agony, struggling in vain for life." Seeming to speak to each individual, she pointed out what distinguished her from all the audience members: "I personally experienced the fatal ushering in of the nuclear age into this world." She paused to let that register with the audience.

Over time, she said, her feelings about that ordeal had changed from sadness to impatience to anger—anger that in thirty years humankind had not come to realize the potential for "total destruction of their planet and the total annihilation of life on it." Most atomic-bomb survivors refused to recount the nightmare to maintain their sanity. She, on the other hand, felt compelled to make the world listen: Hiroshima, Nagasaki, and Bikini should not be forgotten. "Surely we owe this to our lost loved ones who disintegrated instantly or who perished in agony," she said, her boldness and passion growing. "Surely we owe this to the future generations of the beloved human community on this planet."

She proceeded to talk about the plight of hibakusha and her disappointment over the attitude toward nuclear weapons taken by her adopted country, Canada. Yet seeing the number of those gathered at the University of York, committed to stopping this insanity, she did not despair. In closing she remarked on Sir Noel-Baker's talk that morning, in which he quoted William Shakespeare, Francis Bacon, and Jean-Jacques Rousseau. She chose to quote an Okinawan villager whose monologue opened the Pulitzer Prize–winning play of 1953, *The Teahouse of the August Moon*:

> Suffering makes man think,
> Thought makes man wise,
> Wisdom makes man free.

She looked out to the hundreds sitting before her and asked, "At what stage of development are we, individually and collectively?"[3] Then she stopped talking, as if waiting for their answer. A hush settled over the audience. Suddenly everyone stood; loud applause filled the room. Leaders in the disarmament movement had been introduced to the survivor who in time would become a star witness for their cause.

Three days later the delegates unanimously accepted the "Declaration of York." It demanded that the use of nuclear weapons be prohibited as a "crime against humanity" and concluded, "Now is the time for the peoples of the world to make their voice heard."[4]

Back in Toronto, Hiroshima-Nagasaki Relived was gearing up for just such an action. It had initiated a coalition of seventeen organizations to sponsor a Citizens' March to Ban the Bomb. On a blustery sixteenth of October, 250 Canadians carrying antinuclear placards marched from the Metropolitan United church to city hall, where Toronto mayor David Crombie welcomed them. A lineup of distinguished religious and academic speakers urged the Canadian government to support a United Nations' disarmament conference; oppose the construction of the American Trident nuclear-submarine base in Washington State, south of Vancouver; and cease foreign sales of CANDU nuclear reactors.

Jim and Setsuko considered the rally a success. "It received extensive and, generally, sympathetic coverage on radio, television and in the press," Jim wrote in their 1976 Christmas letter.[5] Yet some reporters dismissed its importance; some derided the effort. "What's This? A Ban-the-Bomb March?" read a headline in the *Toronto Star*.[6] "Ban-Bomb Signs, Protest Songs, Rally Reminiscent of the Sixties," reported the *Globe and Mail*.[7] The demonstration may have brought back memories of those times of unrest as participants sang "When the Saints Come Marching In," but they didn't have a Joan Baez or a Bob Dylan, chaffed a journalist. One participant was reported to have lamented, "Let's face it, nuclear arms proliferation [and] love and peace were trendy ten years ago. Now everyone is protesting things like wage and price controls, rent hikes and pay cuts."[8]

In an opinion piece titled "Postscript for the Few," columnist Dick Beddoes described the event in a way he may have thought entertaining to his readers even though it was demeaning to the protestors. "No newsboys yelled 'EXTRA,'" his article began. As the demonstrators walked to city hall, he said he heard two women discussing furniture styles: "I like Danish modern if it isn't too modern." He noted a car radio blaring, "Reds win first game of World Series." A drunk panhandler solicited spare change from participants. "How can we ban the bombs?" he reported one of the "peaceniks" asking. "We can't even ban the bums."[9]

Setsuko and Jim ignored the barbs. When asked if they thought they could change the policies of the superpowers by their "little efforts," Jim replied, "a movement has to begin somewhere."[10] Rousing Canadian and U.S. citizens to action, however, proved difficult. Many still justified the necessity of atomic weapons from a political perspective. Hiroshima-Nagasaki Relived needed to persuade the public to view the use of nuclear arms through a moral lens instead. "I put that responsibility at the core of my very experience," Setsuko said.[11]

Starting with the younger generation might be more effective, Jim reasoned. The required curriculum for most Canadian high schools and universities did not cover the atomic bombings. As always, Setsuko appreciated Jim's valuable strategic insights. So she began to tell students her story. She wanted them to comprehend what it meant to live in the nuclear age. "Study the facts, read, don't accept what anyone says," she advised them. "Debate among yourselves, write to your leaders, express your concern."[12] That strategy, however, depended on individual teachers inviting her into their classrooms. Instead, the entire system needed to take responsibility. Serving as the social worker for the

Metropolitan Toronto School Board at the time, Setsuko set out to convince decision-makers—the school board trustees—of its importance. She arranged for university faculty and ministers to attend a board meeting where she could present the historical, social, and moral issues surrounding nuclear weapons. As a result, progressive trustees formed a special committee to review the curriculum. When more conservative trustees joined the group, however, progress halted, and Setsuko had to start over. With her remarkable perseverance, she never wavered, devoting twenty years to the Toronto School Board.

In late May 1978, Setsuko made her first trip to the United Nations. As a nongovernmental organization (NGO) representative, she was attending the UN General Assembly's First Special Session on Disarmament. Her excitement mounted as she approached the eighteen-acre United Nations Plaza, located on Manhattan Island, overlooking the East River. Flags of the member states lined the edge of the headquarters complex, dominated by the thirty-nine-story Secretariat Building. Most impressive was the General Assembly Hall. Inside, its concave sides supported a seventy-five-foot ceiling, capped with a shallow dome. Delegates were assigned tables, arranged in large semicircles, facing the rostrum, which held the speaker's podium and where the secretary-general and the president of the General Assembly sat. Above them hung the UN emblem, a world map encircled by branches of an olive tree. Representatives from 145 countries gathered inside this hall to consider the slow progress in disarmament. This was the group who had to be persuaded to condemn the use of nuclear weapons.

For Setsuko the highlight of that Special Session came on May 26, when Prime Minister Pierre Trudeau addressed the assembly. He outlined what he termed a "strategy of suffocation," which included four measures to halt and eventually reverse the nuclear-arms race, aiming his comments at the United States and the Soviet Union. Canadian and U.S. newspapers carried his speech, described by one historian as "an impressive example of an intellectually coherent critique of the existing nuclear disorder and a practical set of measures that, if taken up comprehensively, could effectively halt the arms race."[13] Furthermore, Trudeau indicated Canada's intent to play a central part in forging the UN agenda for arms control. Setsuko felt proud of her prime minister. "He agitated American leaders," she said. "But he certainly got a lot of respect from around the world."[14] The "Final Document" from the United Nations General Assembly's First Special Session on Disarmament stated that even though the ultimate goal continued to be complete disarmament, "the immediate goal is that of elimination of the danger of a nuclear war and the implementation of measures to halt and reverse the arms race."[15]

Now that Trudeau had drawn Canadians' attention to the cause Setsuko championed, her schedule filled with speaking engagements at churches, schools, and civic groups. She received interview requests from local television and radio stations, as well as the *Toronto Star* and the *Globe and Mail*. Although she hoped these requests indicated the media's commitment to educating the public about the consequences of nuclear warfare, she knew that reporters sought engaging personal stories. That's what sold newspapers.

In August 1981 Setsuko traveled to Japan for the 1981 World Conference Against Atomic and Hydrogen Bombs. It was a success, drawing a large international audience and culminating in the reaffirmation of a Peace Declaration by Hiroshima's mayor, Takeshi Araki. What a shock when the ceremonies were interrupted by news that the United States had just tested another nuclear weapon at the Nevada test site—on August 6 of all dates. Adding to what Setsuko called a "callous indifference," President Ronald Reagan went on to announce—on the anniversary of the Nagasaki bombing—that the United States was proceeding with the production of a neutron bomb.[16]

One night during this intense period of hope mixed with despair, Setsuko received a call from a Japanese woman in Kobe. Her husband, Mr. Santo, had read in a Tokyo newspaper the story told by a Japanese Canadian hibakusha of her rescue thirty-six years earlier. It sounded familiar. Could they meet? Setsuko agreed.

"It was a sweltering August morning," Setsuko later told a reporter from the *Toronto Star*, "as I stepped out of the train at Kobe Station and searched for a man in a suit." In the midsummer humidity, most commuters dressed lightly, so she had no trouble identifying a sixty-year-old man wearing a gray suit.

"Are you Mr. Santo?" she asked. He nodded, trying to hide his emotions. They bowed. Setsuko introduced herself and said she was pleased to meet him. "We have met before," he whispered. He was the soldier who, on August 6, 1945, had helped her crawl from the rubble of the collapsed Army Headquarters.[17]

Setsuko spent the afternoon with Mr. Santo and his wife. From his diary he read descriptions of the "rosy cheeked" girl he had seen leading her group that morning and the look of joy on her bloody face when she crawled free. He had never returned to Hiroshima. "As we said our farewells," Setsuko recalled, "I was overcome with the sudden realization that if it had not been for this man, I would have been horribly burned alive like so many of my classmates."[18] Because she had been saved, she felt she had an obligation to help make certain it never happened again. "I came home to Canada," she said, "feeling inspired and more committed than ever to the cause of disarmament and peace."[19]

Although Setsuko wanted to talk to the press about the deliberations of the World Conference Against Atomic and Hydrogen Bombs, the media expressed more interest in how she met the man who had rescued her from the flames. Whenever she complained to Jim about her loss of privacy, he replied, "If we want the press coverage, this is the price you have to pay."[20] Although other members of Hiroshima-Nagasaki Relived offered to speak to reporters, Setsuko was fast becoming a media draw.

Not everyone applauded her efforts, however. To combat the rising tide of antinuclear advocacy in the United States, the government began to cast activists as communists, and Setsuko became a target for their hatred. In 1981 she spoke in Cleveland, Ohio, at a meeting of the National Council of Churches, a distinguished ecumenical partnership of thirty-eight Christian faith groups. Pleased that her presentation had been well received, she wasn't surprised to find a crowd waiting as she and the other speakers walked out the front door. Then came the shock: "Commies, go to Moscow," they yelled.[21] As she proceeded guardedly past that hostile group, someone spat on her.

Even more disturbing was a potential calamity at Ottawa's National Gallery in 1982, when Setsuko addressed its patrons at the opening of *Hiroshima: Drawings of Survivors*.[22] The exhibition included one hundred works by eyewitnesses of the first atomic bombing—a dramatic display that revealed the catastrophic event far better than could mere words. After her remarks Setsuko excused herself. She had to catch a flight to Des Moines, Iowa, where she was scheduled to address a group of ministers the next morning. Hundreds were still sitting in the audience, she later learned, when a commotion erupted from a bomb threat. The National Gallery was evacuated, leaving the exhibit by atomic-bomb survivors as well as ninety-three thousand permanent works from around the world and many of Canada's greatest artistic treasures in the hands of a possible malcontent. Although no bomb detonated, Setsuko felt a chill down her spine. Speaking out against nuclear weapons had become more dangerous than she had imagined, even in her own country.

Setsuko arrived at Toronto's Pearson Airport just in time for her flight to Chicago en route to Des Moines. At U.S. Customs and Immigration, a young border-services officer took her passport and without a word started to walk away. "Please come back quickly," she called after him. "I have to make a connection through Chicago." He returned after her flight had left. "You can now enter my country," he said, tossing the passport back at her. "My country is full of peaceniks. We don't need another one." Furious and teary-eyed, Setsuko called Jim and said she was coming home. In his patient and tender way, he said, "Remember six hundred church ministers are waiting for you in Iowa. Those people will be speaking in churches. Thousands of people will get your message. This is an opportunity you don't want to miss."[23] Jim was right; she needed to calm down and go on to Des Moines.

But Setsuko did not calm down. She called Kay Macpherson, a friend and leader of the Canadian Voice of Women for Peace. Macpherson had been delayed at the border on her way to the United Nations. Setsuko supposed they both had been subject to more strenuous screening because of the McCarran-Walter Act, a ruling used to prevent entry of political agitators into the United States. When Setsuko reached her, Macpherson was being interviewed by CBC News. She handed the phone to the reporter. That night Setsuko Thurlow's picture flashed on Canadian television as the six o'clock news broadcast the incident. It was after midnight when Setsuko reached Des Moines. Exhausted and with nowhere to go, she lay down on the floor in a waiting area and slept. At nine o'clock the next morning, she was standing in front of six hundred ministers. When she related the incident at the border, the group expressed chagrin and sent a letter of complaint to U.S. Customs and Immigration. (Months later it responded: Mrs. Thurlow had been late for her flight.)

From Des Moines Setsuko flew to New York City to join the June 12, 1982, rally held during the United Nations Second Special Session on Disarmament, at which President Ronald Reagan was scheduled to speak. "The vast parade and rally," reported the *New York Times*, "organized by a coalition of peace groups, brought together pacifists and anarchists, children and Buddhist monks, Roman Catholic bishops and Communist Party leaders, university students and union members."[24] Almost a million demonstrators from as far away as Bangladesh, Zambia, and Japan carried placards in dozens of languages. Police officers wore necklaces of folded paper cranes, the Japanese symbol of peace adopted by the disarmament movement. Chanting, clapping, and singing, protestors marched from the United Nations Plaza to Central Park's Great Lawn, where they heard speeches from leading activists, interspersed with music by James Taylor, Joan Baez, and Linda Ronstadt. Setsuko's spirits soared. At this, the largest antinuclear protest in American history, people from around the world were demanding a freeze in the arms race and reduction of all nuclear weapons.[25]

At this, his first UN appearance, President Reagan lashed out at the Soviet Union: "The decade of so-called détente witnessed the most massive Soviet buildup of military power in history." He did not discuss his previous decision to update the U.S. nuclear arsenal, and he dismissed Premier Trudeau's strategy of suffocation. The UN Special Session ultimately ended in a stalemate. There was one particular achievement: "The greater participation of NGOs and research institutes," wrote the former UN director of Disarmament Affairs, "not only increased their involvement in disarmament questions, but enhanced their stature. It is now possible for them to play a larger role and increase their effectiveness, both at the UN and in their local branches."[26] Setsuko Thurlow was excited to participate in that effort.

Two weeks later, on June 27, the Toronto Youth Corps, a Catholic youth organization, filled Varsity Stadium for an address by Mother Teresa. Setsuko Thurlow had been asked to speak first, to galvanize the audience with her story.

She stood a head taller than the tiny, frail nun in her blue-trimmed white sari of India's lowest caste. And she wore a bright-green silk dress; her nails were polished red. By now speaking to twenty thousand didn't faze her. When she stood at the microphone, stillness settled over the stadium. The crowd sat riveted as she invoked the sounds and sights from August 6, 1945:

> Mother Teresa, when I was a 13-year-old school girl, my city of Hiroshima was destroyed in a moment, blinded by the flash, flattened by the blast, burned by the scorching heat, contaminated by the radiation of the atomic bomb. In the twilight, under the swelling mushroom cloud, with flames and smoke rising all around, I saw the blackened and burned, dead and dying covering the ground and heard the cries for help from those pinned in the debris and being burned alive. The low, agonized voices of the dying pleading for water still ring in my ears. I saw multitudes of survivors, grotesque figures terribly mutilated with parts of the body missing, eyes liquefied, and strips of flesh hanging like ribbons from their bones, sometimes collapsing in heaps by the wayside. Thus my city of 400,000 became desolation, heaps of ashes and rubble, skeletons and blackened corpses.

Having gotten their attention, Setsuko expanded on Mother Teresa's message of peace, deriding governments that developed and accumulated nuclear weapons. "Even when they are not used," she told the crowd, "these weapons cause us to live in fear. Their control by a small number of decision makers holds us hostage and robs us of the freedom to control our own destinies."[27]

In stark contrast to this firebrand, Mother Teresa addressed the crowd with quiet reverence, sharing her message of peace, love, and justice.[28] At the rally's end, musicians led the crowd in singing a well-known hymn by John Michael Talbot, which captured Mother Teresa's charge:

> Here I am, Lord.
> Is it I, Lord?
> I have heard You calling in the night.

I will go, Lord,
If You lead me.
I will hold Your people in my heart.[29]

For Setsuko the song underscored what Reverend Tanimoto had taught her when she was still a teen seeking to resolve her spiritual dilemma. While Mother Teresa emphasized personal faith and works, Setsuko talked about Christian social activism. Twenty thousand had come to hear Mother Teresa, feeling blessed by her presence. Likely, many left with Setsuko Thurlow's story on their minds.

In July Setsuko traveled back to Japan, where she planned to conduct a psychosocial study of the bomb's long-term psychological effects on hibakusha. Ten days after she departed for a five-month stay, Jim developed chest pain and during his evaluation was found to have diabetes. Although hospitalized for two weeks, he minimized the problem and insisted Setsuko continue her research. She stayed on in Japan, although with some reluctance. Thus began a lifelong pattern: Jim repeatedly downplayed his medical issues, making sure her quest to abolish nuclear weapons took precedence.

From her numerous interviews of survivors, Setsuko found a common thread: most hibakusha had vowed to make sure their loved ones had not died in vain, yet grief thwarted their efforts to turn that vow into action. "Thousands of the victims have buried their pain so deeply that they won't talk about it," she told a reporter. "It's never too late. That pain has to come out." Most physicians had emphasized their medical recovery only. At last they could talk to someone who understood and shared their grief. "It is the dark corners of the mind that need exploring," Setsuko said.[30]

Those five months gave Setsuko precious time to spend with her mother. Sharp as ever at age ninety-five, Shigeno Nakamura still lived independently. She and her husband, Benkichi, had always encouraged their spirited, strong-willed youngest child. Accompanying her father to business meetings and banquets had sharpened Setsuko's mettle, which now served her well. And Shigeno, having taught Setsuko she was born to serve, must have felt proud of her daughter. Yet she never complimented her. Long ago Setsuko had accepted that to be the Japanese way.

Back in Toronto, members of Hiroshima-Nagasaki Relived were starting to make some headway. The Board of Health consulted them about an upcoming report, *Public Health Consequences of Nuclear Weapons and Nuclear War*. The Toronto City Council distributed it to all households and held a referendum in the November 8, 1982, municipal election, asking voters, "Do you support nuclear disarmament?" "Yes," answered 79 percent. Two months later the council designated Toronto a nuclear weapons–free zone. "This has been a momentous year for all of us," Jim and Setsuko wrote in their Christmas letter. "But before we congratulate ourselves," they cautioned, "let us remember that not one nuclear warhead has been dismantled, and the nuclear arms race continues its mad pace."[31]

If Hiroshima-Nagasaki Relived had helped designate their city as a nuclear weapons–free zone, efforts by Father Massey Lombardi, director of the Office of Social Action in the Catholic archdiocese, brought even further international attention. Having persuaded the mayor to build a peace garden in Toronto, he asked Setsuko to assist him and to serve as the negotiator in Japan. She returned to Hiroshima, met with Mayor Takeshi Araki, and arranged for Father Lombardi to bring back an ember from their Flame of Peace.

On March 5, 1984, former prime minister Pierre Trudeau turned the first sod for Toronto's Peace Garden with great celebration. Located in front of city hall, the 1,800 square-foot oasis included a pavilion, a fountain, a pond, and plantings. Six months later Pope John Paul II lit an eternal flame with the ember from Hiroshima and poured a vial of water from Nagasaki's Nakashima River into the Peace Garden's pool. The eternal flame represented hope; the water represented faith in the renewal of life.[32] And, on October 2, Queen Elizabeth II formally dedicated the Toronto Peace Garden as a lasting expression of the city's commitment to peace. Still, Setsuko Thurlow's efforts did not always prove to be this rewarding. Just three months earlier she had faced a formidable Massachusetts judge.

15 Watchman

I have made you a watchman for the people . . .
so give them warning.

–Ezekiel 3:17 (New International Version)

"Demonstration Erupts at 'Avco 7' Trial," read a headline in the *Boston Globe* on December 14, 1983.[1] "Massachusetts Trial Turns into Emotional Forum on Nuclear Weapons," reported the *Hartford Courant*.[2] They were referring to Setsuko Thurlow, who had disrupted the Lowell District Court in Massachusetts when she yelled, "People are still dying" just a few feet from Judge Edward Viola's face.[3]

It had all started with an urgent phone call from Boston—a request for Mrs. Thurlow, as a hibakusha, to testify for the defense of seven religious activists charged with trespassing and malicious damage. Using fake identification cards, they had entered the Avco Systems Division, located in Wilmington, Massachusetts, where reentry vehicles for MX and Pershing II missiles were produced. In attempts to delay their fabrication and deployment, the seven had smashed computers and essential manufacturing equipment with hammers; they spilled blood on blueprints and other company documents.

This would not be the first time Setsuko had been asked to stand up for activists in court. In 1977 she had testified for the defense at the trial of thirty-seven anti–Trident submarine protestors in Seattle's U.S. District Court. The group, which included eight children, had illegally entered the Trident base at Bangor, Washington, to have a picnic in celebration of the human family. Charged with trespassing, they pleaded not guilty, arguing that their action should be judged by a higher law. To that end the defense team called three expert witnesses:

a former Trident missile engineer at Lockheed Corporation, who confirmed the Trident to be a first-strike weapon, designed to initiate a nuclear war; an international law expert from Princeton University, who deemed the program illegal according to the Nuremburg principles forbidding nuclear aggression; and Setsuko Thurlow, who was to attest to its inhumanity. Over the public prosecutor's objection, Judge Walter McGovern allowed Thurlow to testify.

In a heavily guarded courtroom, Setsuko underscored two crucial aspects of nuclear weapons that violated international law: their indiscriminate mass killing power and the prolonged effects of radiation on human lives. Although the defendants were found guilty of criminal trespass, her work with the protestors was such an inspiring experience that she agreed to serve as a witness whenever possible.

Antinuclear activists knew they would be facing difficult times when Ronald Reagan became president. His Strategic Defense Initiative worsened the tense relationship with the Soviet Union. In 1983 the United States began deploying Pershing II and ground-launched cruise missiles in Europe. Public fear of a nuclear exchange increased, as did the number and intensity of antinuclear protests—and the exasperation of many judges.

In December 1983, when Setsuko traveled to Lowell, Massachusetts, to testify at what the press called "the Avco vandalism trial," little did she know it would be presided over by the most overtly hostile judge she had yet faced.[4] From the start Setsuko was impressed by the dedication of the seven defendants: a grandmother to twenty-nine children, a psychiatric nurse who helped Vietnamese refugees, a teacher fired for her activism, a woman who grew up under German occupation, a Vietnam veteran, and two who worked with underprivileged youths in New York City. One defendant told how she had been transformed from being a "comfortable suburban housewife" to a peace advocate after she had heard prominent activist and Jesuit priest Daniel Berrigan speak at Trinity College several years earlier. Quoting Ezekiel, he summoned each student to action: "You are the watchman, and the blood will be on your hands."[5]

As the jury filed into the courtroom, they saw the defendants, lawyers, and supportive spectators, including Father Berrigan, with hands joined in prayer. Judge Edward Viola presided. To justify their act of civil disobedience, the defense team called on several distinguished individuals. Retired navy admiral Gene La Rocque pronounced the probability of nuclear war to be at dangerous levels. Former assistant to the secretary of defense, Daniel Ellsberg, affirmed the likelihood of a nuclear war from the delegation of command or an accident. Princeton University law professor Richard Falk argued that the secrecy surrounding nuclear weapons had undermined American democracy, citing the Nuremberg Principle regarding citizens' responsibility to oppose policies that violated international law. And Boston University history professor Howard Zinn called civil disobedience a vital part of democracy.

Next the defense lawyers summoned Setsuko Thurlow. As she approached the witness stand, Judge Viola halted the proceedings. A rapid exchange took place at the bench between the judge, district attorney, and defense counsel, after which Judge Viola said he would not accept Mrs. Thurlow as a witness: Hiroshima had been bombed thirty-eight years earlier. She heard him use phrases such as "appeal for sympathy" and "prejudiced point of view." Furthermore, he described her proposed testimony as "putting a thumbtack in a wall with a sledgehammer."[6] Recounting how people die in a nuclear attack, he contended, was "irrelevant to the trial."[7] Setsuko became infuriated; she considered the judge's behavior akin to denying the suffering of A-bomb survivors. Still positioned next to the witness stand, she exploded. "It has nothing to do with our lives?" she shouted at Judge Viola. "What are you saying? People are still dying today!"[8]

Judge Viola ordered her to be seated. Defendants and their supporters started hissing. Setsuko stood her ground, glaring at him. One of the defendants, John Schuchardt, a Vietnam veteran, suddenly jumped up, put his arm around her shoulder, and started to sing, "We Shall Not be Moved."[9] One by one the rest of the accused joined them. Judge Viola pounded his gavel and ordered a recess. After a day of deliberation, the jury reached the verdict of guilty. Sentenced to several months in jail, the seven defendants were escorted out of the courtroom in handcuffs.

"Late on a dreary, chilly, rainy day," Setsuko later wrote, "exhausted physically and emotionally, I left Lowell for Boston."[10] There a conference titled "New Trends in Missile Systems" had commenced at the Park Plaza Hotel.

Four hundred citizens were demonstrating outside; seventy had already been arrested. The scene heartened her: the courts may have tried to squelch the antinuclear movement, but it was expanding. Between 1983 and 1984, police detained over eight thousand protestors for acts of disobedience.[11]

Despite Setsuko's time-consuming antinuclear efforts and Jim's ongoing work with Hiroshima-Nagasaki Relived, they considered their family life idyllic: two delightful sons, a home with a swimming pool in the Don Mills suburb, after-dinner ping-pong matches, a sailboat moored on Lake Ontario, symphony tickets, cross-country skiing, and educational trips to Greece, Spain, and Morocco. As their activism escalated, however, family interactions seemed limited to dinner-table conversations, usually centered on current events. More and more Setsuko made headlines: leading a peace march, challenging a legislator, disrupting a courtroom, confronting an immigration officer. How did their teenage sons, Peter and Andy, feel about that? For years Jim had stressed the vital importance of their mother's work. So when one of their friends referred to her as a "wild activist," the boys just laughed.[12]

Once Peter and Andy began their college education at the University of Toronto, dinnertime discussions on political, economic, and social concerns became more heated. Setsuko and Jim found these debates stimulating. They referred to them as family council meetings. By the mid-1980s, both sons had moved to Vancouver to pursue postgraduate work, Peter in economics and Andy in chemical engineering. Setsuko and Jim covered over the swimming pool with a Japanese garden, and Jim sold the sailboat. As his health began to decline, he said he had to temper his urge to sail by constructing model ships. Still, the sea called to him, and he and Setsuko enjoyed the relaxation they found on a cruise.

While Setsuko was advocating disarmament at academic, religious, and civic institutions around the globe, Jim directed the history department at the Don Mills Collegiate Institute and played a major role in Hiroshima-Nagasaki Relived. At the same time, he maintained a stable home life. No matter what crisis occurred in Setsuko's work, Jim was always there—listening to her, calming her, loving her. If Setsuko hesitated, saying, "I can't do that," he replied, "Oh yes you can." Every paper she wrote, he edited; every speech she composed, he checked. To maintain credibility she knew her comments, written or spoken, must be precise, and she always could count on Jim: "Do you think I can say this? Is that appropriate? Is this accurate?" Setsuko considered her husband a "living encyclopedia." He bolstered his wife's antinuclear platform and gave her the confidence to challenge international leaders and address large and sometimes hostile audiences. "For everything I have received, whether an honor or an academic degree," she later said, "Jim deserved half of it."[13]

An increasing number of engagements in the mid-eighties kept Setsuko on the road, from Vermont to Detroit to New Orleans. Rather than representing any one particular advocacy group, she worked as an independent activist. Like Ezekiel's watchman, she told her story as a warning, hoping an enlightened public would force leaders to make decisions that would reduce the chance of precipitating a nuclear holocaust. Among the requests she hoped would get broad coverage was the Easter Pilgrimage for Peace.

A leader of one of England's major Christian disarmament groups had invited Setsuko to join the event, supported by Britain's largest antinuclear organizations, the Campaign for Nuclear Disarmament. The pilgrimage would start on Palm Sunday, April 15, 1984. Thurlow would speak at the main gate of Greenham Common, the site of a U.S. Air Force base, eighty miles west of London, where women had kept a vigil for over two years. Then she would join the pilgrims in their walk, which would end in London eight days later, on Easter weekend.

In their holiday letter that year, Jim described Setsuko's experience: "Behind the British police with their ferocious dogs could be seen the squat, menacing silos," he wrote, "with their devastating contents of cruise missiles, eventually to be the equivalent of 1,500 times the horror of Hiroshima." It was with a "sickening shock," he continued, "that Setsuko realized how much of England's green and pleasant land was enclosed by vicious razor wire and dedicated to preparations for nuclear war."[14] Unfortunately, her participation was cut short when she was hospitalized with severe fatigue. Afterward, she sent the group's leader a poem written by her friend, Sadako Kurihara, to share with the women of Greenham Common:

Red cyclamen flower blooming by the window
Symbolizing a new year.
But another clock shows three minutes to midnight.
As for mothers is there nothing they can do
But wait for the end of time
Kissing their children farewell?
In Europe Pershing IIs are deployed;
In Asia the battleship "New Jersey"
Will arrive loaded with cruise missiles.
In order to guard their children's future
To protect the earth from cold, darkness, desolation,
As radioactive particles block out the sun,
Women of Europe
Surround the base
With a human chain.
Let the sun shine over children's heads
Let the children chase butterflies,
Dragonflies and cicadas in forest and field.[15]

Having quickly regained her vigor, Setsuko accepted seventy speaking engagements in 1985. Jim had another "mild" heart attack, his second hospitalization for cardiac issues in six months. He brushed aside her concern and insisted Setsuko not cancel anything, especially her commitment in Budapest.

In the summer of 1985, Setsuko once again stepped onto the international stage, invited to address the Fifth World Congress of the International Physicians for the Prevention of Nuclear War (IPPNW). Founded in 1980 by American cardiologist Bernard Lown, an early developer of cardiac defibrillation, and Soviet cardiologist Evgeni Chazov, IPPNW set out to educate the world about the medical and environmental consequences of atomic bombing. "Nuclear war would be the final epidemic," they warned.[16] In June 1985 eight hundred physicians from sixty countries were meeting in Budapest with the goal of formulating a "medical prescription" that called for the cessation of all nuclear testing.[17] (The organization would be awarded the Nobel Peace Prize six months later.) Dr. Lown had seen an interview with Setsuko Thurlow broadcast by CBC; he thought her testimony would lend urgency to their task in Budapest. Setsuko had a different idea: she planned to talk to this gathering of physicians about the emotional state of hibakusha.

For years non-Japanese researchers wrote and talked about hibakusha as subjects of interest, bringing back memories of the Atomic Bomb Casualty Commission. One of the first to document survivors' psychological damage was Robert Jay Lifton, an American psychiatrist who was recognized in academic circles as a prominent psychohistorian, an expert on the relationship between historical change and the psychology of the individual. In his six-hundred-page book, *Death in Life: Survivors of Hiroshima*, published in 1967, he expounded on the hibakusha's state of mind. Extrapolating from interviews of seventy-five survivors, conducted seventeen years after the bombing of Hiroshima and Nagasaki, he explored the psychological significance of "psychic numbing," "impaired mourning," and "survival guilt."[18]

Thurlow had critiqued his work back in 1982 at the annual meeting of the American Orthopsychiatric Association in San Francisco. She had credited Lifton with conducting the first detailed study of survivors. "As Lifton noted," she said, "psychic closing off, the cessation of normal human feelings in the face of massive death and suffering of the most grotesque and horrible kind, was a common experience of the survivors." For years Setsuko had wondered why she felt nothing when she had given water to scores of dying people on August 6 or as she had watched her sister and nephew being cremated. And although the psychic numbing diminished over time in some survivors, Lifton had described a chronic state of despair and denial in many. That explained why few hibakusha told their stories or became involved in antinuclear activism. Setsuko also appreciated Lifton's insights on "impaired mourning" and how, even years later, a particular stimulus related to the bombing could provoke an emotional outburst.[19]

She was disturbed, however, by Lifton's emphasis on the prevalence of "survivor guilt." He did not seem to understand that, in Japanese culture, consciousness of wrongdoing is more commonly associated with a sense of shame. Yet, she said, "hibakusha thought if . . . a professor at a famous university, an expert, said this, it must be right."[20] She could not identify with that emotion. Of course she felt pain and anguish whenever she thought about her loved ones, but she did not feel responsible. "I am unaware of feeling guilty . . . at having had to leave my friends to be burned alive, since I know clearly there was nothing I might have done to save them. . . . The time I feel guilt is when I stop speaking of the issue of nuclear war."[21]

More disturbing to her on behalf of all hibakusha was one of Lifton's final conclusions: "*Hibakusha* could, in certain activities such as peace movements, assume the aura of the spiritual elite who have 'known' death, and then returned to teach others the secret of mastering it."[22] She questioned how a non-Japanese researcher could draw such a conclusion on the innermost sentiments of hibakusha based on a few survivors' testimonies, most told through a translator. These were the insights she decided to address at the IPPNW meeting in Budapest.

Setsuko knew others had similar opinions about *Death in Life*. A reviewer for the *New York Times* wrote that, although Lifton had created a coherent conceptual framework, his "stretching for overarching principles" by comparing hibakusha to victims of Nazi concentration camps and the Black Death seemed "more pretentious than profound."[23] A number of Japanese historians, social workers, and well-informed citizens found it offensive, an unbalanced depiction of survivors. So, Setsuko thought, who better than a group of physicians to whom she should convey these concerns.

More often than not, Setsuko's speeches evoked standing ovations. This one elicited a muted response; furthermore, the topic was not addressed in the study groups that followed. Setsuko had wanted to impart a more balanced, compassionate insight into the anguish suffered by victims of a nuclear attack. Somehow she had missed the mark. Of course the response would be tepid, she later reasoned. Robert Lifton was a distinguished academician; she was a Canadian social worker. And, after all, the thrust of the meeting was to energize this esteemed group of physicians and to formulate a "medical prescription" that called for cessation of all nuclear testing.

Setsuko felt humbled to have been asked to address the IPPNW and thrilled to meet some of the world leaders in the antinuclear movement. Still, it gave her pause. What was her role in the antinuclear movement—a survivor who told an impassioned, jolting story to lead off meetings, a living example, a case in point? At times her insights seemed to be discounted; she may have been in the room, but she didn't have a seat at the international antinuclear activist table.

Kenzaburo Oe, the Japanese Pulitzer Prize–winning author of *Hiroshima Notes,* had written about the many victims who remained silent. Then he spoke of another group: "people who take the misery inflicted upon them by the atom bomb and convert it from a passive into an active force . . . in the movement against nuclear arms."[24] Among this smaller group stood Setsuko Thurlow. Yet she was beginning to feel like Jim's sailboat, slipped off its moorings, adrift in the water.

16 Indifference Is Not an Option

> Indifference . . . is the strongest force in the universe. It makes everything it touches meaningless. . . . It lets . . . monstrous injustice go unchecked. It doesn't act. It allows.
>
> –Joan De Vinge, *The Snow Queen*

Setsuko had returned from the IPPNW World Congress in Budapest impressed with its members and their commitment yet personally disappointed. She began to question her part in the global antinuclear movement. At least she had a group of like-minded professionals back in Toronto, Hiroshima-Nagasaki Relived (HNR). Eleven years had passed since its inception. They had been successful in bringing antinuclear issues to the forefront in Toronto. Then, at their November 16, 1986, meeting, to Jim and Setsuko's surprise, the cochair brought up a new agenda item—HNR's future. Participants were aging; several had retired and were moving out of the area. Perhaps time had come for younger antinuclear activists to assume this responsibility. A motion was made that Hiroshima-Nagasaki Relived become primarily a consultative group. The motion passed, despite Jim and Setsuko's exception.

As Jim began to wind down Hiroshima-Nagasaki Relived's activities, he and Setsuko reexamined their lives. His position at Don Mills Collegiate Institute and her two decades as the Toronto School Board's social worker, in addition to their extensive antinuclear efforts, had limited their time for travel, the symphony, their Japanese garden, family, hobbies, and friends. Jim began to talk about their possible retirements. In her mid-fifties Setsuko still had some unfinished business.

Setsuko and Jim had applauded Prime Minister Pierre Trudeau's policy of multiculturalism, which stressed integration over assimilation for Canadian immigrants. Yet from her years as a social worker for the Ontario Crippled Children's Centre and the Toronto Board of Education and as a field instructor for the University of Toronto's School of Social Work, Setsuko had become well aware of the limited services for Japanese immigrants. A survey conducted by the Multicultural Coalition for Access to Family Services had identified a critical gap in assistance provided to the twenty thousand people of Japanese ethnocultural background living in Toronto. How could she retire and relax in her garden or sit at her easel, choosing the right shade of green for her painting? Setsuko could not ignore the situation; dispassion was alien to her emotional makeup.

At first she focused on assessing the services needed by those who could not comprehend or speak English, most of them newcomers. She attended an immigrants' group meeting, where she talked about empowering them to recognize their rights and to seek professional help when needed. "We are doing well. Everybody is doing well," they replied. Typical of Japanese, she thought. Even if they were hungry, they wouldn't admit it. Next she approached government agencies for resources to meet the needs of these immigrants. "The Japanese community is rich," they told her. "Look at Sony. Look at Toyota."[1] Having met resistance inside and outside the Japanese community, Setsuko knew a great deal of advocacy work would be required. Negotiating with the government for funding meant political action, in which the more established Japanese Canadian population did not want to get involved. It would take someone bold—someone like her.

Setsuko assembled a group of interested human-services professionals to address this critical issue. Their stated goals included providing psychosocial counseling to Japanese-speaking individuals in their own language, expediting the adjustment of newly arrived individuals by helping them integrate into the community, and educating them about and facilitating their use of available resources. They planned to begin by providing an intake-and-referral service, a list of Japanese-speaking mental-health practitioners, and support groups—

all publicized in Japanese newspapers. Finally, they would solicit volunteers and seek financial assistance from the greater Japanese Canadian community.

Japanese Family Services of Metropolitan Toronto (JFS) was launched and incorporated as a nonprofit in 1989, with Setsuko Thurlow as executive director, an eleven-member board of directors, a small staff, and a host of volunteers. The first year they raised funds largely from community organizations. They provided 1,300 counseling sessions to individuals and families and conducted fifteen educational programs.[2] "Japanese Family Service Honoured by Consulate General of Japan," *Nikkei Voice* announced in their third year of service.[3] Japanese consular agents stationed in Toronto gave the group public recognition, featuring Setsuko Thurlow. JFS was providing the services they should have and didn't. "Setsuko was characteristically polite," recalled Ralph Garber, a former dean of social work at the University of Toronto, "but very sharp in her criticism of the establishment, asking why they weren't doing more."[4] The organization thrived mainly through the efforts of a handful of dedicated individuals. Besides her administrative duties as executive director, Thurlow provided most of the individual guidance sessions—all on a voluntary basis. "You can see that although Setsuko has left the Toronto Board of Education," Jim told friends, "she has certainly not retired."[5]

Setsuko regretted leaving her clients when, in April 1992, her mother, at age 105, fell ill. She flew to Hiroshima to find Shigeno had lapsed into a coma and no longer responded to her youngest daughter. She died soon thereafter. Gone was the exceptional woman who had maintained her equanimity despite hardship and unthinkable loss and who had fostered her daughter's curiosity and resourcefulness, watched her defy Japanese societal norms, and let her fly free. A devout Buddhist, Shigeno had stressed humility and Setsuko's moral duty as a samurai descendant to care for those less privileged than her. She would have been pleased to learn of her daughter's work with JFS.

Although Jim was enjoying his retirement, he devoted considerable time to the group, for the most part writing funding applications. That effort soon had to be curtailed for health reasons. On their thirty-eighth wedding anniversary, Setsuko came home to find Jim in bed, unable to move. He had suffered a stroke and spent the next month in the hospital learning to function despite residual left-sided weakness. Once discharged, he sought to recuperate at their favorite vacation site in Cuba—sitting under the palm trees, looking at the long stretch of white-sand beaches. Setsuko returned refreshed; Jim returned with pneumonia. Then, just as they prepared to celebrate the 1994 new year, Jim developed severe chest pain and underwent quadruple coronary bypass surgery.

Despite all her trips to the hospital and concern for Jim, Setsuko didn't let assistance to Japanese immigrants slip. Then, in 1994, the Ontario government, in response to large federal and provincial deficits, began cutting funds for education, health care, and social services. Although JFS was applauded for providing assistance to more than a thousand people each year, funding became tenuous. "Japanese Family Service on Verge of Closing Its Doors," read headlines in the *New Canadian* on September 5, 1996.[6] Four months later, to Setsuko's dismay, JFS began to transfer its clients to other agencies. She had devoted ten years to this effort.

"This year has been a unique milestone in Setsuko's life," Jim wrote to family and friends. "For the first time in her adult life she is experiencing the joy and relief of being in control of her own time. . . . Picture her curled up in an easy chair, losing herself in a Japanese novel."[7] Knowing Setsuko as they did, most could never picture her curled up in an easy chair. She shifted her energy to her antinuclear efforts.

While trying to keep JFS afloat, Setsuko had accepted numerous speaking engagements. Among the most significant was an invitation from the International Citizens' Assembly to Stop the Spread of Nuclear Weapons, which was hosting an NGO meeting in parallel with the UN Review Conference on the Nuclear Non-Proliferation Treaty (NPT), scheduled for April 17–May 12, 1995. This landmark international treaty, which had commenced in 1970, sought to inhibit the spread of nuclear weapons. All signatories had agreed to pursue negotiations relating to disarmament as outlined in Article VI: "Each of the Parties to the Treaty undertakes to pursue negotiations in good faith on effective measures relating to cessation of the nuclear arms race at an early date and to nuclear disarmament, and on a treaty on general and complete disarmament under strict and effective international control."[8]

Unfortunately, Article VI was subjected to different interpretations, impeding progress. The UN reviewed the NPT every five years, and at the 1995 conference the parties agreed to extend the treaty indefinitely. Even though the NPT was touted as a major step in limiting the spread of nuclear weapons, critics pointed out the slow pace of nuclear disarmament and the senselessness of persistent reliance on the doctrine of deterrence, with its underlying assumption that the fear of mutually assured destruction by nuclear weapons in retaliation would persuade enemies of the futility of using them. Among those vocal critics were Setsuko and Jim Thurlow.

The Riverside church, located in Manhattan not far from Columbia University, was a perfect site for the NGO meeting. Built by John D. Rockefeller Jr. in 1930, the magnificent church was modeled after a thirteenth-century French cathedral. Since its inception the Riverside church was known as a hub for activism. Martin Luther King Jr. spoke there in 1967, Nelson Mandela in 1990. The NGO meeting was hosted by former senior minister Reverend William Sloane Coffin, a renowned civil rights and antiwar activist who had resigned his position at the Riverside church to lead the 170,000-member antinuclear organization SANE/FREEZE.[9]

On April 21 Setsuko began with her personal testimony. This was the first time that many in the assembly had heard a hibakusha speak, and they were clearly moved. She was no longer content, however, to serve as the opening act. Because she did not represent any specific antinuclear organization, Setsuko felt free to say what she wanted to say, not what someone else expected her to say. So, after she related the horror of the first atomic bomb through her own story and talked about the psychosocial oppression during the U.S. occupation, she changed direction, surprising the audience with what to many activists was a new point of view. The Japanese were victims, but at the same time they were victimizers of millions of people of Asia. "We have to have that perspective," she believed. "We are not just saying, 'Poor me, poor me. They did that to us.' We were just as guilty." On the cenotaph in the Hiroshima Peace Memorial Park, she proceeded to say, was an inscription that read, "Rest in peace; the mistake will not be repeated." They were all in this together. For the sake of humanity, she said, they must pursue a "cultural transformation away from our obsession with violence and war."[10]

She ended with a targeted entreaty: "I appeal to you, my American friends, to use your power as citizens with the vote to influence your government to come out of the mentality of nuclearism and negotiate at the NPT review conference for a world that is safer for future generations."[11] This plea echoed the powerful words from her friend Sadako Kurihara's poem, "America: Don't Perish by Your Own Hand!":

> We vowed
> that the mistake would not be repeated.
> It is the United States that must take the vow.
> O America, you with the atomic bombs
> to burn out Hiroshima a million times over:
> don't perish by your own hand!
> When a million Hiroshimas explode
> in the U.S.A.,
> Americans
> won't have time to think, "Ah, Hiroshima,"
> before they vanish into the air.[12]

"Only Americans, and not we outsiders," Setsuko concluded, "have the power to influence your government which has had control of the biggest nuclear arsenal in the world and which has actually used nuclear weapons on living citizens."[13]

Setsuko received a rousing, standing ovation, and, when she stepped back from the podium, Reverend Coffin gave her a big hug. "What an important thing you said," he commended her. "I want you to go around the world and share that message." As she returned to her seat, so many participants were congratulating her that Setsuko barely noticed the young Japanese woman who handed her a thick parcel. "Please read this on your flight back to Toronto," she said.[14]

17 Reframing the Narrative

Remember your humanity, and forget the rest.

–"Russell-Einstein Manifesto"

On August 6, 1995, Setsuko stood at the foot of the Acropolis, watching the late afternoon sun cast a glow over Athens. She was attending a service commemorating the fiftieth anniversary of the atomic bombing of Hiroshima. The solemnity could have overwhelmed her, yet when she saw the determination on the faces of the Japanese youths around her, dedicated to peace without nuclear weapons, she was suffused with hope. Four months earlier, after her speech at the Riverside church, a young Japanese woman had given her a packet of information and asked her to read it on the plane ride home. It introduced Setsuko to a relatively new antinuclear effort—Peace Boat.[1]

Setsuko was not familiar with this Japan-based NGO. She learned that Peace Boat had been convened in 1983 by a group of university students, led by Yoshioka Tatsuya of Waseda University, in response to the Japanese government's attempts to conceal the atrocities their military had perpetrated during World War II. They had pooled their resources, rented a boat, and traveled throughout northeast Asia, investigating the persecution of populations in the name of Japanese imperialism. What they found sickened them: accounts of death marches, widespread rape, torture, and human experimentation. Thus began a grassroots endeavor aimed at forgiveness and reconciliation.[2]

That first trip had been such an illuminative and productive experience that the Peace Boat group decided to continue its efforts, and the number of participants increased. On board they engaged in educational activities, and at ports around the world they provided humanitarian aid while raising awareness on issues of human rights, peace, and environmental sustainability. They started with a chartered boat and ended up with a cruise liner. For 1995 Peace Boat planned a worldwide trip to display a photographic exhibition of the atomic bombings and of Unit 731, which emphasized the victim-victimizer concept—a concept that resonated with Setsuko. She cherished the idea of planting the seed of antinuclear advocacy in the next generation. And the thought of traveling the world thrilled her. The material in that packet captivated Setsuko, and, by the time she landed in Toronto, she was committed.

In June Setsuko boarded the Peace Boat as a resource person and spent two months on a voyage from Tokyo to Shanghai, Ho Chi Minh City, Singapore, Sri Lanka, Eritrea, Port Said, Athens, Marseilles, and Casablanca. The group took part in antinuclear symposia and press conferences to educate people around the globe about the obliteration of Hiroshima and Nagasaki.[3] The exchange of ideas proved mutually beneficial for the passengers as well as for the people at each port. Jim called Peace Boat an "international floating learning community."[4] Setsuko found the most uplifting aspect of the trip to be the resolution and dedication of the students on board. The Thurlows believed the way forward toward a nuclear-free world was to educate young people, and Setsuko was doing just that.

Back home Setsuko contributed to the production of several films in connection with the fiftieth anniversary, the most successful of which was *Our Hiroshima,* a documentary made by Canadian filmmaker Anton Wagner, who interspersed Setsuko Thurlow's vivid, eyewitness account with archival footage from Hiroshima and Nagasaki. In doing so he brought to life the reality of the unimaginable havoc wreaked by one bomb. Photos of a woman praying over a mound of skeletons and a young man disfigured by keloids flashed on the screen as peace activist Ursula Franklin asked, "Does anyone have the right to do this to another human being?"[5] The film detailed Canada's pivotal role in the development of the atomic bomb, a piece of history to which most Canadians were still oblivious. On the screen Thurlow recalled when she first moved to Toronto and found most Canadians apathetic with regard to nuclear weapons. In *Our Hiroshima,* which circulated widely, she called on her adopted country to raise its voice to advocate for nuclear disarmament.

On May 11, 1998, India tested a weaponized nuclear explosion. Seventeen days later Pakistan detonated its first nuclear weapon in response. The Doomsday Clock was reset from 14 to 9 minutes to midnight.[6]

Meanwhile, Setsuko had become more active in what Jim called her "speaking circuit."[7] She addressed audiences across Canada and the eastern United States at high schools, colleges, churches, peace rallies, and even a golf-a-thon. Interspersed were their long-awaited travels together: an extended tour of eastern Europe, a Caribbean cruise, a fifth visit to Cuba. They had more trips planned, but Jim's health fluctuated, prompting them to sell their family home and move into a condominium not far from the hospital. When Jim became more robust, he encouraged Setsuko to reengage with Peace Boat.

In the summer of 2001, she joined the group as they took medical supplies to Cuba, then traversed the Panama Canal to El Salvador to assist in rebuilding after an earthquake. What Setsuko admired most about the 650 passengers, composed mostly of young adults, was their appetite for learning and energy for action. She envisioned her husband joining her on future Peace Boat trips. Jim, the lover of ships and seas and foreign lands, Jim the consummate teacher: together they could help change the world.

On September 11, 2001, the Thurlows were appalled and sickened by the tragic events in New York, Washington, and Pennsylvania. What if it had been a hydrogen bomb? New York City would no longer exist. A few weeks later, Setsuko felt exhausted and was hospitalized with a rapid, irregular heart rate and fluid accumulation in her lungs—symptoms of heart failure. She was sixty-nine years old. Her doctor recommended she curb her hectic schedule.

As soon as she could clear her calendar—September of the next year—Setsuko booked a Mediterranean cruise with Jim. He decided to leave his heavy BiPAP machine at home, and his overwhelming fatigue from difficulty sleeping limited their enjoyment. Setsuko tried again in the spring of 2004, with an extended cruise in the Caribbean, Atlantic Ocean, and Mediterranean. They got as far as Sint Maarten when Jim developed acute abdominal pain, and their trip had to be aborted. The next winter Jim was hospitalized for five months. At one point he suffered a respiratory arrest and after resuscitation did not even recognize Setsuko. "We live each day with thankfulness for the gift of time," she wrote to friends and family after he recovered.[8]

By June 2006 Jim's health had improved, and he urged Setsuko to join Peace Boat as it traveled from New York to Central America and on to Vancouver for the World Peace Forum, a newly established global platform for peace activists to present their initiatives. Although she felt uncomfortable leaving Jim for three months, he pushed her. "You have special gifts for young people," he told her, "so I want you to go and to do my portion of the responsibility."[9] He planned to spend those months rehabilitating at the Seniors' Health Centre and assured her he would become much stronger. Their younger son, Andy, a specialist in power-generation technology and wastewater treatment, relocated from Vancouver to the Toronto area to watch over his father.

On October 9, 2006, headlines announced that North Korea had tested a nuclear weapon for the first time. The Doomsday Clock was moved forward: 5 minutes to midnight.

Upon her return from the Peace Boat voyage, Setsuko learned she had been awarded membership in the Order of Canada. She was surprised, given how outspoken she had been about the Canadian government's stance on nuclear weapons and the widespread apathy among its citizens. This, the highest honor conferred on a Canadian, had been established by Her Majesty Queen Elizabeth II in 1967, in recognition of outstanding achievement, dedication to the community, and service to the nation.

Setsuko, Jim, and Andy traveled to Ottawa for the investiture at Rideau Hall, the official residence of the governor-general. On the night before the event, Setsuko spoke at a reception co-hosted by the Parliamentary Network for Nuclear Disarmament and Physicians for Global Survival. She called it an undreamed-of privilege to speak in the Parliament buildings and took that opportunity once again to give her firsthand testimony of the physical and emotional trauma suffered by the citizens of Hiroshima. On October 25, 2007, she was escorted onto the stage in Rideau Hall, where Governor-General Michaëlle Jean read the citation: "A survivor of one of the most pivotal events in modern history, Setsuko Thurlow has displayed great courage and leadership, sharing her experiences in order to sensitize us to the consequences of armed conflict on civilian populations and to promote lasting peace."[10] As the medal was attached to her lapel, Setsuko looked out at Jim: membership in the Order of Canada belonged to him too.

Jim did not want to miss any of the festivities; still, his energy began to wane. He could not sit through the celebratory luncheon or accompany Setsuko to the Japanese ambassador's residence, where the ambassador and his wife received her with flowers and champagne, expressing great national pride. He was resting up for the formal banquet and ball. Setsuko wore a stunning gown made from a black silk kimono with her family crest embroidered on the sleeve; Jim looked distinguished in his tuxedo. Partway through the evening, as he stood beside his vibrant wife, Jim appeared to wilt. Setsuko insisted they return to the hotel before the dancing began.

Setsuko had not planned to join Peace Boat's 2008 Global Voyage for the Abolition of Nuclear Weapons. The trip would entail almost four months away from Jim. After a pacemaker had been placed, however, he felt much stronger. With his ever-present equanimity, winsome smile, and soft, loving eyes, he reassured Setsuko that he would be fine and looked forward to some relaxation at the Seniors' Health Centre. Andy would visit on a regular basis. Besides, this would be a unique experience for her: one hundred hibakusha had been invited to give testimonies around the globe. She should not pass up this special opportunity to spend time with them.

The Peace Boat itinerary included twenty-three ports, among them Da Nang, Vietnam; Kochi, India; Massawa, Eritrea; Izmir, Turkey; Barcelona, Spain; Callao, Peru; Papeete, Tahiti; Auckland, New Zealand; Rabaul, Papua New Guinea; and Sydney, Australia. Also on board would be 650 young people, eager to learn and spread their hopes for a more peaceful world. The coordinator of the 2008 voyage was thirty-nine-year-old Akira Kawasaki, a nuclear-disarmament specialist from Tokyo, with whom Setsuko formed an enduring friendship.[11]

Hibakusha had been invited to help with Peace Boat's antinuclear agenda by telling their stories to the world. Many of them had never revealed the trauma they had experienced and, as a result, had suffered from psychological isolation. In a 1987 article for an academic publication, Setsuko Thurlow had written, "I think when we lose our loved ones, we go through a certain period of grieving during which we need the support of the people around us who understand what we are going through." As an example, she told of being besieged by flashbacks. Jogakuin's chaplain had recognized the need for her and her classmates to share their grief. He set up discussion groups, which helped them grapple with their distress. Most hibakusha were not so fortunate. "At the time, when they needed the emotional support," Setsuko wrote, "the political and social milieu was a very restrictive one. You were not supposed to talk about it."[12]

Before long Akira noticed that Setsuko spent a great deal of time with the hibakusha, inviting individuals to her cabin for what to many became a sort of peer counseling session. There she listened to and reflected on their struggles. She used her social-work skills to provide solace and enhance their healing. At first reluctant to talk about their experiences, with encouragement from Setsuko, many broke their silence.

In the series of lectures on board the Peace Boat, Setsuko told the audience that anger was an important motivation for her—anger not just about the decimation of Hiroshima and Nagasaki but also about the discriminatory behavior she had suffered when she moved to North America. Akira recalled that when she shared those painful experiences, she did not say, "We should keep calm; we should be polite and keep peaceful," as did many pacifists, especially Japanese. She expressed her indignation, which seemed to augment her courage and resolve.[13]

Peace Boat members met with local community groups at each site and conducted joint programs. At many ports Setsuko was a major speaker, highlighted in newspapers or on television. What impressed Akira Kawasaki most was that, even with that attention, her main focus on that voyage was listening to hibakusha. A documentary titled *Flashes of Hope: Hibakusha Traveling the World* chronicled the voyage and drew attention to what was becoming an important part of the global antinuclear movement.[14]

As they approached Turkey, Akira told Setsuko that the Japanese Foreign Ministry had requested she join a four-member delegation from Peace Boat to address the First Committee of the Sixty-Third UN General Assembly on behalf of Japan. Setsuko's first thought was that she didn't have the appropriate clothes to wear. Then she concentrated on the content of her speech. "If you want me just to talk about human misery," she told the ministry representative, "it is not satisfying to me." He faced a dilemma: they wanted Mrs. Thurlow, among the most articulate of hibakusha, to represent Japan and tell her heartrending story. Yet they had heard her criticize the Japanese government for hiding under the U.S. nuclear umbrella. They were asking her to play the prototype hibakusha role again. Not this time, she resolved: "We have to go beyond that. It is our responsibility." They conceded, "You are free to say whatever you think best."[15]

The United Nations General Assembly First Committee had been formed at the time the UN was established in 1945. As one of the six major committees of the General Assembly, it considers all disarmament and international security matters. On October 7, 2008, the head of Japan's delegation, the ambassador extraordinary and plenipotentiary, Sumio Tarui, spoke to the First Committee. "Japan reaffirms its firm determination to continue to play a leading role in promoting disarmament and nonproliferation," he began, "as a nation that has dedicated itself to peace after World War II." He said he thought it "high time" that international political leaders made a commitment to "nuclear disarmament, nuclear non-proliferation, and the peaceful uses of nuclear energy."[16] His words pleased Setsuko.

On October 27 she addressed the First Committee. She may have told her story to many groups, but this was different. This was the United Nations; this was the First Committee. These were the people she needed to persuade to change the discourse on nuclear weapons from a strategic narrative to a humanitarian narrative. In the five minutes allotted, she began with her own story, as the Japanese ministry had requested, expanding it to recount even more horrendous details of the massive human suffering inflicted by the atomic bomb. Then she moved on to the future. "Humanity and nuclear weapons cannot coexist," she said, intensifying the pitch and tone of her voice. "And the only way to have security and peace is through the total abolition of nuclear weapons. We must stop squandering our money and brain power on maintaining and continuing to develop the most immoral and destructive instrument of homicide known to humanity."[17] At that point many UN representatives must have realized this was not the last time they would hear from Setsuko Thurlow with her rallying cry: "Humanity and nuclear weapons cannot coexist."

The Peace Boat contingent spent ten days in New York, interacting with other NGOs and UN officials. The highlight for Setsuko was a UN symposium at which Henry Kissinger and other notable diplomats spoke. She had applauded the opinion piece on the abolition of nuclear weapons that he had coauthored with George Shultz, William Perry, and Sam Nunn, published in the *Wall Street Journal* the previous year. She agreed with them that reliance on nuclear weapons for deterrence was "increasingly hazardous and decreasingly effective" and that the Nuclear Non-Proliferation Treaty had not yet accomplished its objective. She had been heartened by their conclusion: "We endorse setting the goal of a world free of nuclear weapons and working energetically on the actions required to achieve that goal."[18] In his holiday letter that year, Jim wrote, "Setsuko still cannot calm down from the excitement of that day, hearing official representatives of many countries echoing the same message of abolition of nuclear weapons that we have been advocating for over sixty years. How empowering."[19]

Despite the excitement, Setsuko missed Jim so much that she was tempted to return home. She had committed, however, to rejoin Peace Boat for two more months, as it continued across the Mediterranean Sea and the Atlantic Ocean, through the Panama Canal, to South America and on to Tahiti. She arrived home just in time to celebrate Jim's eightieth birthday.

With her five-minute UN address, Setsuko had made an indelible mark. Soon thereafter she was invited to attend the International Commission on Nonproliferation and Disarmament, a joint initiative of the Japanese and Australian governments to reinvigorate efforts toward nuclear nonproliferation and disarmament. Composed of high-ranking officials from fifteen countries, the commission held its second meeting in Washington DC in February 2009. Among the participants were U.S. vice president Joseph Biden; former secretary of defense William Perry; chair of the Committee on Foreign Relations, Senator John Kerry; a leading member of Japan's House of Councillors; the deputy chair of the Duma Defense Committee; the former prime minister of

Norway; China's permanent representative to the UN; and the leader of the Liberal Democrat Party in the United Kingdom's House of Lords.[20] Setsuko considered it a great privilege to communicate with many of them during post-presentation discussions and dinner conversations.

Two months later President Obama made his Prague speech in which he boldly stated, "as the only nuclear power to have used a nuclear weapon, the United States has a moral responsibility to act. We cannot succeed in this endeavor alone, but we can lead it, we can start it. So today, I state clearly and with conviction America's commitment to seek the peace and security of a world without nuclear weapons."[21] At last a U.S. president was listening to those who had witnessed the atomic bomb firsthand. Setsuko would press him repeatedly to fulfill his promise.

When the documentary *Flashes of Hope: Hibakusha Traveling the World*, in which Setsuko had a prominent role, premiered at the UN General Assembly First Committee in November 2009, it was deemed a powerful film. Setsuko was presented to the emperor and empress of Japan on their visit to Toronto that year. They expressed appreciation for her work with Japanese Family Services and her call for the abolition of nuclear weapons.[22] Furthermore, the Speaker of the House of Representatives of Japan requested a discussion with her on nuclear-disarmament issues during his upcoming trip to Canada.[23]

Setsuko knew Jim longed to breathe in the salty air and fall asleep to the rolling motion of the sea. She had postponed such a trip for too long. So in February 2010 they embarked on another Caribbean cruise. Plagued by chronic fatigue and loss of balance, Jim viewed the sights at the ports of call from a wheelchair. Setsuko realized this might be their last voyage together, yet that thought remained unspoken. At least she could let Jim dream.

After they returned home, Jim seemed to recover somewhat and again urged Setsuko to continue her antinuclear work. Japanese peace organizations began to appreciate the international star in their midst. "We want Setsuko Thurlow to speak on our behalf," became a common refrain.[24] She was invited to present at the 2010 International Anti–Atomic and Hydrogen Bomb Conference in Hiroshima's Prefectural Gymnasium on August 6. There she stressed to the thousands in attendance the imperative that survivors convey their message to the younger generation, who must carry on with the task of pushing for global nuclear disarmament. After that, for the first time in twenty years, she attended the annual memorial ceremony. "It was a special emotion-provoking experience," she wrote to family and friends, "to be with fellow survivors to pray for the souls of loved ones." While in Hiroshima, Setsuko visited her sister Yukiko, who was suffering from advanced Parkinson's disease. She succumbed to her illness soon thereafter. Their older sister, Fumiko, had died eight years earlier. Now all six of Setsuko's siblings were gone. "I am the custodian of their memories," she wrote.[25]

Setsuko and Jim were preparing for Christmas when they received the best of holiday gifts: on December 22, 2010, the U.S. Senate gave its advice and consent to ratify the New Strategic Arms Reduction Treaty (New START). On April 8 President Barack Obama and President Dmitri A. Medvedev of the Russian Federation had signed the treaty, which further reduced their strategic nuclear arsenals. Now, with U.S. Senate approval, it would enter into force in the new year. A lot was happening in nuclear disarmament, and Setsuko was excited to be part of the effort.

Then, on Christmas Eve, Jim fell for the fourth time that month, and she watched an ambulance take him away. She couldn't imagine spending Christmas without Jim. To her delight paramedics brought him home the following day. After that he was confined to a wheelchair; his legs could no longer support him. Yet he kept encouraging her. "I want to be there," he said of disarmament efforts, "but since I cannot be there doing it, I want you to do my part of the job."[26]

Jim was hospitalized at North York General Hospital with pneumonia several times during the winter, but Setsuko never believed she might lose her dear husband. She expected him to recover, as he always had. But he no longer had the strength to keep going. On the evening of April 5, 2011, Jim Thurlow died. The sustaining light in Setsuko's life for fifty-eight years had flickered and gone out.

18 Point of No Return

> The point of no return was not necessarily the edge of the precipice: it could be the bottom of the valley, the beginning of the long climb up the far slope, and when a man had once begun that climb, he never looked back to that other side.
>
> –Alistair MacLean, *HMS Ulysses*

Whenever Setsuko entered their condominium, she could still feel Jim's presence. Reading her mail on the living room sofa or eating at the dining table, she could see Jim's photograph. In most other snapshots, he looked right at the viewer; his smile and eyes expressed kindness and affection. In this black-and-white photo, posted on his obituary and displayed on a pedestal in their home, Jim's face is turned from the camera, his lips set, as if he is gazing into a different place.

Jim's friends and colleagues reminisced about his integrity and modesty, his quiet wisdom, his students' admiration. His obituary cited James Thurlow's service to Toronto's Japanese community and commitment to nuclear disarmament: "He was a man of global vision and local action."[1] What it didn't say was that he had fostered and cherished the woman who would become one of history's most vocal, persistent, and effective antinuclear activists.

Over kitchen duty in Bibai, Jim had fallen in love with a young woman who had vowed to help abolish nuclear weapons, and Setsuko had married the man who shared that resolution. "He gave me all the energy and time I needed," she said of their fifty-six years together. "There were many moments when I couldn't take it emotionally, writing speeches late at night. I just couldn't have coped by myself. He was always there for me." Her work had required personal sacrifices: birthdays missed, concerts unattended, exercise classes cancelled, books unread, paintings unfinished. That price had not been too high. On the other hand, she said, "I had some sense of regret that I took a lot of time away from my husband. I wanted to start a new chapter with him, but that chapter never came."[2] Setsuko felt lost without Jim—her sounding board, editor, private historian—her great love. Their son Andy adjusted his life to become what Setsuko called her "tower of strength."[3] Soft-spoken and devoted, he willingly responded to his mother's bidding. Her older son, Peter, lived in Abu Dhabi, where he served as fiscal policy adviser for the government of the United Arab Emirates. He seldom returned to Canada.

In September 2011 Setsuko traveled to Nishinomiya, Japan, for a celebration of Jim's life at Kwansei Gakuin University, where he had taught. After that she visited friends and family in Hiroshima. Painful memories of the devastation caused by the atomic bomb prompted her to reaffirm her vow: "I am committed to share the warning of Hiroshima until my last breath."[4] Still, with her vitality deflated, she wondered how she could resume those efforts without Jim. Setsuko needed to imagine what he would say if he were still alive: "You must never feel consumed or immobilized by regret or guilt. Didn't I always urge you to put the abolition of nuclear weapons front and center in our lives? You cannot stop now. One day you will prevail." Even after his death, Jim gave her the strength to carry on.[5]

Interacting with the younger generation had never failed to energize Setsuko, and so it was no surprise how important Hibakusha Stories became in revitalizing her. Kathleen Sullivan, an educational consultant to the United Nations Office for Disarmament Affairs, had teamed up with Robert Croonquist, a longtime teacher and director of Youth Arts New York, to create Hibakusha Stories in 2008. Its stated mission was "to pass the legacy of the atomic bombings of Hiroshima and Nagasaki to a new generation of high school and university students to empower them with tools to build a world free of nuclear weapons."[6] Sullivan and Croonquist invited survivors of these catastrophic events into their classrooms to inform students about the current dangers by sharing testimonies, thus filling a gap in their education. Within ten years they would reach thirty-two thousand students and provide extensive staff development in disarmament education. Sullivan had first heard Setsuko Thurlow's testimony at an NGO workshop. "She was captivating," she recalled. "I instantly loved her."[7] Setsuko's perfect English, her ability to connect with the audience, and the power of her conviction impressed Croonquist and Sullivan. So when they launched Hibakusha Stories in New York City, they sought to engage the fiery Japanese Canadian.

Thurlow had joined Hibakusha Stories in 2010. Straightaway, she noted how most young people either seemed oblivious to nuclear weapons or considered them inevitable: an assumption she set out to help change. During Jim's illness she had to curtail her activities with the group. Eight months after his death, Sullivan encouraged Setsuko to reengage with Hibakusha Stories. She knew the healing power of youth. Setsuko returned to New York and, with two other hibakusha, visited twenty schools, reaching out to 1,600 students. Setsuko's story touched her young audience; in turn, their eager faces rejuvenated her. Her goal was not to create a troop of activists but to stimulate them to challenge the status quo and to read and form their own opinions. While she enlightened them about nuclear weapons, she imparted lessons on deprivation and courage, displaying the resilience of the human spirit. "A story of hope," one student called her testimony.[8]

Before long Kathleen became Setsuko's self-appointed secretary. She kept her calendar, responded to correspondence, helped to shape speeches, and accompanied her on international travels. Wherever they went, Setsuko enjoyed the local cuisine and absorbed the atmosphere. Despite their thirty-five-year age difference, they shared a zest for life. Like Setsuko, Kathleen had been born into privilege as the daughter of a wealthy chemical corporate CEO. She had become engaged in activism at a young age when her mother, whom she described as a "left-wing, radical Catholic," took her to an antinuclear march in Cleveland.[9] For decades Kathleen worked with environmental activist Joanna Macy on nuclear guardianship, which called for community-controlled management of radioactive waste. Resolute and passionate about her work, Kathleen, like Setsuko, felt comfortable challenging those in positions of power.

In annual letters to her family, Setsuko referred to Kathleen as a friend and an emotional support.

On January 3, 2012, Setsuko celebrated her eightieth birthday. "Time to slow down a bit," she wrote to friends.[10] She looked forward to joining an Aquafit class, using her new sewing machine, organizing her files, and writing. That was not to be. By year's end she had spoken at Princeton University, the University of Chicago, and Georgetown University; visited Costa Rica, where she was named the Peace Ambassador by the University for Peace, a UN-supported institution; and received a Queen Elizabeth II Diamond Jubilee Medal for her major contributions to her community and country. And that year the international effort to ban nuclear weapons took off.

In 1970 the UN Treaty on the Non-Proliferation of Nuclear Weapons (NPT) had entered into force, signed by 191 states, including the five permanent members of the United Nations Security Council (P5): China, France, Russia, the United Kingdom, and the United States—all of whom possessed nuclear weapons. At first the UN deemed the NPT successful as measured by the reduced number of states that sought to acquire nuclear weapons and the declining rate of proliferation. Still, the P5 retained their arsenals, and the United States continued to commit their nuclear weapons to defend members of the North Atlantic Treaty Organization (NATO), as well as Japan, South Korea, and Australia, in the event of a nuclear attack. Furthermore, nonsignatory states were not required to comply with the treaty. The 2005 Review Conference of the NPT had been marked with discord and lack of consensus. Progress toward nuclear disarmament seemed to have stalled.

Setsuko Thurlow's frustration was increasing. Now more than four decades since the NPT had commenced, she saw no tangible progress. The deterrence theory seemed to monopolize disarmament considerations. Even at so-called peace meetings, the agenda consisted of nuclear-weapon counts by country and type, along with scientific explanations of their operations and power. Deliberations on moral, ethical, social, and psychological aspects were secondary. "So much effort was being diverted to learn about fighting systems," Setsuko bemoaned, "instead of looking at what this means to my life, my family, my neighborhood, to the globe."[11] She felt troubled. In that she was not alone.

Disheartened by the slow progress in nuclear disarmament, seventy-five-year-old Malaysian obstetrician Datuk Dr. Ron McCoy, former co-president of the International Physicians for the Prevention of Nuclear War (IPPNW), had concluded that they needed a different tactic. The International Campaign to Ban Landmines, founded by peace activist Jody Williams, had led a successful effort to prohibit the use of landmines. In 1997, despite substantial opposition, 122 states signed the Anti-Personnel Mine Ban Treaty. Why not model their approach?

In 2005 McCoy contacted colleagues and proposed a new organization, which he called the International Campaign to Abolish Nuclear Weapons (ICAN). Health-care and peace workers in Australia, including co-founders Bill Williams, a general practitioner who served Aboriginal communities; Tilman Ruff, a public-health professor at the University of Melbourne; and Dimity Hawkins, a researcher on victims of nuclear testing, were among the first to respond with enthusiasm: "We wanted to reignite a global conversation and passionate action around a simple idea: Can you imagine a world free of nuclear weapons? I can." Ban treaties had controlled not only landmines but also cluster munitions as well as biological and chemical weapons. Nuclear weapons should be added to that list, they argued. They were the sole weapons capable of destroying all humankind. An international law that made them illegal became ICAN's goal. "We need a determined worldwide movement to outlaw and abolish nukes," said co-founder Bill Williams. "We need to build the wave of public opinion into a mighty crescendo: a massive, surging irresistible force which carries us all the way to absolutely zero nukes. Without it, even the most inspirational of leaders will falter."[12]

ICAN had launched its campaign in April 2007. From the start it envisioned itself as a global, collaborative effort—an umbrella organization. By 2010 it had established headquarters in Geneva and, starting with two major antinuclear groups—Mayors for Peace and IPPNW—had acquired almost five hundred partners. Among them were Hibakusha Stories and Peace Boat. ICAN leadership was now shared by three co-chairs: Tilman Ruff, one of the co-founders;

Akira Kawasaki of Peace Boat; and Rebecca Johnson, a British peace activist and strategist, director of the Acronym Institute for Disarmament Diplomacy. ICAN leaders knew nuclear-weapon states would oppose their efforts, so they focused on the weapon-free nations. Signatories to NPT themselves, most of them were rankled by the small group of countries who blatantly disregarded the goal of disarmament, which had been agreed on in that treaty. As a cornerstone for its campaign, ICAN emphasized the catastrophic human consequences of nuclear war, as epitomized by survivors' testimonies. Thus hibakusha became a centerpiece for its crusade.

Time had come to shift the official narrative from deterrence to humanitarian consequences, as Setsuko Thurlow had been advocating for years. The concept of deterrence was abstract. Thurlow's depictions of human suffering were tangible: strips of skin hanging like ribbons, eyeballs blown from their sockets, facial features melted like lava, stomachs burst open, precious children transformed into chunks of charred flesh. Such words helped stigmatize nuclear weapons in efforts to cast their use as a crime against humanity.

A crucial milestone for ICAN's campaign was obtaining the active support of the International Committee of the Red Cross (ICRC). This global network of eighty million people, for the most part volunteers, had been established in 1863 by Civil War nurse Clara Barton to ensure humanitarian protection and assistance to victims of armed conflict and other violent situations. As a rule, discussions between Red Cross leadership and individual nations remained confidential, outside of political contexts. Such had been the case with nuclear weapons, even though Marcel Junod, working for the Red Cross, had been the first foreign physician to enter Hiroshima. Yet in 2010, ICRC president Dr. Jakob Kellenberger, stated publicly that deliberations on nuclear weapons needed to refocus on people and the future of humankind.[13] With that he led the International Committee of the Red Cross into the center of the ongoing global controversy. A force of eighty million had been summoned to action.

Another major step toward the abolition of nuclear weapons was taken by UN representatives from Norway, Mexico, and Austria at the Sixty-Seventh Session of the General Assembly, held in October 2012. Increasingly concerned that a minority of states controlled humankind's future, they and eleven other representatives called for creation of a UN Working Group to draft specific plans to achieve a world free of nuclear weapons. A large majority of states agreed, and on October 12, the UN General Assembly adopted Resolution L46, which convened an Open-Ended Working Group (OEWG) "to develop proposals to take forward multilateral nuclear disarmament negotiations."[14] The nonnuclear states had begun to revolt.

To reframe nuclear weapons as a humanitarian issue and gain momentum, advocates convened three stand-alone intergovernmental conferences. They started in Norway. On March 4, 2013, the Norwegian government hosted the first conference on the humanitarian impact of nuclear weapons, referred to as the Oslo Conference, with ICAN as its civil-society partner. Representatives from 127 states, the United Nations, civil-society groups, and the International Committee of the Red Cross gathered for two days in Oslo.

Norway's minister of foreign affairs, Espen Barth Eide, served as chair. In his welcoming statement, he said that for decades heads of states and scientists had been debating the power of nuclear weapons and their potential deployment. This conference, he announced, would take a different starting point—the humanitarian consequences of their use. Over the next two days, attendees would explore the immediate and long-term results from the discharge of these weapons of mass destruction and assess if governments and aid organizations could handle the attendant human catastrophe.[15]

Eide insisted the meeting be fact-based, with presentations by experts in specific areas. As a NATO member, the Norwegian government wanted to forestall the perception that it had a different agenda. So consideration of a ban treaty did not appear on the conference program. Nevertheless, the P5—China, France, Russia, the United Kingdom, and the United States—declined to participate in the Oslo Conference. They said they were already cognizant of the dangers of nuclear weapons. Furthermore, they warned Chairman Eide that this conference could derail the efforts of the Nuclear Non-Proliferation Treaty, which they considered the most judicious approach to limiting nuclear arms. He clarified that conference organizers did not intend to pursue a substitute for the NPT. At least two of the nuclear armed countries, India and Pakistan, sent representatives, as did Canada and Japan, both under the U.S. nuclear umbrella.

In the first session, specialists provided concrete descriptions of a nuclear-weapon detonation and its immediate effects on individuals and infrastructure, dramatized by a video taken in the aftermath of Hiroshima. The scale of destruction surprised many attendees. The second session covered widespread and long-term consequences for public health, food, security, and the environment. On the second day, international authorities and leaders of humanitarian organizations reviewed requirements for an adequate response and the current state of preparedness. A picture of futility emerged. Many delegates emphasized that only by eliminating nuclear weapons could such a calamity be prevented. In his chair's summary, Eide underscored the devastating aftermath with which neither states nor humanitarian organizations could cope and stressed that a nuclear explosion would impact populations worldwide and not be constrained by national borders. He did not, however, use the term "ban treaty."

Setsuko was not able to attend the Oslo Conference. When she read the agenda, two aspects disappointed her. First, not one hibakusha had been asked to speak at a conference with "Humanitarian Impact" in its title. And, second, its main purpose seemed to be dissemination of facts. She understood that, as a member of NATO, the Norwegian government did not want to signal a ban treaty as the conference goal. On the other hand, ICAN was starting to build a case to delegitimize nuclear weapons. Although the P5 assumed a discussion on nuclear weapons would be pointless without their participation, their dismissive posture enhanced the momentum for pursuing the humanitarian approach. The Mexican government offered to host a follow-up conference early the next year. Most delegates left Oslo feeling that something momentous was happening. Reflecting back on the conference, one attendee said, "Oslo changed everything."[16]

Meanwhile, the United Nations Open-Ended Working Group, created to develop proposals to take forward multilateral nuclear-disarmament negotiations, met throughout the spring and summer of 2013. In the fall they submitted their report to the UN. In her summary Beatrice Fihn, a peace activist with the Women's International League for Peace and Freedom, who later would assume leadership of ICAN, wrote that it resembled a "laundry list of every single proposal that has ever been made." Its major outcome had been to embolden those states that did not have nuclear arms to assume their rightful role in promoting nuclear disarmament. "The traditional power dynamics between nuclear-armed and non-nuclear weapon states are changing," she concluded.[17]

On February 12, 2014, Setsuko Thurlow flew to Nuevo Vallarta for the second conference on the humanitarian impact of nuclear weapons—the Nayarit Conference. She had boarded Air Canada under gray skies and snow flurries and disembarked to find a tropical paradise. Located just north of Puerto Vallarta on Mexico's west coast, Nuevo Vallarta had been developed as a resort community in the state of Nayarit, with five miles of white-sand beaches edging the turquoise-blue ocean. Setsuko checked into the Paradise Village Hotel. Set among natural lagoons, the resort offered a spa, golf course, two large pools with waterfalls, and unique culinary experiences. Its natural beauty stood in stark contrast to the task at hand—safeguarding humankind from annihilation.

Delegations from 146 states, the United Nations, the International Committee of the Red Cross, and over 120 representatives from other civil-society organizations participated. Again, ICAN played a major role coordinating the NGOs. And the nuclear-weapon states continued their boycott of this second conference on the humanitarian consequences of nuclear arms. Manuel Gómez Robledo, Mexico's vice minister for multilateral affairs and human rights, served as conference chair. In his welcoming comments, he said that over the next two days, they planned to build on what they had learned in Oslo. The agenda included the challenges of a nuclear detonation to economic growth and sustainable development, public-health impacts, and the risk of an accidental nuclear explosion—all focused on the humanitarian consequences. With that in mind, the organizers devoted most of the first morning to testimonies from hibakusha: three Japanese men, two of whom were leaders of the Japan Confederation of A- and H-Bomb Sufferers (Nihon Hidankyo); a Nagasaki teenager who spoke about her parents and grandparents; and Setsuko Thurlow.[18]

As she prepared her ten-minute talk, Setsuko felt torn. The Nayarit Conference organizers hoped to attract nuclear-weapon states. Although they wanted the world to hear firsthand what had happened to individuals from Hiroshima and Nagasaki, the organizers did not want the end point to appear to be a total ban of nuclear weapons. Thurlow perceived a double agenda; she was to educate yet, at the same time, not alienate. Behind the podium hung the emblem for the second international conference—an eight-foot-high drawing of a child standing on a precipice. To the right were green trees with three birds flying in the sunshine; to the left were three charred trees, three bombers, and a mushroom cloud against a black sky.

If Setsuko had been cautioned not to confront nuclear-weapon states, she disregarded the advice with her opening words: "Dear colleagues from around the world engaged in the urgent task of abolishing nuclear weapons."[19] Then she told her story. ICAN co-chair Rebecca Johnson had insisted Thurlow be on the podium. "Setsuko was catching them by the throat and the heart and the eyes and the ears with her testimony," she said. This was not the first time Johnson had heard her talk: "Whenever she speaks, I look out at the people listening, and I see those faces change as I'm sure my face changed when I heard her the first time and every time thereafter."[20]

Setsuko didn't stop with her testimony, however. She explained how survivors came to feel that no one should ever experience the "inhumanity, illegality, immorality, and cruelty of the atomic bombing." They had a moral imperative to abolish nuclear arms. She paused. Then her voice became more forceful as she charged forward, directing her admonition to those somewhat passive, unengaged states and those under the umbrellas of nuclear-weapon states. She condemned the "lack of political will for disarmament" and called the situation an "unacceptable reality." She pointed to the failure to ratify the Comprehensive Test Ban Treaty, which had been adopted by the UN General Assembly back in 1996; the noncompliance in fulfilling the legal obligation of Article VI in the Treaty on the Non-Proliferation of Nuclear Weapons; the failure to achieve a nuclear weapons–free zone in the Middle East; and the continued modernization of nuclear weapons. They must plot a new course. "The time has come for non–nuclear weapons states and civil society to initiate a nuclear weapons ban for the sake of humanity," she urged. Then she looked into the audience and issued a challenge to each one sitting there: "You and I, together, we can. We must."[21]

Prolonged applause followed as everyone stood. Yet clapping could not express the depth of feeling she evoked. Who was this eighty-two-year-old Japanese Canadian? Many had never heard her speak. Her passion, her command, stunned the audience. She defied the power of recalcitrant states and impugned their long-standing arguments. She exhorted those who tiptoed around them. She beseeched those who had wearied of the effort. And she set the tone for the Nayarit meeting as she summoned each individual to action. Later that day a man with a white beard approached her. He said he had never heard an antinuclear advocate speak with such clarity and spirit. That man was Dr. Ira Helfand, co-president of the International Physicians for the Prevention of Nuclear War and a member of ICAN's Steering Group. In Setsuko he may have just found ICAN's voice, its animating force going forward.

After the hibakushas' testimonies, speakers in the first working session reviewed the key findings from the Oslo Conference, highlighting the devastating effects on human health and the inadequate response capabilities. That was the first time Setsuko heard Beatrice Fihn, an impressive young Swedish lawyer, speak about civil society and the humanitarian approach to nuclear weapons. She would become ICAN's first executive director five months later. That afternoon the second working session tackled global effects of a nuclear-weapon explosion on the environment, climate, and infrastructure. Finally, the third session addressed the repercussions of a nuclear detonation on global public health. At the evening reception, held at the Paradise Village golf course, Setsuko mingled with international leaders, many of whom looked forward to meeting this outspoken hibakusha.

On the next day, the fourth working session introduced a new topic—the risk and threat of an accidental detonation of nuclear weapons due to human or technical error. This topic was considered a remote possibility or not considered at all by much of the public, and the revelations jolted the audience. Patricia Lewis of Chatham House, an independent policy institute headquartered in London, presented results from a new study, titled "Too Close for Comfort." She reported sixteen cases of near misses due to technical errors and misperception to demonstrate the importance of what she called the "human judgment factor" in nuclear decision making. Given the lax safety and security measures, the current nuclear-weapon count of seventeen thousand should raise concerns, she concluded; they posed an unacceptable peril.[22]

Perhaps the most frightening presentation came from investigative journalist Eric Schlosser, author of *Command and Control: Nuclear Weapons, the Damascus Accident, and the Illusion of Safety*, published the previous year. He spoke via video. As he moved from theoretical to real-life situations, he underscored the likelihood of a catastrophic mistake. Those who had not read his book sat horrified as he told about a nuclear mishap that could have obliterated Arkansas. The incident had occurred back in 1980 and appeared on the list of thirty-two reported "Broken Arrows," defined by the military as any incident in which a nuclear weapon is lost, stolen, or inadvertently detonated.

Titan II, the largest U.S. intercontinental ballistic missile (ICBM), stood 103 feet tall, with a nine-megaton thermonuclear warhead inside its nose cone. Eighteen ICBMs had been hidden in missile silos throughout rural Arkansas. Among them was Launch Complex 374–7, located near Damascus, fifty miles north of Little Rock. At 6:30 p.m. on September 18, two missile repairmen were checking the pressure on the missile's stage 2 oxidizer tank. The senior airman was using a socket wrench to unscrew a pressure cap when he accidentally dropped the nine-pound socket. It fell seventy feet and ricocheted off the missile shell with such force that it created a leak. Rocket fuel started spraying out. Once emptied, the stage 1 fuel tank could collapse and cause the rest of the eight-story missile to fall and rupture, in turn setting off a nuclear explosion. Its warhead was six hundred times more powerful than the bomb that had destroyed Hiroshima. Specialists from the Little Rock Air Force Base were summoned immediately. Arkansas's governor, Bill Clinton, was told that the situation was under control, not that they were on the brink of a catastrophe.

In the early hours of Friday, September 19, senior airman David Livingston volunteered to enter the silo in a heroic attempt to turn on an exhaust fan. The Titan II exploded, ejecting the second stage and the warhead. Livingston was fatally wounded; twenty-one other air force personnel were injured. At daybreak, after several frantic hours of searching, the air force retrieved the warhead from a shallow ditch not far from the silo. Its safety mechanisms had prevented a nuclear discharge.

In his best-selling book, which would be a finalist for the 2014 Pulitzer Prize for History, Schlosser concluded that, although the United States had among the most developed nuclear weaponry at the time, it had such deficiencies in regulation and monitoring as to pose a threat to itself as great or even greater than that from other countries. Japanese poet Sadako Kurihara had presaged this years earlier when she wrote: "O America, you with the atomic bombs / to burn out Hiroshima a million times over: / don't perish by your own hand!"[23] Schlosser laid bare the perplexing dilemma any country that had acquired nuclear weapons confronted: how to command and control weapons of mass destruction so as not to be destroyed by them. Most attendees agreed with ICAN's conclusion that "the continued possession and deployment of nuclear weapons is a reckless and unsanctionable gamble with the future of humanity and the planet."[24] To date they had been lucky. It was just a matter of time before their luck ran out.

Organizers dedicated the remainder of the day to open discussions, in which delegates from over half of the states spoke. Most echoed Setsuko Thurlow's challenge: "The time has come for non-nuclear weapons states and civil society to initiate a nuclear weapons ban for the sake of humanity." Several countries, including the Netherlands, Turkey, Australia, Germany, and—to Setsuko's dismay—Canada, thought banning nuclear weapons would not lead to their total elimination and at the same time would erode their state's security. They preferred the NPT approach with its gradual action plan. They cautioned that a proposed ban would antagonize the nuclear-armed states, who once again had boycotted the conference, driving them further from a multilateral process. Still, over fifty states called for the total elimination of nuclear weapons, and Austrian foreign minister Sebastian Kurz announced that the Austrian government would host the third conference on the humanitarian impact of nuclear weapons in Vienna. "The sense of momentum established in Nayarit was palpable," wrote ICAN leaders, citing the poignant testimonies from the hibakusha as a "powerful reminder of the urgency and overwhelming importance of the need to ensure that these weapons are never used again."[25]

At the end of the day, the conference chair, Manuel Gómez Robledo, reminded attendees what Eide, the chair of the Oslo Conference, had warned:

"The effects of a nuclear weapon detonation are not constrained by national borders." As more countries deployed an increasing number of nuclear arms, the risks of accidental, mistaken, or unauthorized use of these weapons increased substantially. The aftermath would be catastrophic. Robledo pointed out that in the past "[chemical and biological] weapons have been eliminated after they have been outlawed. We believe this is the path to achieve a world without nuclear weapons." The time had come to initiate a diplomatic process, he concluded, with humanitarian consequences at the center of their efforts. "Nayarit is a point of no return."[26]

19 Confronting Truman

> Truman was opening the door to the possible annihilation of the species, and he knew it.
>
> –Peter Kuznick, "The Bomb Sends a Message to the World"

In 2014 Setsuko Thurlow traveled to eight countries, crossing the Atlantic Ocean three times and the Pacific once, totaling over thirty thousand miles, mostly in the winter. She was eighty-two years old. Low-back pain from arthritis required her to use a cane or wheelchair. Still, she insisted on sitting in economy class.

The year had started with a keynote address at the second conference on the humanitarian impact of nuclear weapons in mid-February. While in Nayarit, she met Breifne O'Reilly, Ireland's director for disarmament and nonproliferation. In his concluding comments, he had said, "It is especially difficult not to be moved by the very powerful and personal testimony of the Hibakusha. . . . They speak with a unique voice on the consequences of nuclear weapons."[1] Afterward, he asked Thurlow to speak at an upcoming symposium, "Disarmament and Non-Proliferation: Historical Perspectives and Future Objectives," to be held at the Royal Irish Academy, whose distinguished members had included Edmund Burke, Charles Darwin, and Albert Einstein. Six weeks after her return from Mexico, Setsuko was on a plane to Dublin.

Setsuko found it refreshing to speak freely at the conference, held on March 28, 2014, with no overt or even subtle restrictions. And she felt pleased that, besides governmental and NGO representatives, this conference included members from the academic community and the military. Standing on the dais in the elegant meeting room of the Academy House, surrounded on all sides by books, floor to ceiling, she acknowledged Ireland's long history in the nuclear-disarmament movement. She paid tribute to the late Seán MacBride, a Nobel Peace Prize laureate, for his significant contributions to Japan's peace movement in the mid-1970s. "With his memory in our hearts," she said, "and to strengthen our own work for nuclear disarmament, let me take you back in time to Hiroshima." Then she told her story to an awestruck audience. After that she reviewed a litany of failed efforts at the hands of nuclear-weapon states, followed by a new point she had begun making in her speeches: "The nuclear weapons states have kept the world as hostages in fear and anxiety while squandering trillions of dollars away from meeting human needs in order to build ever more destructive weapons of mass destruction." The media highlighted one particular statement from her speech: "We believe that humanity and nuclear weapons cannot coexist."[2]

The press found Thurlow engaging. On a tour of Oscar Wilde's home, a reporter began to explain that Wilde was one of their most esteemed writers, to which Setsuko replied that she had enjoyed reading his works since college and had selected him for her senior thesis. After that people approached her at the hotel or on the street and asked, "Are you the one who wrote about Oscar Wilde?"[3] And they appreciated her antinuclear efforts. One evening at a farm-to-table restaurant, four men approached her and asked, "Are you that lovely lady from Hiroshima that was in the paper this morning now?"[4] She nodded. Teary-eyed, they thanked her for speaking out on Ireland's behalf.

Of particular fun for Setsuko was the time she and Kathleen Sullivan spent with British peace activist Rebecca Johnson and her partner, Heena. Like Setsuko, Rebecca was an ardent antinuclear champion, yet both had a sense of fun. Johnson recalled the evening the four went to a famous old pub in Dublin. When they entered the crowded taproom, they had difficulty bringing Setsuko's wheelchair inside. "I think I just saw you on the telly," a customer said. "She's the woman from Hiroshima."[5] Amid oohs and aahs, the patrons made way and brought the four ladies pints of Guinness. Setsuko proudly held up her pint for a photograph.

Setsuko returned to Toronto in time to see the enchanting array of cherry trees in bloom. A Japanese ambassador had gifted two thousand to the people of Toronto in thanks for their kindness to Japanese Canadians who had relocated there after World War II. Setsuko had barely unpacked when she began planning for her next trip, albeit with some vexation. She felt she had been coerced into participating in the Annual Truman Legacy Symposium.

Setsuko had met President Harry Truman's grandson, Clifton Truman Daniel, back in 2011, when Kathleen Sullivan invited him to join Hibakusha Stories. She had advertised him to Setsuko as a freelance journalist who aspired to create a world without nuclear weapons. Setsuko was reluctant to meet him. Despite that, Kathleen involved Clifton in their work. She said she considered him like a brother, listing him as a team member on their website, pushing Setsuko to welcome him. Kathleen scheduled a number of joint panels and interviews, bringing attention to Hibakusha Stories with programs such as "Clifton Truman Daniel with Hiroshima and Nagasaki Survivors," which aired on CSPAN's History Channel. Kathleen continued to thrust them together. She told Setsuko that Clifton adored her and was writing a screenplay about her life to elevate her story. He wanted her to speak at the Annual Truman Legacy Symposium, to be held at the Harry S. Truman Little White House in Key West on May 16–17, 2014. Setsuko said she had no interest in having President Truman's grandson "elevate her story."[6]

Exhausted from her travels and with two upcoming international trips, Setsuko wanted to cancel, but she felt obligated to attend as a participant from Hibakusha Stories. And Sullivan reminded her that Clifton served as the honorary chair of the board of trustees of the Harry S. Truman Library Institute. The symposium topic—on which Setsuko had strong opinions—was President Truman's decision to use the atomic bomb. A panel would debate whether or not his decision about "which innocents to save," as he phrased it, was morally sound.[7] Members of Hibakusha Stories were developing a list of speakers when they learned that the board of trustees already had set the program, which included two historians who had served on the Nuclear Regulatory Commission and a Catholic priest. Setsuko disapproved and suggested historian Peter Kuznick, author of *Rethinking the Atomic Bombings of Hiroshima and Nagasaki: Japanese and American Perspectives*, to balance the panel discussion. Clifton told her it was too late. Too late for someone as radical as Kuznick, Setsuko thought. Added to that she had not been invited to participate in either of the two panels.

This growing star of the worldwide antinuclear movement, this survivor who inspired standing ovations, this keynote speaker alongside Pope Francis for the upcoming third conference on the humanitarian impact of nuclear weapons, was scheduled to give public comments on behalf of Hibakusha Stories from a small makeshift stage on the Truman Little White House lawn the evening before the formal program began. If this was how she was to be treated, Setsuko felt free to speak her mind—no political niceties for the largely Truman-loving audience. And she would take as much time as she needed to make her points.

Setsuko began with her own story, usually guaranteed to get the audience's attention. She didn't stop there. She recounted how in time some historians, addressing the motives behind Truman's decision to drop the bombs, rejected the American myth of lives saved, calling it a political, not a military, decision. Filmmaker Oliver Stone and American University professor Peter Kuznick's best-selling book, *The Untold History of the United States*, published in 2012, and the twelve-part documentary film series that followed, rebutted the Truman apologists who claimed the decision to drop the bomb was to prevent casualties—up to a half million, the president was told at one point. In truth, as these revisionist historians contested, Truman's goal was to subdue the Russians and deny them their anticipated territorial and economic concessions. "With the understanding of the historical perspective," Thurlow told the audience, "the survivors saw themselves as pawns in the opening moves of the Cold War rather than as sacrifices on the altar of peace." She proceeded to quote noted historian Richard Falk, who wrote that the atomic bombings should have been appraised as atrocities so that "Hiroshima is understood to have been on the same level of depravity and in many ways far more dangerous to us as a species and as a civilization than was even Auschwitz."[8] In other words, history should consider President Harry Truman a war criminal. "Setsuko eviscerated Harry Truman on the lawn of the Little White House," Kathleen Sullivan observed.[9] She did not receive her usual standing ovation.

On May 17 the symposium officially started, with a panel who debated Truman's decision to use the atomic bomb. Moderator J. Samuel Walker, author of *Prompt and Utter Destruction: Truman and the Use of Atomic Bombs against Japan*, published seventeen years previously, called the president's decision to use the atomic bombs the "most contentious debate in all of American history." He didn't think they would settle the argument on that day but hoped to "lower the volume of ill will that has all too often been a prominent part of this controversy." He noted the two poles of thought—the traditional interpretation that the atomic bomb was necessary to get Japan to surrender and avoid an invasion, which would have cost hundreds of thousands of American lives; and the revisionist interpretation that Japan was trying to surrender, and Truman used the bomb to intimidate the Soviet Union. He said that most *scholars*—using that designation numerous times—most *scholars* agreed with the traditional interpretation. He went on to say he hoped they could conduct their arguments at the symposium in a "civil manner" with "no eruptions."[10] That statement was likely directed at Setsuko Thurlow, given her comments the night before on the Truman Little White House lawn.

The first speaker, lawyer and historian Richard B. Frank, had written *Downfall: The End of the Imperial Japanese Empire*, published in 1999, in which he concluded, "It is fantasy, not history . . . to believe that the end of the war was at hand before the use of the atomic bomb."[11] Winner of the Harry S. Truman Book Award, Frank now reviewed the events leading to unconditional surrender, focusing on the casualty toll as the reason to end the war expeditiously. With respect for Setsuko Thurlow, he said, "We heard last night very movingly and very appropriately from two survivors of the atomic bombings. I believe it is extraordinarily important that we always keep in mind the horrendous nature of those weapons that hangs over us to this day." But he went on to say, "you have to understand just how utterly God-awful the war was." An estimated quarter million people perished every month, mostly Asian noncombatants. "This is the context in which all of this takes place," he ended. "This is the context in which we can sit back and make judgments."[12]

The next panelist, Reverend Wilson Miscamble, a professor and priest at the University of Notre Dame, had authored *The Most Controversial Decision:*

Truman, the Atomic Bomb, and the Defeat of Japan, in which he concluded that Truman was trying to stop the brutal war in the Pacific. He contended that without the bomb Japanese losses would have been greater. "Hard to believe when one hears the testimony of survivors," he said with a brief hand gesture in Setsuko's direction. He then proceeded to describe Truman almost as a saint who rescued the peoples of Asia, saying, "The losses in Hiroshima and Nagasaki . . . pale in significance" when compared to twenty-four million dead from the Japanese "rampage." He talked of starvation, beatings, beheadings, "a charnel house of atrocities." Truman had written that he "didn't like the idea of killing all those kids," Miscamble continued. Those who call him immoral should look at the Japanese leaders: "neo-samurai" who with their "banzai spirit engaged the whole population in a kind of kamikaze campaign." It required incredible control from Thurlow to keep from interrupting Father Miscamble as he condemned the entire Japanese population using language hardly befitting of a priest. He then spoke of Truman's Christian views, grounded in the Ten Commandments and the Sermon on the Mount.[13]

The third panelist, Robert Norris, was a senior fellow for nuclear policy with the Federation of American Scientists and author of *Racing for the Bomb: General Leslie R. Groves, the Manhattan Project's Indispensable Man,* which was out of print at the time. He had concluded that the use of the atomic bomb was Leslie Groves's decision, not Truman's. The president's only position was not to interfere with Groves. "President Truman was not involved in the decision to use the bomb as subsequent literature has alleged," Norris argued. "He should not be blamed."[14] To Setsuko's chagrin the panel had not engaged in a debate; they had presented a consensus, reinforced with scattered vitriolic rhetoric.

As the camera panned the audience, it picked up the most well-known hibakusha worldwide frowning. If it could have broadcast her thoughts, the public would have heard what she later said privately: "I groaned as I listened to them. Oh my gosh, they are slipping down into the valley of Tennessee or North Carolina or West Virginia, as if they have never been to the main road and have read outdated history textbooks. These were the kind of people teaching young people. I was heartbroken."[15]

The three presentations finished early, leaving an hour for questions from the audience. As individuals stood at the microphone, the moderator, J. Samuel Walker, seemed not to notice Thurlow. He continued to call on others, to whom the panelists gave long-winded answers. With less than five minutes left in the session, he said, "And now we have a final question from a special questioner."[16] He did not introduce her by name or recognize her as a hibakusha. In a loud, clear voice, Setsuko said, "As I listen to you people, I realize that you seem to share a similar view and perspective. I was thinking that in this country there are many other historians and other experts who do have very different viewpoints on the issue you are talking about, and I think it would be a great service to American citizens to have this kind of symposium, staffed by the people with a different perspective. And not only American people, but I think there are a lot of Japanese historians, Japanese experts who have a very different viewpoint. . . . Wouldn't it be wonderful if we can organize a symposium of this nature?"[17] Walker answered that he based his invitations on their scholarly work, not their ideology or their position on the bomb. Setsuko probably had to bite her tongue to stop from pointing out to Frank that his *scholarly* work was thirteen years older than that of historian Peter Kuznick, whom they had declined to invite.

Setsuko then asked why none of the panelists had mentioned the U.S. government report on the strategic bombing survey that had concluded that Japan had already been beaten, making the bomb unnecessary. Professor Frank replied, "I can't say strongly enough how much empathy I have for you and your fellow survivors. . . . It is an enormous tragedy." He went on to say that evidence that the Japanese were on the cusp of surrendering is lacking, and, after a scholarly analysis, the strategic bombing report, in his view, had been "thoroughly trashed."[18]

In ending, the panelists pointed out that no military figure had opposed the bomb before it was dropped. Frank said that Truman's chief of staff, Admiral William Leahy, did advise the president: "The bombs will not work. I'm an expert on explosives. They will not work."[19] He and the other speakers gave a hearty laugh, which concluded the panel—hardly appropriate for Frank, who minutes before had expressed "empathy" for Setsuko and her fellow survivors.

Many in the audience echoed the laugh; others gave an embarrassed chuckle. Thus concluded the discussion on Truman's earthshaking decision to use the first atomic bomb.

Setsuko left Key West feeling manipulated, belittled, disheartened, and angered. Through her work with Hiroshima-Nagasaki Relived, Peace Boat, and Hibakusha Stories, she had been trying to educate young people about the tragedies, both past and future, from nuclear weapons. This encounter with these "scholars" underscored what many students in the United States were being taught. And she had just experienced the kind of polemic she knew they would face in trying to persuade the United States to relinquish its nuclear weapons. By the time she reached Toronto, the cherry blossoms had fallen.

In the fall Setsuko flew to Japan to receive the Kiyoshi Tanimoto Peace Prize. Established to commemorate the spirit of Reverend Tanimoto in his devotion to Hiroshima's A-bomb survivors, it is awarded to individuals who promote peace worldwide. The chair called Setsuko Thurlow's appeal for the abolition of nuclear weapons, extending over half of a century, extraordinary. She felt touched to receive the award named for her beloved pastor. A few days later, the mayor of Hiroshima presented Setsuko with an official letter, naming her a Hiroshima peace ambassador.

From Japan Setsuko flew sixteen hours across two continents to reach Oslo. There she began a Scandinavian tour with Kathleen Sullivan prior to the third conference on the humanitarian impact of nuclear weapons, to be held in Vienna. As a guest of the Norwegian People's Aid, she attended a series of events with young parliamentary leaders, students, and the general public. She traveled on to Sweden, where, invited by the 1985 Nobel Peace Prize winner, International Physicians for the Prevention of Nuclear War, Setsuko addressed parliamentarians and was interviewed extensively by reporters from television, radio, and newspapers.

Most noteworthy was her appearance on *Skavlan*, one of Europe's longest-running talk shows with an estimated three million viewers, hosted by journalist Fredrik Skavlan. Over the years his guest list had included a host of celebrities, from political leaders Bill Clinton, Kofi Annan, and Tony Blair to Nobel Peace Prize laureate Malala Yousafzai to entertainers Adele, Justin Bieber, and Andrea Bocelli to the sports figure Pele. Skavlan's guests on December 5, 2014, included Sweden's prime minister, Kjell Stefan Löfven; the 2014 winner of the Nobel Prize in Physiology or Medicine, May-Britt Moser; British comedian John Cleese, best known for *Monty Python's Flying Circus*; and Setsuko Thurlow. What a contrast a politician, scientist, comedian, and antinuclear activist made. John Cleese, who led off the guests, told the audience, "I'm not allowed to make jokes tonight," which of course made them laugh.[20]

After introducing Setsuko Thurlow as a Hiroshima survivor, Skavlan asked where she was when the atomic bomb was dropped. Just a few feet from Skavlan, she looked directly at him and began her oft-told narrative. Although she had recounted it hundreds of times by then, her storytelling was as fresh as if this was her first account, filled with drama and animation. It appeared that Skavlan had not been prepped thoroughly. He looked incredulous, almost sick, as she described stomachs burst open, body parts missing, and people holding their eyeballs in their hands. He interrupted the terrifying tale with simple questions such as "Did you hear any sound? What did Hiroshima look like?" As with most reporters, it was easier for him to focus on buildings than on people. Setsuko didn't ease up and proceeded to describe the catastrophe she found on the army training ground. When the camera scanned the other guests, the scientist and prime minister sat riveted; John Cleese looked down and twisted his fingers during the entire interview as if waiting for the punchline that never came. "Do you think that the people who have not experienced what you have experienced are able to grasp the consequences of nuclear weapons, of a nuclear detonation?" Skavlan asked.[21]

"They certainly could," she replied, "if they put their minds to the issue and are interested in finding out what kind of world we are living in. Then you can read, you can think, you can talk. Yes, you can use your imagination." She went on to say that hibakusha were recalling their experience around the world because it is not just something that happened seventy years ago; it has continued. "At that time there were only two bombs which were used on Hiroshima and Nagasaki. We thought it was a catastrophic situation. But now we have sixteen to seventeen thousand nuclear weapons. . . . But most of the people have their heads in the sand."[22] This was a natural segue to talk about ICAN's work and a possible ban treaty. Instead, Skavlan changed direction and asked about her social-work career.

Setsuko was disappointed with the interview. She found Skavlan ill-prepared, unaware of the imminent, groundbreaking third conference on the humanitarian impact of nuclear weapons to be held in Vienna in three days. The political leaders and activist groups seemed pleased with her comments, however. She was captivating, a natural storyteller. No wonder she was asked to give keynote addresses at so many major conferences. Others could give facts and figures, but she had the narrative, and she told it in such a way that she placed the listener there with her at that unspeakable moment. If anyone could reach the public and make a case to ban nuclear weapons, it was Setsuko Thurlow.

A highlight of the Scandinavian tour for Setsuko was meeting American historian and journalist Eric Schlosser, author of *Command and Control.* When they spoke together at Stockholm University and other events, he was deeply moved by Setsuko's testimony. And Setsuko found him to be an impressive thinker—and charming, with an urbane sensibility. As her traveling companion Kathleen Sullivan often observed, when Setsuko interacted with luminaries and fellow activists, they expressed awe at her intellect and wide range of interests. And like so many others, Eric Schlosser was clearly taken with her. He thought Setsuko remarkable on so many levels. "In the most superficial sense," he said, "her stamina is incredible, her life force extraordinary, and for her to be radiating a positive and inspiring energy after what she experienced is extraordinary. To live through that and find a way to adapt is one thing, but then to take that experience and to give meaning to it for others in an effort to prevent it from ever being repeated—that's remarkable."[23] Together they moved on to the third conference on the humanitarian impact of nuclear weapons.

20 Moving toward Zero

When it comes to nuclear weapons, there is no after.

–Beatrice Fihn, *Bulletin of the Atomic Scientists*

As Setsuko Thurlow stood in front of Vienna's Hofburg Palace, the cold rain could not obscure its grandeur. Built by the Babenbergs in the thirteenth century, it is among the largest palace complexes in the world. In this magnificent royal seat, monarchs once held court; heads of states made historic decisions; and Hayden, Mozart, and Beethoven presented world premieres. Here the third international conference on the humanitarian impact of nuclear weapons would commence the next day, December 8, 2014, with representatives from 158 states; the International Red Cross and Red Crescent Societies; and civil-society groups, most notably ICAN, which was central to the meeting's organization.[1]

In attempts to attract nuclear-weapon states to Vienna, the Austrian organizers had assured them that the intent was not to write a ban treaty to replace the UN Treaty on the Non-Proliferation of Nuclear Weapons (NPT) but rather to compile the essential elements from the three humanitarian conferences for the 2015 NPT Review Conference. Thus Great Britain and the United States, including umbrella states Canada, Japan, Australia, and the Republic of Korea, agreed to attend, along with India and Pakistan. Given their participation, media coverage would be greater than in either Oslo or Nayarit. At the same time, civil-society organizations, especially ICAN, were pressing the organizers to commence a diplomatic process toward negotiating a nuclear-weapon ban.

On the morning of December 8, the rain stopped, and the sun was shining. First responders from the Austrian Red Cross greeted attendees as they entered the palace. They wore gas masks and hazmat suits, simulating a nuclear emergency, and tested delegates for radioactive contamination. The conference chair, twenty-eight-year-old Sebastian Kurz, Austria's youngest foreign minister, opened the conference. "We all agree that the world would be a better one without nuclear weapons," he said. "It is high time to move from words to real action!"[2]

The first of two keynote speakers, Setsuko Thurlow took the stage in the palace's largest state room, the Festsaal, its rich red carpets and magnificent chandeliers creating an imperial ambience. As a young teen, watching helplessly as thousands of women and children died around her, Setsuko could never have imagined that one day she would take center stage in an imperial palace at an international effort to prevent people everywhere from suffering a similar fate. Ambassador Alexander Kmentt, the Austrian diplomat in charge of organizing the Vienna Conference, had told her he needed someone to open the conference with a powerful speech, and he knew he could count on her.

Standing at the podium, Setsuko took a moment to look out at the nine hundred participants as if planning to address each individually. "It gives me great satisfaction," she said, "that these conferences have renewed the focus on the humanitarian dimension of nuclear weapons, the fundamental issue yet long neglected by the shifting of the world's attention to the doctrine of deterrence in the name of national and international security." Then she told her story, as fresh and as painful as if she were telling it for the first time. She said she spoke for all hibakusha whose mission was "to warn the world about the reality of the nuclear threat and to help people understand the illegality and ultimate evil of nuclear weapons."

The Austrian organizers may have assured the nuclear-armed states that the intent was not to write a ban treaty to replace the NPT, but Setsuko Thurlow had made no such promise. Instead of tiptoeing around the issue at hand, she pointedly asked the audience, "How much longer can we allow the Nuclear Weapon States to continue threatening all life on earth?" Her voice rose to a crescendo as she resolved, "Here in Vienna let us move forward, courageously," setting the upcoming seventieth anniversary of Hiroshima's and Nagasaki's bombings as the appropriate occasion to prohibit and eliminate nuclear weapons. "Let us start this process, beginning with negotiations on a ban treaty, here and now in Vienna."[3] A momentary hush was followed by resounding applause, signaling agreement among those sitting in the Festsaal.

Archbishop Silvano Maria Tomasi followed Thurlow with a message from Pope Francis. His Holiness emphasized that the discussion of nuclear weapons previously focused on their power, not the suffering they inflict, a theme Setsuko had been reiterating for years. Recognizing the "prophetic voices" of the hibakusha, Pope Francis extended a special greeting to them. "Military codes and international law," he said, "have long banned peoples from inflicting unnecessary suffering. If such suffering is banned in the waging of conventional war, then it should all the more be banned in nuclear conflict." He emphasized that the Creator made one human family—adding a spiritual dimension to the debate—and the survival of that family depended on eliminating nuclear weapons. In closing His Holiness urged governments and civil society "to ensure that nuclear weapons are banned once and for all, to the benefit of our common home."[4] With that Pope Francis put the full weight of the Catholic Church behind the global movement to condemn nuclear weapons.

The morning session began, much as had the Nayarit and Oslo Conferences, by addressing the short- and long-term consequences of nuclear explosions on the world's health, environment, climate, and food supply. Moving on to the history of nuclear-weapon testing, victims from the Marshall Islands, Australia, and Utah bore witness to the devastating health effects and long-lasting environmental radioactive contamination from such trials. Ninety minutes of open debate followed.

The afternoon session focused on risk drivers for the detonation of nuclear weapons—deliberate or inadvertent—including human error, miscalculation, miscommunication, and technical lapses. Eric Schlosser caught the audience's attention as he related several real-life, hair-raising scenarios. Having titled his presentation "The Most Dangerous Machines," he told attendees that, after six years of research for his book *Command and Control*—which included interviews with former missile crew members, air force generals, and Pentagon officials—he had come to realize that "nuclear weapons really are not symbols of national power or symbols of national prestige. Nuclear weapons are machines, they are manmade machines, designed by human beings, maintained by human beings, and the reason that that is important is that all machines eventually go wrong."

Throughout history scientific and industrial experts had made incredible advances but had often failed to regulate the subsequent technologies. Schlosser gave a number of examples. Cars from top automakers were being recalled because airbags had killed a number of passengers. Malaysia flight 370, a Boeing 777, which had vanished thirty-nine minutes after taking off from Kuala Lumpur, was still missing nine months later. During the Cold War, the United States wanted to have nuclear weapons that were always available for immediate use but that would never explode by accident. They repeatedly chose "always" over "never," he said. Although the Pentagon had released a list of thirty-two "Broken Arrows" (defined as serious nuclear-weapon accidents), Schlosser had found more than a thousand that had occurred in one eighteen-year period. He proceeded to disclose some frightening cases.

Around midnight on January 23, 1961, a few days after John F. Kennedy gave his inaugural address, a B-52 bomber on routine surveillance mission from an air force base in Goldsboro, North Carolina, started losing fuel rapidly. As it spiraled toward the earth, it began to break apart. On board were eight crew members, five of whom survived by making parachute landings. The B-52 carried two four-megaton hydrogen bombs. On one the centrifugal force yanked a lanyard, which a crew member would pull to release the bombs in an attack situation, and it proceeded through arming steps to detonate. The final switch, later found to be faulty, aborted a thermonuclear explosion hundreds of times more powerful than that in Hiroshima. An estimated twenty-eight thousand would have been annihilated in the Goldsboro area, and radioactive fallout would have spread up the East Coast, affecting millions. "So we were lucky," Schlosser said.

He then recounted how the engines of a B-52 bomber, parked at a Grand Forks air force base, caught fire when a maintenance worker forgot to replace a nut on a fuel strainer. Imagine the captain's panic, knowing the fire would detonate the twelve nuclear weapons on board. Luckily a strong wind blew the flames away from the bomb bay. A crew member later told Schlosser that if they had been assigned to a different parking space on the runway, the wind could have blown the flames toward the bomb bay, exploding the weapons and obliterating the fifty thousand people of Grand Forks. "In that case," Schlosser told the astonished audience, "the difference between safety and catastrophe was the assignment of a parking space."

Recounting another anecdote, Schlosser told the audience that two years later fifty minutemen missiles went offline for an hour, blocking the ability of the launch crew to communicate with them. The cause was later found to be a loose computer chip. What if it hadn't been a loose computer chip but a cyber-attack or a hacker who could launch a missile? "Again and again," he informed the audience, "I was told by the people I interviewed we were lucky to get out of the Cold War without a nuclear detonation." He paused for a moment and repeated his warning: "The problem with luck is that eventually it runs out."[5]

Subsequent presentations that afternoon dealt with possible scenarios from a nuclear explosion and preparations for handling the aftermath. The last scheduled speaker, Rudolph Mueller, deputy director of the UN Office for the Coordination of Humanitarian Affairs, reviewed a study conducted by the United Nations Institute for Disarmament Research. The detonation of nuclear weapons not only would produce a humanitarian disaster, it determined, but also would blast large amounts of radioactive material into the atmosphere, imperiling populations far distant from the detonation site. "The study reminds us," he concluded, "that until we achieve a world free of nuclear weapons, these devices will continue to pose the risk of catastrophic consequences for humanity."[6]

The formal program for the first day had ended with a stark picture of doomsday. For the interactive debate that followed, Robert Croonquist took Setsuko from the overly crowded Festsaal into the annex room, where she more easily could view a simulcast of the debate. Most speakers underscored the futility of relief operations after such a catastrophic event; several physicians warned, "Don't count on us. There is nothing we can do."[7] Toward the end of the debate period, the Japanese ambassador, Toshio Sano, stood to speak. He said that after listening to all the lectures and speeches, he thought, "We shouldn't be so pessimistic. How do we know we can't rebuild from this kind of thing?"[8]

He thought they should be considering how to be better prepared to cope with such a situation. "Very interesting point to end on," the conference chair said, "but we are over time, and we have our wine reception now. Everybody have a lovely evening."[9]

Taken aback, Setsuko asked Kathleen Sullivan, "What? What did he say?" As she was repeating his statements, Kathleen grabbed the wheelchair. She knew Setsuko had to confront him, so she started wheeling her from the annex room down the long hallway to the Festsaal. When reporters saw Mrs. Thurlow moving at a rapid clip, they started following. Setsuko had great appeal for the Japanese media because she never hesitated to speak her mind, regardless of a person's power or position. "Don't get angry," she was telling herself as they flew past people leaving the meeting. "Just find out exactly what he said. That's the first thing." At the conference-room entrance, she directed Kathleen to stop. She got out of the wheelchair and, using her cane more for emphasis than support, approached the Japanese ambassador. He was already surrounded by a group of reporters, who stepped aside as Setsuko Thurlow approached. "I would like to ask you a question," she said, with no preliminaries. "I was in another room when I saw you, but I couldn't quite hear you. Show me your speech." Looking at it, she charged, "Did you really say that?"

He took a booklet out of his inside pocket. "This is a UN document," he told Setsuko, "and see on this page, we have agreed in case of disaster, we will do our best to rescue and protect dying people. We have that responsibility, and that's what I think we should be doing. But all these people are so pessimistic."

"Yes," she replied, "but we have been hearing those up-to-date scientific, scholarly presentations. Do you mean to oppose these?"[10] As her stance became more confrontational, he became more defensive, and the press drew closer, their recording devices a few feet away. As a parting shot, she told him that, as a survivor of Hiroshima, she found his comments offensive. *Asahi Shimbun* and other Japanese newspapers carried a photo of the encounter—a hibakusha challenging the Japanese government at a major international conference.

Exhausted by such an intense day, most attendees headed for the reception and a much-needed drink before boarding buses to the Gartenbau Movie Theater to view the prescreening of a documentary titled *The Man Who Saved the World.* The graphic account of this little-known moment in history was unnerving. Most attendees had seen photos of Hiroshima and Nagasaki; most had heard the painful words of Setsuko Thurlow and other hibakusha. Now, for two hours, they became immersed in Stanislav Petrov's story, likely instilling terror into the hearts of all those sitting in the Gartenbau Theater.

Stanislav Petrov, a forty-four-year-old lieutenant colonel in the Soviet Air Defense Forces, seemed an unlikely hero, more thoughtful and mild-mannered than militaristic. He served as part of a highly specialized team that managed their new early warning system, Oko, designed to detect ballistic missile attacks. He happened to be the duty officer in charge on September 26, 1983, when, in the early morning hours, an alarm sounded. The United States had launched a nuclear-armed intercontinental ballistic missile, directed at the Soviet Union, the system warned. "Launch" flashed on a large overhead screen. Rigorously trained, Petrov and his team had clear instructions as to how to proceed. He was to call his superior, who would notify the top Soviet leadership. In a matter of minutes, they had to determine whether or not to initiate a retaliatory strike. Would the United States have initiated a sudden, unprovoked attack? Tension between the two countries had reached a peak three weeks earlier when the Soviet military shot down a Korean Air Lines plane that had strayed into its airspace. All 269 passengers and crew, including 62 Americans and a U.S. congressman, perished.

Petrov was staring at the screen when the alarm blared again, announcing that a second missile had been fired. Both would reach the Soviet Union within twenty minutes. The warning system indicated the reliability of the alert to be at the highest level. Still, he did not pick up the phone; he seemed frozen in place. A minute passed, and the siren sounded again. A third missile had been launched, then a fourth, then a fifth. The overhead screen registered "missile strike." The rest of the team was horrified that their duty officer continued to peer at the screen. Despite clear-cut protocol, Petrov did not act; he had the nagging feeling that this warning arose from a computer glitch, not a true attack. He proceeded to contact the satellite-radar operators, who were watching for U.S. missiles using the old technology. Nothing had appeared on their screens. Even though per protocol the new early warning system took precedence over the radar system, Petrov didn't quite trust it. Besides, if the United States had initiated an all-out attack, he asked himself, why did they launch only five missiles?

Petrov's team looked back and forth between the flashing red screens and their leader, who seemed paralyzed. "There was no rule about how long we were allowed to think before we reported a strike," he later said in the documentary. "But we knew that every second of procrastination took away valuable time, that the Soviet Union's military and political leadership needed to be informed without delay. All I had to do was to reach for the phone, to raise the direct line to our top commanders—but I couldn't move." If he was wrong, much of the Soviet Union soon would be obliterated by five mushroom clouds. "Nobody would be able to correct my mistake if I had made one," the audience heard him say. If this was an erroneous warning, and he notified his superiors per protocol, the military would likely barrage the United States with missiles, triggering a nuclear war. He made his decision. He did not call. Twenty-three minutes passed. Nothing happened. Stanislav Petrov had averted a nuclear holocaust and probably saved the world.[11]

Lieutenant Colonel Petrov had been correct in suspecting a computer malfunction. A later investigation determined that Soviet satellites had mistakenly identified sunlight reflecting on clouds as engines of intercontinental ballistic missiles. In the meantime Petrov received an official reprimand for making mistakes in his logbook. Because he had committed a dereliction of duty, he was reassigned to a lesser post—a scapegoat. Petrov's role in averting a nuclear war did not become public until after the dissolution of the Soviet Union. In 2006 he traveled to New York to receive a World Citizen Award at the United Nations.

In the documentary Petrov's final thoughts about the event were chilling: he noted that he was the only duty officer who had a civilian education. "My colleagues were all professional soldiers; they were taught to give and obey orders," he said. "They were lucky it was me on shift that night."[12] Participants from the Vienna Conference had just heard the most cogent reason for banning nuclear weapons.

On December 9 the morning session delved into a new topic—nuclear weapons and international law. Speakers pointed out that, as opposed to biological and chemical weapons, no comprehensive, universal legal norm prohibited the possession, transfer, production, or use of nuclear weapons. Furthermore, the moral and ethical questions raised by these weapons transcended legal discussions. One speaker drew comparisons with the moral assessment of torture.

The remainder of the day was devoted to position statements, made by over a hundred states and international organizations. Based on the risks and humanitarian consequences revealed and emphasized by the conference, moving from data to individuals, from hypothetical to actual, most non–nuclear-weapon states supported prompt movement toward nuclear disarmament. Great Britain, the United States, and its umbrella states acknowledged the consequences yet continued to argue the importance of deterrence for their national security, preferring a step-by-step approach as outlined by the NPT. Eric Schlosser challenged the concept of deterrence. He called it a "psychological threat to annihilate the population of another country."[13] If they couldn't accept the suffering nuclear weapons would cause, how could they accept the concept of nuclear deterrence? Discouraged but not surprised that her homeland, Japan, and her adopted country, Canada, sided with this position, Thurlow felt heartened that an increasing number of states urged prompt enactment of a legal ban on nuclear weapons.

At 6:15, after two intense days of analysis and debate, Sebastian Kurz, the conference chair, returned to the podium to summarize the proceedings and deliberations. He thanked contributors, especially hibakusha, saying how they "exemplified the unspeakable suffering caused to ordinary civilians by nuclear weapons." Building on the discussions at Oslo and Nayarit, he said they had reached several key conclusions. The humanitarian consequences from the use of current-day nuclear weapons, unconstrained by national borders, would be more catastrophic than previously thought: they might even threaten the survival of humankind. Any risk of a nuclear explosion, whether intentional or not, was unacceptable. Although no legal measure prohibited their use, the increasing awareness of the repercussions of these weapons raised profound ethical and moral questions.

Delegations had expressed various ways to advance the nuclear-disarmament agenda, he went on to say. Having assured the nuclear-weapon states ahead of time that the intent was not to script a new ban treaty, Kurz ended by saying, "The overwhelming majority of NPT States Parties expects that the forthcoming 2015 NPT Review Conference should take stock of all relevant developments, including the outcomes of the conferences on the humanitarian impact of nuclear weapons, and determine the next steps for the achievement and maintenance of a nuclear-weapon-free world."[14]

With the chair's summary as the last agenda item on the program, attendees were surprised when Ambassador Kurz introduced Austrian deputy foreign minister Michael Linhart. He informed the audience that Austria had determined to move beyond the chair's summary. Considering all the evidence presented at the three humanitarian conferences—Oslo, Nayarit, and Vienna—Austria pledged to promote the protection of civilians against risks arising from the presence of nuclear weapons and to cooperate with all stakeholders to "stigmatize, prohibit and eliminate nuclear weapons."[15]

"The place went wild," Setsuko said. "It was incredible." Sitting next to her was Haruko Moritaki, whose father, Ichiro Moritaki, a leader in Japan's antinuclear movement, had inspired young Setsuko. They jumped up and started hugging and crying. "Both of us had such joy," Setsuko said.[16] Representatives from nuclear-armed and umbrella states remained seated. The Oslo, Nayarit, and Vienna Conferences on the humanitarian impact of nuclear weapons had clarified the central issues. Now it was up to participants in the NPT Review Conference, scheduled four months later, to take the next steps to achieve a world free of nuclear weapons.

At that moment in time, fourteen countries held a total of approximately 16,300 nuclear weapons, with 1,800 on high alert, ready for immediate use.

21 Moral Indignation

The world is impatient.
I demand to the leaders of all nations:
ban nuclear weapons, ban nuclear weapons now!

–Setsuko Thurlow, Nuclear Non-Proliferation Treaty Review Conference

"On the cenotaph in Hiroshima's Peace Park," Setsuko Thurlow told the assembly, "is an inscription that reads, 'Rest in peace; the error will not be repeated.'" This had become a vow for survivors, determined that no one ever again should suffer what she called the "inhumane, immoral, cruel, and indiscriminate effects of nuclear bombs."[1] Having given weight to each of these four words, her vehemence awakened those in the audience, from 161 states and 107 nongovernmental organizations, lulled by the reassuring yet passive words from so many that week. Once again she was speaking at the United Nations, this time at the 2015 Review Conference of the Parties to the Nuclear Non-Proliferation Treaty (NPT). The NPT had been in force since 1970 with the goal of limiting dissemination of nuclear weapons, achieving nuclear disarmament, and promoting the peaceful use of nuclear energy. A review conference was held every five years to ensure progress toward attaining these objectives. The action plan agreed on at the 2010 NPT Review Conference suffered failure of fulfillment, as had so many before it.

Four days earlier, in his opening statement at the conference on April 27, 2015, UN secretary-general Ban Ki-moon of South Korea had pronounced the elimination of nuclear weapons a top UN priority, with the NPT as the essential basis for achieving this goal. Furthermore, he pointed out that positioning humanitarian considerations at the center of disarmament deliberations had "injected a moral imperative into a frozen debate." He thanked hibakusha for bringing this message forward: "I defy anyone to look into the eyes of these courageous and resilient individuals and say you know better what nuclear weapons bring. They are here as a sober, living reminder of the horrific humanitarian consequences of nuclear weapons and of the urgent need for their abolition."[2] He summoned leaders to abandon their shortsighted political posturing and fulfill the obligations entrusted to them by communities around the world. The secretary-general's charge boosted the fortitude that non–nuclear-weapon states and NGOs needed to persevere in the coming weeks.

Under the leadership of the meeting's president designate, Algerian ambassador Taous Feroukhi, the first four days of the NPT Review Conference were devoted to a general debate in the plenary session, which gave every nation the opportunity to make a statement. Of particular interest to Thurlow was that of U.S. secretary of state, John Kerry. He spoke of their shared vision of a world without nuclear weapons and enumerated his country's disarmament endeavors. He mentioned deterrence, a concept Setsuko loathed; he did not mention an outright ban. Although he predicted it would "probably" take years to reach their objective, he advised against seeking "shortcuts." Still, he assured them that the United States was "serious."[3]

Kerry's comments frustrated Setsuko. Six years earlier, in his acclaimed Prague speech, President Barack Obama had professed his commitment to create a nuclear-free world. Still, U.S. leaders clung to a step-by-step approach. So when it was her turn to speak at the end of the first week, leading off the civil-society presentations, Thurlow expressed her annoyance with them. She announced that reporters just had revealed that the United States had "shamelessly" pressured officials from Norway and Japan to refrain from signing Austria's pledge, now reframed as the "Humanitarian Pledge." And Japan had complied with the United States, even though Prime Minister Shinzo Abe had avowed his commitment to the elimination of nuclear weapons. "In international politics," Thurlow continued, "this kind of arm-twisting tactic or sabotaging behavior may be common among the nuclear-weapon states and nuclear-dependent states, but from the perspective of the majority of the people of the world, such shady diplomacy is nothing but repugnant." Never hesitant in speaking truth to power, she pointed out that President Obama and Prime Minister Abe had negated what they had touted as their special roles. For those who thought she had overstepped some intangible line of decorum, she had more sharp words:

> Each and every one of you NPT member delegates agreed to Article VI of this Treaty "to pursue negotiations in good faith on effective measures relating to cessation of the nuclear arms race at an early date and to nuclear disarmament." You are part of the decision-making body for the fate of the human community and your responsibility is grave. Please break away from the non-productive past record on disarmament. After all, the NPT is 45 years old. The world is impatient. . . . I demand to the leaders of all nations: ban nuclear weapons, ban nuclear weapons now![4]

Setsuko Thurlow had delivered a powerful punch as delegates approached the weekend break.

The second week of the NPT conference entailed tackling the stated objectives in three specific committees. Main Committee I considered nuclear disarmament. The nuclear-armed and nuclear-supportive states resisted setting a specific schedule and defaulted to platitudes and ambiguous expressions. They deemphasized humanitarian consequences, stating that no new pertinent information had emerged. Main Committee II debated nonproliferation, safeguards, nuclear security, and implementation of the 1995 resolution of the Middle East to set up a nuclear-weapon–free zone. Israel, although not an NPT member, disputed such plans. Main Committee III addressed peaceful uses of nuclear energy. With committee meetings marked by acrimony and intimidation and with opposing sides clearly delineated, the state parties could not reach a consensus. So a select group moved outside of the UN to a private room, from which civil-society groups were excluded, to draft a compromise final document for the conference.

At the May 22 plenary session, conference president Feroukhi presented the draft. "Anti-democratic and nontransparent," some delegates called it.[5]

"The NPT is a treaty of the nuclear-armed states," concluded a prominent ICAN member.[6] A former UK secretary of state for defense, bemoaning his part in designating the five permanent members of the UN Security Council (P5) at its inception, said, "I did not expect that they would become a cartel."[7] The South African ambassador admonished the parties to the NPT for descent into minority rule, similar to what they had in South Africa under apartheid. Non–nuclear-weapon states compromised and supported the draft so as not to scuttle the NPT, the only binding commitment to disarmament by nuclear-weapon states. Despite that concession, the United States, the United Kingdom, and Canada, in support of Israel's opposition to a Middle East nuclear-free zone, refused at the last moment to sign the final draft, calling it unrealistic and unworkable. After five weeks of intensive work, no meaningful progress on nuclear disarmament had been made. "A month of statements. A month of finger-pointing and sometimes name-calling. A month of too much caffeine and too little sunshine," summed up Ray Acheson, director of Reaching Critical Will.[8] "In short," Setsuko said, "the NPT Review Conference was a failure."[9]

A consequential outcome from the conference did ensue, however, one that had not been on its agenda: 107 states, which comprised most of the NPT state parties and the majority of countries worldwide, endorsed the Humanitarian Pledge, committing states to stigmatize, prohibit, and eliminate nuclear weapons. ICAN had promoted it throughout the conference. A *Washington Post* reporter called the endorsement an "uprising."[10] After spending a month on a political rollercoaster, Setsuko told friends she came home "exhausted but invigorated."[11]

The year ended with epochal news from the UN: on December 7, 138 nations voted in favor of General Assembly Resolution 70/33. An Open-Ended Working Group (OEWG), in which all member states could participate with optional consulting from NGOs, academia, and industry, would be convened by the UN in Geneva. It would address concrete legal measures, provisions, and norms for achieving and maintaining a nuclear-weapon–free world. As expected, the nuclear-armed states had refused to participate in the discussion of the resolution. Nevertheless, the force of ICAN proved too strong. This coalition of NGOs in one hundred states, with their remarkable advocacy skills, had educated delegates about the components of and expectations for a ban treaty.

The first of three OEWG meetings took place in February 2016. Setsuko did not attend, given the frigid winter weather. She did agree to address the second OEWG conference in Geneva. On May 4 she began with her moving testimony, after which she unfurled a large yellow banner displaying the names of 351 classmates who had perished. They weren't just numbers, she told the audience, they were "young lively girls, laughing and chattering" who suddenly were obliterated. "Each one has a name and was loved by someone." The banner created a powerful visual reminder of the humanitarian impact of the atomic bomb.

Her somber, respectful tone then changed. Tired of the repeated hectoring and attempted bulldozing by the nuclear-armed and nuclear-supportive states, she let loose. She lambasted the Japanese government for repeatedly stating, "as the only nation to have suffered nuclear bombs, we must be at the forefront in taking action for disarmament," while at the same time endorsing the U.S. step-by-step approach. She said hibakusha, as well as the majority of the Japanese population, felt abandoned by their leaders. Thurlow had even harsher words for President Obama, who planned to visit Hiroshima in three weeks. She reminded the audience how in 2009, at his first visit to Prague, he had said, "as the only nuclear power to have used a nuclear weapon, the United States has a moral responsibility to act." Yet the U.S. government had not even sent a representative to the OEWG meetings. "Where is the moral responsibility or leadership in that?" she asked.[12]

While Setsuko continued with prior engagements in Europe, President Barack Obama made his historic visit to Hiroshima, the first sitting U.S. president to do so. On May 27, 2016, he spoke at the Memorial Peace Park. Again Thurlow was besieged by the media: Should he have made an apology? Setsuko replied she was grateful he had accepted the invitation; it took courage. "A forced apology is meaningless," she said. "It has to be the President's decision."[13] If he chose not to make amends, she understood, considering the upcoming presidential election.

In private she expressed her disappointment with President Obama's speech. "Seventy-one years ago, on a bright, cloudless morning, death fell from the sky," he had begun, "and the world was changed."[14] "What?" she exclaimed. "Death didn't 'fall from the sky'; they dropped a bomb on us."[15] Although he made some dramatic statements, such as how Hiroshima and Nagasaki should be known as the "start of our own moral awakening" and how they must have the courage to pursue a world without nuclear weapons, the president went on to predict, "We may not realize this goal in my lifetime."[16] Setsuko may have accepted his lack of apology for the atomic bombings, but she considered the latter comment unacceptable. And she determined to challenge this notion.

Thurlow saw an opportunity to reach out to President Obama ten days later, at the annual meeting of the Arms Control Association, an independent organization dedicated to the elimination of threats posed by the world's most dangerous weapons. She had traveled to Washington DC to accept their highest honor, the Arms Control Person of the Year. Broadcast on C-SPAN, the meeting addressed global nuclear challenges and potential solutions for the next U.S. president. It featured two keynote speakers—eighty-four-year-old Setsuko Thurlow and thirty-eight-year-old Benjamin Rhodes, President Obama's deputy national security adviser for strategic communications. Rhodes had accompanied him to Hiroshima and helped write his speech. Setsuko requested a private conversation with him.

After her testimony the moderator called for questions, which allowed Thurlow to expound on the NPT and President Obama's nuclear policy. She pointed out that, under NPT Article VI, nuclear-weapon states had the legal obligation to work toward disarmament, yet they had not fulfilled that commitment forty-five years after the treaty had been agreed on. "We are not going to wait anymore," she said. Civil society, the Red Cross, and non–nuclear-weapon states were working together to create a legally binding instrument to prohibit and eliminate nuclear weapons. In Hiroshima President Obama had said abolition of nuclear weapons probably wouldn't happen in his lifetime. "We can't afford to wait," she said; they could and should eliminate nuclear weapons now. When she was asked about Obama's budget for nuclear weapons, she replied, "I don't even call it a weapon. I call it a device of mass murder." Furthermore, she considered it a "crime" to deprive the public of funding for proper education and medical care "based on the foolish notions of deterrence and security."[17]

Prominent Princeton University physicist and a member of the Arms Control Association's board of directors, Zia Mian knew of Thurlow's work through ICAN. He didn't appreciate until this meeting how "fierce and indignant" she could be. And he gained insight into what he thought motivated her: she had what English historian and antinuclear activist E. P. Thompson called "the nerve of moral indignation." It's not about "how could you do this to me?" It's about "how could you do this?"[18]

In his presentation Ben Rhodes reviewed President Obama's accomplishments in a calm and measured manner, defending the NPT as well as the U.S. nuclear modernization project. He said he considered the work of the Arms Control Association and civil-society groups essential. After all, the government and its citizens had the same goal—a world without nuclear weapons. They just differed in their tactical approach.[19] Afterward Thurlow met with Rhodes—briefly and privately—even though reporters snapped photos through the French doors and tried to lip-read their conversation. Her main objective was to give him a letter to deliver to President Obama. He accepted it graciously.

Thurlow's letter did not begin with a note of appreciation for his visit to Hiroshima or compliments on his heartfelt speech. Instead, she wrote that many had asked what she would have said had she met him face-to-face during his historic visit. She said she would have told him the story of her four-year-old nephew, Eiji, transformed into a charred, blackened, and swollen child who died in agony. She reminded the president that he had said, "We have a shared responsibility to look directly into the eye of history and ask what we must do differently to curb such suffering again." His words seemed to echo those of former German president Richard von Weizsäcker, who had said, "We Germans must look truth straight in the eye. . . . There can be no reconciliation without remembrance." Here was the difference, she continued: Germany had erected memorials to the victims at Auschwitz and other camps; the United States had preserved the top-secret sites at Los Alamos and Oak Ridge as a "celebration of that technological achievement."

She quoted the president as touting their "moral imperative to abolish nuclear arsenals" as he stood in front of the cenotaph for A-bomb victims. "Why then," she asked, "with all due respect to you, Mr. President, is the US government boycotting the United Nations disarmament negotiations born of the Humanitarian Initiative, the most significant advance for nuclear disarmament in a generation?" She called him out for "inexcusably" boycotting the three conferences on the humanitarian impact of nuclear weapons. She reminded him that in his speech he had said, "That is why we come to Hiroshima. So that we might think of people we love." She asked him to reframe his "profound sentiment," understanding that the people they love are under the constant threat of annihilation because of the very existence of nuclear weapons and the U.S. policy of deterrence. Then she cranked up her rhetoric even more. "You, Mr. Obama," she wrote, "the only sitting US President to visit Hiroshima, came accompanied by a duty bound officer with the nuclear briefcase, should you need the codes to command a remote missileer to insert a floppy disc as a prelude to the end of life on earth."[20] In conclusion she pointed out that he had the power to lift the threat of nuclear war. This could be his legacy. How did the 44th President, who had written, "a sense of empathy is at the heart of my moral code," feel when he read Setsuko Thurlow's letter?[21] She didn't know. She never received a reply.

In August 2016 the Open-Ended Working Group held its third session in Geneva. Prompted in part by the disastrous NPT Review Committee results from the previous year, the group recommended that the UN General Assembly convene a conference in 2017 to negotiate a legally binding instrument to prohibit nuclear weapons. Setsuko was thrilled. After years of frustration, thwarted at almost every turn, the movement was accelerating toward its goal—a ban treaty.

On October 3 the UN General Assembly's First Committee, responsible for international security and disarmament, began its annual meeting. "This week, delegations to the UN General Assembly could help shift the course of history," reported Ray Acheson, the director of Reaching Critical Will and a member of ICAN's Steering Group. The First Committee sometimes seemed like a "recycling facility for statements and resolutions" under discussion for decades while "armaments rise and bombs continue to fall," she wrote in *First Committee Monitor*. Nevertheless, she had high expectations for the 2016 annual meeting: "This year is different. This year we have L.41."[22]

L.41, the UN resolution that had resulted from OEWG's recommendation, was called "dangerous," "delusional," "polarizing," and "illegitimate" by nuclear-weapon states.[23] British and French officials urged European Union members to vote no; U.S. officials pressured NATO members to do the same. On October 27, 2016, despite these efforts to scuttle the resolution, 123 nations voted in favor of L.41, the landmark resolution to begin negotiations in the new year on a legally binding instrument to prohibit nuclear weapons. Only 38 nations voted no, and 16 abstained: "a sea change" supporters called it.[24] "I am experiencing a tremendous feeling of euphoria," Setsuko wrote in her Christmas letter to friends. "The world has at long last listened to the Hibakusha's persistent plea."[25]

On March 25, 2017, Setsuko found herself surrounded by almost a thousand Muslim men when she entered London's Baitul Futuh Mosque. She had come to the famed mosque to receive the Ahmadiyya Muslim Prize for the Advancement of Peace. Although she was initially reluctant to participate, once she learned about the importance of the prize to the Muslim community and that the mayor of London, members of Parliament, and representatives from the Canadian and Japanese embassies had been invited, she gracefully accepted. Awarded for her efforts to disarm nuclear weapons, Thurlow received a copy of the Quran, an engraved crystal globe, and £10,000, which she planned to share with ICAN. In her acceptance speech, she called the Ahmadiyya Muslim community an enlightened role model for the world, emphasizing their commitment to peace and justice.[26]

Setsuko was packing to fly back to New York for the United Nations conference to negotiate a nuclear-weapon ban treaty when ICAN contacted Kathleen Sullivan. Thurlow had been selected to speak at the opening session, and they needed a copy of her comments as soon as possible. In the crowded airport waiting area, with reporters from Japan's public broadcaster NHK snapping photos, she dictated her extemporaneous remarks to Kathleen, who sent them on to ICAN.

"Ready, Set, Go: Time to Ban the Bomb," wrote Ray Acheson in the *Nuclear Ban Daily* on March 27, 2017. "Today we begin negotiations of a treaty banning nuclear weapons. We all know the determination and creativity it took to get here. Decades of activism. . . . Endless engagement with nuclear-armed states. . . . Millions of people marching in the streets. Commitments made and broken. Pleas from survivors. . . . Countless UN resolutions. . . . Three humanitarian impact conferences. Two open-ended working groups. One Humanitarian Pledge. And then, a historic resolution in the UN General Assembly last October."[27]

Now delegates from 130 states as well as 220 international organizations and civil societies commenced crafting the long-awaited treaty. The conference was scheduled in two segments: March 27 to 31 and June 15 to July 7. Ambassador Elayne Whyte Gómez, permanent representative of Costa Rica to the UN Office in Geneva, had been elected president of the conference—a wonderful choice, Setsuko thought. A professor at National University of Costa Rica, Whyte Gómez had a scholarly approach to problem-solving, and she hailed from a country that had abolished armed forces in efforts to achieve peace. Added to that she had experience working with large international organizations. Articulate, gracious, and composed, Whyte Gómez had no doubt that when the conference ended, they would have a document to which all members would agree and of which all would be proud.

How much could they accomplish in the first five days? At the NPT Review Conference, almost nothing had been achieved in a month. President Whyte Gómez, however, had a well-scripted plan of action. The three humanitarian conferences and the OEWG meetings had provided the requisite background knowledge and identified underlying principles as well as areas of commonality. From the start she established agreed-on rules of procedure from which she did not deviate. Still, she acknowledged every voice and encouraged participation from civil-society groups. Discussions were characterized as taking place in a constructive atmosphere with a collaborative spirit—refreshing compared with those at the NPT Review Conference.[28]

There were some vacant seats, among them those for representatives from the nuclear-armed states, as well as many nuclear-supportive states. "U.N. Ambassador Haley Opposes International Ban on Nukes," read a headline in *Politico*.[29] Flanked by ambassadors from France and the United Kingdom, Nikki Haley told reporters that their job was to protect their citizens. In a deprecating tone, she questioned whether states that supported a ban on nuclear weapons actually understood the global threat: "You have to ask yourself, are they looking out for their people?"[30] Her words reflected the stance of the newly inaugurated U.S. president, Donald Trump, regarding nuclear weapons: "If we have them, why can't we use them?"[31] ICAN director Beatrice Fihn gave Haley's rebuke a positive spin: "It was really quite a big sign that we were onto something very important if the US government would have to protest outside the negotiating room."[32] Questioned about the boycott, Whyte Gómez told the press, "When there is a negotiation process in a room and there are very divergent opinions, it is much more difficult to bring the positions closer together."[33] Their absence allowed the delegates to keep on track.

From the start Whyte Gómez made certain the humanitarian imperative remained ever-present as an inspiration for the ban treaty. And who better to set the stage than Setsuko Thurlow. "We hibakusha have worked tirelessly for decades," Thurlow told the august group, "for the total elimination of these devices of mass murder and cross-generational radioactive violence." In a low pitch, she spoke of the vow she and many hibakusha had made to their loved ones that their deaths would not be in vain. Then her voice rang through the hall as she commanded them: "Your task . . . is to establish a clear, new, international standard . . . to declare, in no uncertain terms, that nuclear weapons are illegitimate, immoral and illegal. . . . Do your job well! This treaty can—and will—change the world."[34]

And they did do their job well. During those first five days, the group agreed on four basic principles: First, the new treaty should strengthen and complement the existing agreements, in particular the NPT. Second, the instrument should not have any loopholes that allowed states to benefit from nuclear weapons. Third, the treaty should be straightforward, prohibiting nuclear weapons explicitly and emphatically. Fourth, it should provide a clear pathway for nuclear disarmament.

As the group moved along with congruity, nuclear-armed states reacted with disdain, accusing them of undercutting international law, obstructing the NPT, crippling international security, and even provoking the buildup and use of nuclear weapons. They continued to stymie participation from NATO allies and those under their nuclear umbrellas. Despite their efforts to derail the effort, delegates kept their collective eyes on the goal. At the conclusion of this first segment, Whyte Gómez congratulated them and predicted, "We are going to adopt this treaty on July 7."[35]

During the intervening ten weeks, Whyte Gómez incorporated all they had agreed on into a draft treaty. When they reconvened on June 15, she planned to work through the draft, article by article, from preamble to conclusion. "Perhaps the most significant addition to the treaty," wrote nuclear-policy expert Alice Slater, "was amending the prohibition not to use nuclear weapons by adding the words 'or threaten to use,' driving a stake through the heart of the beloved 'deterrence' doctrine of the nuclear-weapons states."[36]

The management of nuclear disarmament generated lengthy debate, as did the clarification of the relationship between this treaty and the NPT. Throughout it all Whyte Gómez maintained her executive mantra: "Keep serenity in all moments and at all times."[37] In the end, under her calm leadership, she attained near-unanimous agreement: In accordance with the new Treaty on the Prohibition of Nuclear Weapons, state parties could never develop, test, produce, acquire, or stockpile nuclear weapons. States could never transfer these weapons, use or threaten to use them, or allow them to be installed on their territory. Those possessing nuclear weapons would remove them from operational status and destroy them as soon as possible. If another state had deposited nuclear weapons on their territory, they would be removed promptly. If a state had tested or deployed a nuclear weapon in another state, they would provide assistance to victims and undertake remediation for environmental damage.

The delegate from the Netherlands argued that the treaty did not allow them to honor their obligations to NATO. The Singapore delegate maintained that the draft treaty did not clarify legalities relating to other agreements. Japan withdrew its representation. On the afternoon of July 6, President Whyte Gómez read the text of the treaty to the delegates. She clarified that she was not reopening it for negotiation unless a majority of states supported a substantive change.

Voting began the next morning, July 7, 2017. Everyone in the UN General Assembly Hall focused on the voting board. Afghanistan, yes; Algeria, yes; Angola, yes. The tension heightened as each state cast its vote. Iran (Islamic Republic of), yes; Iraq, yes; Ireland, yes. Like a group of marathon runners, they could see the finish line in sight. Zimbabwe, yes. At 10:46 a.m. the Treaty on the Prohibition of Nuclear Weapons was adopted, with 122 votes in favor, 1 against (Netherlands), and 1 abstention (Singapore). The treaty would be open for signature at UN Headquarters on September 20. Ninety days after the fiftieth state ratified it, the ban treaty would enter into force.[38]

Cheers and applause rang through the hall. President Whyte Gómez asked Setsuko Thurlow to have the final words. "I've been waiting for this day for seven decades," she began, "and I am overjoyed. . . ."

> This is the beginning of the end of nuclear weapons. I remember back in 2014, when many of us met in Nayarit, Mexico. The conference chair said, "This is the point of no return." We will not return to the failed nuclear-deterrence policies. We will not return to funding nuclear violence instead of human needs. We will not return to irreversibly contaminating our environment. We will not continue to risk the lives of future generations. To the leaders of the countries across the world, I beseech you: If you love this planet, you will sign this treaty. Nuclear weapons have always been immoral; now they are also illegal. Together let us go forth and change the world.[39]

She bent her head for a moment's prayer to all hibakusha. She had fulfilled her pledge to them. Then she stood, bowed briefly, and joined the audience in joyous applause.

In closing Whyte Gómez recognized Setsuko Thurlow's major role, recalling her comments at the start of the conference: "Those of us who survived became convinced that no human being should ever have to experience the inhumanity and unspeakable suffering of nuclear weapons." Now, just over three months later, they had a treaty prohibiting those weapons. She looked up at Setsuko and said, "Thank you for not letting us rest."[40] Then, with a broad smile, Elayne Whyte Gómez pounded the gavel on the adoption of the Treaty on the Prohibition of Nuclear Weapons.

Reporters from around the world rushed to get comments from Setsuko Thurlow. "Is the *New York Times* here?" she called out above the din. "Is the *Washington Post* here? I don't think so." She challenged the reporters, "You media people, do your part. Pressure them . . . [and] act with us. It is a shared responsibility—yours and ours."[41]

That evening Beatrice Fihn, Ray Acheson, Tim Wright, Kathleen Sullivan, and other ICAN members were joined by diplomats and activists at a nearby bar to toast their success. A bright beam of light seemed to shine on the woman many considered the conscience of the antinuclear movement—Setsuko Thurlow. She could not stop smiling. Presidents Barack Obama and Donald Trump, Prime Ministers Shinzo Abe and Justin Trudeau, and many other leaders of the nuclear-armed and nuclear-supportive states may have considered Thurlow an elderly Hiroshima survivor. Little did they know, they were facing a formidable opponent, a woman with the fervor and tenacity of her ancestors. And she was not done yet.

22 Glory

> I refuse to accept the cynical notion that nation after nation must spiral down a militaristic stairway into the hell of nuclear annihilation.
>
> –Martin Luther King Jr., Nobel Peace Prize speech

"We do not intend to sign, ratify, or ever become party to it," announced UN ambassadors from France, the United Kingdom, and the United States in reference to the UN Treaty on the Prohibition of Nuclear Weapons (TPNW), the Ban Treaty for short.[1] Two days earlier, on July 7, 2017, it had been adopted by a considerable majority of member states. The treaty prohibited developing, testing, transferring, and stockpiling nuclear weapons as well as threatening their use. Those states possessing such weapons must remove and destroy them expeditiously. And they must provide assistance to persons harmed by their discharge, even if inadvertently. In their press statement, the three UN ambassadors went on to say that the treaty was not compatible with the policy of nuclear deterrence, which they deemed crucial in maintaining international peace and security. Their legal obligations with regard to nuclear weapons remained unchanged. Finally, they noted that most of the nuclear-armed and nuclear-supportive states also had refused to engage in the negotiations.

Although some international newspapers reported that the treaty was a success—"History Was Made"; "Treaty Is a Milestone"; "We Did It!"—news from those countries opposed to the TPNW was limited and understated.[2] On the day the United Nations passed the Ban Treaty, as reporters surrounded Setsuko Thurlow, she had called out, "Is the *New York Times* here? Is the *Washington Post* here? I don't think so." She had challenged the reporters, "You media people, do your part. Pressure them . . . [and] act with us. It is a shared responsibility—yours and ours."[3] She had anticipated the U.S. media's lack of attention to this, the first multilateral treaty to prohibit *and* eliminate nuclear weapons. The *Washington Post* ran a two-sentence announcement, the sixth posting in the "World Digest" section, after "Ex-Gitmo Inmate Gets Apology, Millions from Canada."[4] And the *New York Times* reported the treaty on page A-7 along with a picture of the American and British UN ambassadors, Nikki Haley and Matthew Rycroft, both of whom had boycotted the meetings, calling the treaty "misguided" and "reckless." The article failed to mention by name any of the 122 states—two-thirds of the UN membership—that had supported it.[5]

Ten days after the historic event, the editorial board of the *Wall Street Journal* printed its "Opinion," on page A-16, titled "The U.N. Bans Nuclear Weapons: So at Least That Problem Is Solved." The opening statement read, "The United Nations banned nuclear weapons this month, in case you hadn't heard, and all the children of the world joined hands and sang together in the spirit of harmony and peace." This flippant, shameful comment disparaged those who had devoted their lives to safeguarding the world from destruction as well as the UN member states that had voted for the Ban Treaty. "If the U.N.'s record holds," the editorial concluded, "this new treaty will take effect right about the time Kim Jong Un launches a nuclear attack."[6]

Among the limited number of earnest articles, few covered the Ban Treaty with such clarity and gravity as did Alice Slater's piece in *The Nation*. "We are witnessing a striking shift," wrote the New York director of the Nuclear Age Peace Foundation, "in the global paradigm of how the world views nuclear weapons."[7] And political scientist Nina Tannenwald's straightforward piece on the Ban Treaty—its provisions, history, significance, and promise—could have enlightened the public had the *Washington Post* published it on its front page instead of on its blog.[8]

Not only did the media fail to apprise the public about this consequential historic event, but also it missed the opportunity to alert people about the catastrophic aftermath of a nuclear detonation, including obliteration of their families and irreversible devastation of the environment. In 1947 Albert Einstein wrote to the Emergency Committee of Atomic Scientists of the obligation to warn citizens of this danger: "In this lies our only security and hope . . . that an informed citizenry will act for life, not death."[9] Editors seemed to think the personal lives of Britain's royal family or the volatile behavior of President Donald Trump would attract a larger readership than descriptions of a possible nuclear Armageddon. Nevertheless, 122 member states, ICAN, numerous other civil-society groups, the International Red Cross, scholars, and religious leaders pressed on.

On September 3, 2017, North Korea conducted its sixth nuclear test, detonating a weapon equivalent to one hundred kilotons of TNT, which Kim Jong Un called a "gift" to the United States. In response UN ambassador Nikki Haley declared that North Korea was "begging for war."[10] Shortly thereafter North Korea tested an intermediate-range ballistic missile, prompting President Trump to threaten Kim in his first address to the UN General Assembly: "Rocket Man is on a suicide mission for himself and for his regime."[11]

The Treaty on the Prohibition of Nuclear Weapons was opened for signature at the UN Headquarters on September 20, 2017. By signing the treaty, a state signaled its intention to become a party to it in the future, but it was not required to begin implementing its provisions. To become legally bound by the treaty, the signatory state needed to deposit its instrument of ratification, which required approval by its parliament or executives. Once fifty states completed ratification, the treaty would enter into force. Advocates understood this would be a lengthy process. Still, on the very day the TPNW opened for signature, fifty states signed. Moreover, the Holy See, then Thailand, then Guyana not only signed the treaty but also submitted their instruments of ratification.

The refusal of Canada, as a NATO member, to recognize the TPNW did not surprise Thurlow. Japan's response disappointed her even more. Although Prime Minister Shinzo Abe had declared just six weeks earlier—on the seventy-second anniversary of the atomic bombing of Hiroshima—that Japan would "firmly advance the movement toward a world without nuclear weapons," he declined to sign the treaty; he preferred the step-by-step approach.[12] Even more frustrating to Thurlow and antinuclear activists worldwide, the news media failed to notify the public about this crucial next step toward the abolition of nuclear weapons. That changed at noon on October 6.

Television cameras focused on an ornate wooden door through which emerged an official-looking woman. "Good morning, everybody," she said, then came straight to the point. "The Norwegian Nobel Committee has decided to award the Nobel Peace Prize for 2017 to the International Campaign to Abolish Nuclear Weapons (ICAN) . . . for its work to draw attention to the catastrophic humanitarian consequences of any use of nuclear weapons and for its groundbreaking efforts to achieve a treaty-based prohibition of such weapons."[13] Berit Reiss-Andersen, chair of the Norwegian Nobel Committee, had just given ICAN the spark it needed to ignite the public. The press would cover the Nobel Peace Prize ceremony extensively; people around the world would hear their message and learn about the Ban Treaty.

In 1895 Sir Alfred Nobel, a wealthy Swedish industrialist and inventor, had stipulated in his will that most of his estate would be allocated to establish five prizes awarded annually to those who, during the preceding year, had "conferred the greatest benefit to humankind."[14] Starting in 1901, each recipient, referred to as a "laureate," received a diploma, gold medal, and monetary award on December 10, the date of Nobel's death. Four prizes—Literature, Physics, Chemistry, and Physiology or Medicine—were awarded in Stockholm. The Peace Prize, selected by a committee of five, appointed by the Norwegian Parliament, was bestowed in a ceremony held in Oslo. As the 2017 Nobel Peace Prize laureate, ICAN joined an esteemed group, which included Elie Wiesel, Lech Walesa, Mother Teresa, Liu Xiaobo, the Fourteenth Dalai Lama, Mikhail Gorbachev, Nelson Mandela, and Willem de Klerk, as well as organizations such as Amnesty International, the United Nations Children's Fund (UNICEF), the International Committee of the Red Cross, and the International Campaign to Ban Landmines, with Jody Williams.

ICAN's leadership called the Peace Prize a tribute to the efforts of "concerned citizens worldwide," underscoring its gratitude to hibakusha, "whose searing testimonies and unstinting advocacy were instrumental in securing this landmark agreement."[15] World leaders, public figures, and faith communities around the world sent congratulatory notes. Twenty-three countries made celebratory remarks at the UN General Assembly First Committee. UN secretary-general António Guterres told the press that the prize recognized "the determined efforts of civil society to highlight the unconscionable humanitarian and environmental consequences that would result if they [nuclear weapons] were ever used again."[16] Mikhail Gorbachev hailed the award designation as a "very good decision" that signified a "world without nuclear weapons—there cannot be any other goal."[17] When asked to clarify whether Canadian prime minister Justin Trudeau planned to congratulate ICAN, his office did not respond.

In press reports the public learned that ICAN stood for the International Campaign to Abolish Nuclear Weapons, a coalition of 468 nongovernmental organizations in one hundred countries, and that it had been striving to eliminate nuclear weapons since its inception in 2007. "A Peace Prize That Honors the Quest," read a headline in the *New York Times*. A member of its editorial board described the award as a "blunt rejoinder to the world's nine nuclear-armed powers and their allies."[18] On National Public Radio, the chair of the Nobel Committee, Berit Reiss-Andersen, credited ICAN with revitalizing nuclear-disarmament efforts that, she hoped, would motivate nuclear-weapon states to continue negotiations. "We are not kicking anybody's leg with the prize," she told a *New York Times* reporter. "We are giving encouragement."[19] She disclosed that the prize included nine million Swedish krona in cash (approximately $1.1 million).

The announcement was not without controversy, however. "This year's Nobel Peace Prize rewards a nice but pointless idea," reported the *Economist*.[20] *The Guardian* quoted Beatrice Fihn as saying that Donald Trump "puts a spotlight on the dangers of nuclear weapons." Having labeled the U.S. president a "moron" in a Twitter post two days earlier, she told *The Guardian* the award warned all nuclear-armed states that they no longer could "threaten to indiscriminately slaughter hundreds of thousands of civilians in the name of security."[21] At last, through media coverage of the Nobel Peace Prize, the public began to learn about the horrors generated by the use of nuclear weapons. And few could make that point with greater effect than Setsuko Thurlow.

A few weeks following the announcement, the ICAN Steering Group requested she join Beatrice Fihn in accepting the Peace Prize and delivering the Nobel lecture. "I am so deeply humbled," Thurlow told the Canadian press.[22] She considered it a privilege to have worked with ICAN campaigners around the world for over a decade. When alone, she wondered, "Why me?" Over the years she had asked herself, "What role am I playing in this campaign? I'm not making political or tactical decisions."[23] Why had ICAN chosen her? Its members considered her an inspiration, a moral compass. Her grim descriptions of human suffering helped stigmatize weapons of mass destruction in efforts to cast their use as a crime against humanity. Her powerful words moved countless individuals, including Pope Francis and the Dalai Lama. Her tenacious advocacy and sharp analysis made her a formidable opponent in confronting heads of nuclear-armed states. Critical historical events need a personal narrative. An eyewitness to one of the cardinal events in the birth of the nuclear age, Thurlow had become the storyteller for Hiroshima.

In six weeks Setsuko would address her largest international audience to date. She needed to make travel plans, choose her clothing, absorb the week's packed agenda, learn the protocol of the Nobel Committee and the royal family, determine how to frame her message, and then write and rehearse the most important speech she would ever deliver. Meanwhile, prior speaking engagements filled her calendar; interview requests and congratulatory notes to which she needed to reply consumed hours each day.

By far the most challenging and stressful aspect of Thurlow's preparation was composing her speech. She would be the first Japanese woman to deliver a Nobel lecture. Millions worldwide would be watching, among them heads of state, historians, religious leaders, antinuclear activists, and nuclear-weapon advocates. This gave her the opportunity to educate, to warn, to plead with people everywhere to stop this insanity and prevent their annihilation. And she had just twenty minutes to do so. To add to the pressure, the ICAN Steering Group had to review her lecture, as she was representing the entire campaign. And the Nobel Committee requested the speech be sent weeks in advance to allow time for translation into numerous languages.

Just as Setsuko began to compose her lecture, a public-relations firm hired by ICAN sent Kathleen Sullivan a speech for Thurlow that they thought a perfect complement to Beatrice Fihn's. Kathleen showed the proposed speech to Setsuko. Although she knew the suggestion that Setsuko read a speech she hadn't written would offend her, it would add urgency to her task. Setsuko's reaction was predictable: What was the matter with telling her own story? It was choosing the additional points she wanted to make and the strict twenty-minute time limit that were stymieing her.

Fortunately, the ICAN Steering Group assigned the task of coordinating the two Nobel lectures to Tim Wright. A bright young Australian with degrees in international relations and law, Wright had been ICAN's first volunteer campaigner and was now its Asia-Pacific director. He had helped coordinate ICAN's participation in the three humanitarian conferences; he had represented the campaign at review meetings of the Nuclear Non-Proliferation Treaty and the First Committee of the UN General Assembly. Before long he would become ICAN's treaty coordinator. And Setsuko had high regard and affection for this kind, self-effacing, talented young man. So Tim Wright with his calm insight and advice from Akira Kawasaki, and Kathleen Sullivan with her boundless energy, set about guiding Setsuko.

As the process dragged on, Kathleen began to fret. "Setsuko is meticulous," Tim noted. "It doesn't matter if she's speaking to students or at an international conference, she thinks carefully about what she wants to say."[24] Always forthright with Setsuko, Kathleen had read, typed, and suggested edits for countless addresses over years of working together. "Obviously this is your speech," she told Setsuko, "but you are speaking on behalf of our campaign. So we need to help you write it, and we need to vet the whole thing."[25] Yet, as Tim observed, "Setsuko was very much in control."[26] And, in time, the best speech she would ever deliver came into being. "Setsuko was pleased," Sullivan recalled. "Tim was pleased. The International Steering Group was pleased. So we sent the speech to Oslo."[27]

On December 6 Setsuko arrived in Oslo, accompanied by her son Andy. The secretary of the Nobel Committee greeted them at the airport with a deep bow and escorted them to the Grand Hotel. It was indeed "grand," with its white-granite facade and clock tower. Built in 1874, the hotel was located on Karl Johans Gate, between the Royal Palace and the Parliament building. It had the distinction of hosting the Nobel Peace Prize banquet and accommodating the laureates in the Nobel Suite. From a balcony overlooking the Karl Johans Gate, Peace Prize winners received ovations from the crowd below after the ceremony. Setsuko said her luxurious suite made her feel almost royal.

Thurlow's schedule listed December 7 as a "free day getting settled, resting, and relaxing."[28] That did not turn out to be the case. Kathleen had arranged for her to read her lecture to a small group, which included Mitchie Takeuchi and Susan Strickler, filmmakers nearing completion of a documentary on Thurlow, titled *The Vow from Hiroshima*. Mitchie, a business consultant in New York City, was a Japanese expat whose grandfather had been the director of the Hiroshima Red Cross Hospital in August 1945. Mitchie had met Setsuko at Hibakusha Stories, and, when they discovered they both had graduated from Hiroshima Jogakuin, a friendship developed. Emmy Award–winning director Susan Strickler had teamed up with Mitchie to co-write and co-produce the documentary. As the film was to culminate in Thurlow's Nobel Prize acceptance speech, they anticipated filming her throughout the week.

When Setsuko read her lecture to the group, she stumbled over words as if this was the first time she had read it. In just three days, she would be front and center on the world stage. Taken aback, Kathleen quietly said, "I think we need to do a lot more practice."[29] Now almost all of Setsuko's unscheduled time was devoted to rehearsing the speech or resting. Kathleen restricted visitors, even son Andy, Mitchie, and Susan. They were staying in a rental house with members of Hibakusha Stories, and most of Setsuko's scheduled activities did not include them. Before long, friction erupted between Kathleen and Susan, who wanted to capture the week's journey on film. At times she felt that Kathleen was trying to sabotage the documentary. Still, Kathleen persisted: Setsuko must have quiet time to rehearse for this pivotal moment. Besides, she worried that her friend seemed indisposed.

On Friday, December 8, Setsuko again spent a large part of the day rehearsing her speech. She perked up when Tim Wright joined them, instilling a tranquil ambience. He suggested the points at which she should hold for applause, with an eye on an imaginary clock so as to keep the time at twenty minutes. He, too, observed Setsuko's diminished energy and attributed it to nervousness regarding the upcoming ceremony. She did attend a dinner party at the Austrian embassy. By the end of the day, her ankles were swollen, and her back ached.

On Saturday morning Setsuko faced another hectic day. First on the agenda was the Nobel Peace Prize 2017 laureate press conference, held at the Norwegian Nobel Institute. Henrik Syse, the vice-chair of the Nobel Committee, had the honor of escorting Thurlow to all official Nobel Prize activities. Son of a former Norwegian prime minister, Syse had interacted with many prominent people over the years. One of the first things he noticed about this world-famous hibakusha was her modesty and appreciation for the arrangements made for her by the Nobel Committee.

Seated on the stage with Thurlow were Berit Reiss-Andersen; Beatrice Fihn; Olav Njølstad, director of the Norwegian Nobel Institute and secretary to the Norwegian Nobel Committee; and Dr. Tilman Ruff, one of ICAN's co-founders. The only spot of color on the stage came from Setsuko's red blouse. Thurlow, Fihn, and Ruff made opening statements on behalf of ICAN and answered questions from the press corps. "Already Setsuko made a deep impression on me and everyone there," recalled Syse. "I realized immediately that this is not just someone crossing out answers or trying to be morally dramatic, but someone who carefully thinks through what she is saying."[30]

That afternoon they rehearsed at Oslo City Hall, site of the Nobel Peace Prize ceremony. Located in the city center, facing the Oslo Fjord, it had a distinctive exterior of oversized red brick, with twin towers and decorative wooden panels by Norwegian artists. An astronomical clock hung at the entrance, and melodies from forty-nine tower bells played throughout the day. The entrance opened into the magnificent Great Hall with its expansive marble floor, embellished by geometric designs and inlaid stone medallions. Henrik Sørensen's famed mural, *Work, Administration, Celebration,* covered the far wall. A stage had been set up beneath it. Three frescoes by prominent muralist Alf Rolfsen decorated the other walls. Setsuko had no time to appreciate them, however. Like so many other wonderful aspects of Oslo, that pleasure would have to wait for another trip.

The Nobel Committee and recipients had an intimate dinner at the Grand Hotel that evening. Syse became increasingly enamored of Setsuko, as she continued to express gratitude for her elegant suite, the dinner, and his constant attention. Later on Setsuko didn't even recall attending the dinner. Her legs had become swollen up to her knees, and she had difficulty finding a comfortable position in which to sleep that night because of increasing back pain.

On Sunday morning, December 10, Setsuko was thinking what a comfort it would be to have Jim at her side. Midmorning a woman came to style her hair and apply makeup. "She charged me $150 just to comb my hair," Setsuko later complained.[31] For the event she had chosen to wear a gown made from one of her mother's elegant black kimonos, decorated with green waves, which symbolized strength and life. As a final touch, she put on a string of pearls. In Japanese culture, pearls bring good health, something she needed at the moment. Yet she was smiling broadly when Henrik Syse arrived at 11:45 to escort her to Oslo City Hall.

Seats for a thousand guests had been laid out in two sections. In front of a wide central aisle stood four special chairs for the royal family. As the television cameras panned the right side of the audience, it picked up distinguished members of ICAN; Elayne Whyte Gómez, who had presided over the TPNW negotiations; and three hibakusha representatives. Other attendees included the mayors of Hiroshima and Nagasaki and the newly appointed Japanese ambassador to Norway. Across the aisle sat Norwegian prime minister Erna Solberg, nicknamed "Iron Erna," leader of the Conservative Party. As a member state of NATO, Norway supported the retention of nuclear weapons and thus declined to sign the TPNW. The press wondered how she would handle the situation during the celebratory Nobel Prize events.

Notably absent were ambassadors from most of the nuclear-armed states. Olav Njølstad, director of the Norwegian Nobel Institute, told the press the decision by some ambassadors not to attend the Peace Prize ceremony was not a boycott. He did note that some embassies would be sending "representatives at a lower level." The ambassadors of India and Pakistan happened to be traveling at the time of the ceremony, and China had not attended a Peace Prize ceremony since Chinese dissident Liu Xiaobo had been awarded the Peace

Prize in 2010. North Korea did not have an embassy in Oslo. To the surprise of some, the ambassadors from Russia and Israel did attend. The Russian embassy stated that even though it hadn't signed the TPNW, it did "share the long-term goal of a world free of nuclear weapons."[32]

The low buzz of conversation ceased when, at precisely 1:00 p.m., four clarion trumpets played a fanfare, announcing the arrival of the two representatives for the laureate—the International Campaign to Abolish Nuclear Weapons. The audience stood as the procession began: Beatrice Fihn, then Henrik Syse, and then Setsuko Thurlow, pushed in a wheelchair by a Nobel Committee member, followed by two other committee members and Olav Njølstad. As they stood on the stage, guests and television audiences got what was for many their first look at Beatrice Fihn and Setsuko Thurlow. Many thought the thirty-five-year-old Swedish lawyer striking. She stood taller than anyone else on the stage, wearing a white sheath with no decorative jewelry. She didn't need any. Her long blond hair pulled back in a ponytail, a broad smile, and bright eyes: she appeared effervescent and self-assured. Wearing an exquisite kimono, Setsuko, now in her mid-eighties, came up to Fihn's shoulders. In a stately manner, her chin raised, she surveyed the audience.

A second fanfare announced the royal family: King Harald V, Queen Sonia, Crown Prince Haakon and Crown Princess Mette Marit. After the performance of a Scandinavian aria, Berit Reiss-Andersen, a distinguished lawyer and Labour Party member, approached the podium to give her presentation speech as chair of the Norwegian Nobel Committee. To begin she said ICAN was receiving the 2017 Nobel Peace Prize in recognition of its role in providing fresh momentum to the movement to abolish nuclear weapons by focusing attention on the catastrophic humanitarian consequences and by spearheading the creation and passage of the Treaty on the Prohibition of Nuclear Weapons. "The devastation of Hiroshima and Nagasaki has taught us that nuclear weapons . . . must never ever be used again," she said, eliciting a brisk audience applause. The camera focused on Prime Minister Erna Solberg, with whom Reiss-Andersen had sparred over the years; her smile looked forced. Reiss-Andersen proceeded to stress how even the limited use of such weapons would kill millions of civilians indiscriminately and damage the environment in unimaginable ways. Furthermore, she reminded the audience that, despite the best security measures and control systems, human beings control nuclear weapons, and humans make errors. Even more threatening, she warned, is the day when terrorists will be able to sabotage those control systems. She called ICAN's work a "remarkable endeavor to serve the interests of mankind."[33]

Reiss-Andersen proceeded to introduce the two speakers who represented ICAN. "Madam Setsuko Thurlow," she began, "you have devoted your life to bearing witness to the events of 6 August 1945. . . . You do not allow us to forget." Turning to Beatrice Fihn, she said, "You are such a splendid representative of the multitude of idealists who forgo an ordinary career and instead devote all of their time and skills to the work of achieving a peaceful world." Reiss-Andersen concluded her presentation with a tribute to all the individuals and organizations within ICAN who had "given the efforts to achieve a world without nuclear weapons a new direction and new vigor."[34] She then asked Thurlow and Fihn to step forward and receive the award on behalf of ICAN.

Beatrice and Setsuko walked across the stage, arm in arm. Reiss-Andersen passed Fihn the eighteen-carat gold medal, engraved on its face with a profile of Alfred Nobel and, on the reverse side, with three men forming a fraternal bond with an inscription that read, "*Pro pace et fraternitate gentium*" (for peace and fraternity among peoples).[35] Thurlow then received the diploma. The picture of a mother holding a child depicted mother love and the wish for the world's children to grow up in peace. During prolonged applause, Beatrice gave Setsuko an affectionate squeeze of her shoulder. She then held out the medal to ICAN members, indicating that it belonged to all of them. A loud cheer arose from the right side of the audience.

For a musical interlude, popular American artist John Legend played a grand piano as he sang "Redemption Song," written by Jamaican singer-songwriter Bob Marley shortly before his untimely death from cancer. In a press conference the day before, Grammy Award–winning Legend had encouraged young people to express concern for nuclear weapons because "this is literally about the future of human survival on this planet."[36] What an appropriate choice "Redemption Song" was. Although applicable to many social concerns, the song had special meaning for ICAN: through enactment of the Ban Treaty, they sought redemption—deliverance from the evils of nuclear weapons. During the performance television cameras caught Thurlow looking upward as if responding to the lyrics: "But my hand was made strong by the hand of the Almighty."[37]

Now Beatrice Fihn stood at the podium, ready to address her largest audience yet about the threat of nuclear weapons. Born in Sweden, she held a bachelor's degree in international relations from Stockholm University and a master of laws from the University of London. She had written numerous articles on humanitarian law, civil society's involvement in diplomacy, and gender viewpoints on disarmament. With over a decade of experience in civil-society mobilization and disarmament diplomacy, she had led ICAN since 2013.

Fihn began by expressing her gratitude in accepting the prize on behalf of over a thousand inspirational people who constituted ICAN. She thanked foreign ministers, UN officials, the Red Cross and Red Crescent staff, and those in academia who had joined them in their efforts to abolish nuclear weapons. Then she took a beat, assumed a somber expression, lowered the pitch of her voice, and launched into her message: "At dozens of locations around the world—in missile silos buried in our earth, on submarines navigating through our oceans, and aboard planes flying high in our sky—lie fifteen thousand objects of humankind's destruction. Perhaps it is the enormity of this fact, perhaps it is the unimaginable scale of the consequences, that leads many to simply accept this grim reality, to go about our daily lives with no thought to the instruments of insanity all around us. . . . Our mutual destruction is only one impulsive tantrum away."

Her lecture was powerful, perfectly constructed as she proceeded to address fear, freedom, and the future. With regard to the use of nuclear weapons as a deterrence, she said that those who possess them are "puffing their chests by declaring their preparedness to exterminate, in a flash, countless thousands of human lives." During the Cold War, this fear had been ever-present. In his 1950 Nobel lecture, William Faulkner had said, "There is only the question of 'when will I be blown up?'" Now fear had been replaced by denial, what Fihn called "blind acceptance," even though the current threat was far greater than that of the Cold War. She warned that mass murder of civilians could result from "carelessness, a misconstrued comment, or bruised ego." Heads nodded; the audience knew those leaders to whom she was referring. In blunt terms she described the instantaneous, disastrous climate change: "If only a small fraction of today's nuclear weapons were used, soot and smoke from the firestorms would loft high into the atmosphere—cooling, darkening, and drying the earth's surface for more than a decade. It would obliterate food crops, putting billions at risk of starvation." Faulkner had challenged people of the world: "Only by being the voice of humanity can we defeat fear; can we help humanity endure." ICAN was that voice.

Fihn's most enthusiastic applause came when she observed, "We must reclaim the freedom to not live our lives as hostages to imminent annihilation. Man—not woman—made nuclear weapons to control others, but instead we are controlled by them." Prime Minister Solberg whispered to her husband with a look that implied sarcasm. The applause grew stronger, as did Fihn's intensity when she enumerated how the nuclear race was escalating. She quoted Nobel Peace Prize laureate Martin Luther King Jr., who called nuclear weapons "the madman's gun held permanently to our temple." How ironic, Fihn said, "These weapons were supposed to keep us free, but they deny us our freedoms."

Turning to the future, she received her longest applause when she thanked Setsuko Thurlow and other hibakusha for speaking out about their painful past to forge a brighter future. "Those who say that future is not possible," she advised, "need to get out of the way of those making it happen." With a dramatic flair, she called on all nations to ratify the Treaty on the Prohibition of Nuclear Weapons. She waited for the vigorous hand clapping to diminish and then enjoined the nuclear-armed states: "The United States, choose freedom over fear. Russia, choose disarmament over destruction. Britain, choose the rule of law over oppression. France, choose human rights over terror. China, choose reason over irrationality. India, choose sense over senselessness. Pakistan, choose logic over Armageddon. Israel, choose common sense over obliteration. North Korea, choose wisdom over ruin."

She continued, "To the nations who believe they are sheltered under the umbrella of nuclear weapons, your enabling of the nuclear states will not make you any less complicit in the destruction of others in your name." The camera picked up Prime Minister Solberg's reaction: she chuckled. Fihn's voice rose to its highest pitch in her final pronouncement: "To all nations, choose the end of nuclear weapons over the end of us. This is the choice that the Treaty on the Prohibition of Nuclear Weapons represents. Join this treaty."[38] An ICAN member was the first to rise, leading a standing ovation.

Fihn's speech, like Reiss-Andersen's, was well organized and eloquent, their legal backgrounds having taught them how to plead a case. Now, after sitting for almost two hours, some audience members appeared restless. One more speech and this from an elderly Japanese woman whose face remained placid throughout the other speeches, who required assistance walking to the podium. Those who did not know Setsuko Thurlow may have expected a respectful bow, grateful appreciation from a demure, soft-spoken woman. She did not bow. She surveyed the audience, almost as if to say to each person, "Listen to me. I am speaking to *you*." Then she took them back to Japan on August 6, 1945, on a ride most would likely never forget.

After thanking the royal family, the Norwegian Nobel Committee, and "the remarkable human beings who form the ICAN movement," she said that today she was speaking for hibakusha everywhere with whom she had "stood in solidarity" for seven decades. As she named some of those "long-forgotten places," she pointed to specific audience members, recognizing "people whose lands and seas were irradiated, whose bodies were experimented upon, whose cultures were forever disrupted." The audience began to focus on Thurlow—no nodding off, no fidgeting on their chairs. And then she accelerated her rhetoric: "We were not content to be victims. We refused to wait for an immediate fiery end or the slow poisoning of our world. We refused to sit idly in terror as the so-called great powers took us past nuclear dusk and brought us recklessly close to nuclear midnight. We rose up. We shared our stories of survival. We said, 'humanity and nuclear weapons cannot coexist.'" She had taken command of Oslo City Hall. "Today, I want you to feel in this hall," she continued, glancing upward, "the presence of all those who perished in Hiroshima and Nagasaki. I want you to feel, above and around us, a great cloud of a quarter million souls." She paused and looked straight out at the audience. "Each person had a name. Each person was loved by someone. Let us ensure that their deaths were not in vain."

And then she told her story: "I was just 13 years old when the United States dropped the first atomic bomb on my city, Hiroshima. I still vividly remember that morning. At 8:15, I saw a blinding bluish-white flash from the window." She briefly squeezed her eyes shut as if reliving the experience. "I remember having the sensation of floating in the air. As I regained consciousness in the silence and darkness, I found myself pinned under the collapsed building. I knew I was faced with death." Then she heard the faint voices of her classmates: "Mother, help me. God, help me,'" Thurlow said, reenacting the moment. The camera focused on the Crown Princess, who sat motionless, a look of pain on her face. "All of a sudden," Setsuko continued, "somebody shook my left shoulder from behind, and I heard a man saying: 'Don't give up. Keep pushing. Keep kicking. You see the sun ray coming through that opening? Crawl towards it as quickly as possible.'" She spoke with the same urgency as had he. No longer was she reading her speech. She seemed to be in the collapsed building, smelling smoke, crawling over glass and splinters, trying to escape. She took a deep breath, lessened her pace, and continued, "As I crawled out, the rubble was on fire. Most of my classmates in the same building were burned to death alive."

After a hushed silence, Thurlow drew a vivid picture that stunned those hearing her story for the first time, even the second time, and every time thereafter: "I saw all around me utter, unimaginable devastation. Processions of ghostly figures shuffled by. Grotesquely wounded people, they were bleeding, burnt, blackened and swollen. Parts of their bodies were missing. Flesh and skin hung from their bones. Some with their eyeballs hanging in their hands. Some with their bellies burst open, their intestines hanging out. The foul stench of burnt human flesh filled the air." She raised her voice, saying, "Thus, with one bomb my beloved city was obliterated. Most of its residents were civilians who were incinerated, vaporized, carbonized—among them, members of my own family and 351 of my schoolmates." Thousands of others would die from delayed effects of radiation exposure, some in the first week, some even today.

"Whenever I remember Hiroshima," she pressed on, "the first image that comes to mind is of my four-year-old nephew, Eiji, his little body transformed into an unrecognizable melted chunk of flesh. He kept begging for water in a faint voice until his death released him from agony." She paused; she sighed. As many times as she had talked about Eiji, it never got easier. "To me," she continued, "he came to represent all the innocent children of the world, threatened as they are at this very moment by nuclear weapons." Some in the audience bowed their heads; others dabbed the tears welling up in their eyes.

Setsuko broke the momentary hush with her cry: "We must not tolerate this insanity any longer." A prolonged applause of agreement followed. With that her ire rose. She called the annihilations of Hiroshima and Nagasaki "atrocities" and "war crimes." And now nine nations threatened to destroy life on earth with these apocalyptic weapons. Her rhetoric sharpened. "The development of nuclear weapons signifies not a country's elevation to greatness," she pronounced, "but its descent to the darkest depths of depravity. These weapons are not a necessary evil; they are the ultimate evil." A wave of agreement followed every statement. She spoke of her great joy at the adoption of the Treaty on the Prohibition of Nuclear Weapons five months earlier. "Having witnessed humanity at its worst," she said, "I witnessed, that day, humanity at its best."

Then she raised her voice and commanded with a strength surprising for an eighty-five-year-old woman: "All responsible leaders will sign this treaty. And history will judge harshly those who reject it. No longer shall their abstract theories mask the genocidal reality of their practices. No longer shall 'deterrence' be viewed as anything but a deterrent to disarmament. No longer shall we live under a mushroom cloud of fear." It was as if a tide was rising in the audience. She admonished leaders of nuclear-armed states and their "accomplices under the so-called nuclear umbrella": their actions were consequential and endangered humankind. "Join this treaty," she beseeched them. "Forever eradicate the threat of nuclear annihilation."

It was the stirring, poignant, ending to her speech that would be quoted repeatedly: "When I was a 13-year-old girl, trapped in the smoldering rubble, I kept pushing. I kept moving toward the light. And I survived. Our light now is the Ban Treaty. To all in this hall and all listening around the world,

I repeat those words that I heard in the ruins of Hiroshima: 'Don't give up. Keep pushing. Keep moving. See the light? Crawl towards it.'" The audience rose in a single ovation as if propelled from their seats by a crashing wave.[39]

Kathleen Sullivan burst into tears. She covered her face with her program. Tim Wright couldn't stop smiling. The ICAN Executive Committee knew she would deliver a compelling speech; that's why they had chosen her. They never imagined how compelling it would be. Yes, she was the heart and soul of the international antinuclear movement. "No matter what political persuasion you are, no matter what you think of the Ban Treaty, you cannot argue with her story," Henrik Syse thought as he stood clapping. The way in which she intertwined her personal narrative and the larger political setting reminded him of several other Nobel laureates, in particular Elie Wiesel and Albert Schweitzer—eyewitnesses and messengers with a reverence for life, who through their narratives helped change the world. "I think," Syse later said, "for those who attended the Nobel ceremony, if they remember one thing, it is her and her speech."[40]

After another musical interlude, the royal family walked up to the stage to congratulate the winners. King Harald approached Thurlow first and thanked her for her message. He held her hand with unexpected tenderness. It seemed like he did not want to let go. A flourish by the trumpets announced the recessional.

That evening, prior to the Nobel Peace Prize banquet, Thurlow and Fihn stood on the main balcony of the Grand Hotel to watch the traditional torchlight parade. Participants walked through the streets of Oslo from the downtown area, past the Parliament building to the Grand Hotel, to show their support of ICAN. Setsuko thought this the highlight of the entire trip. Waving to the enthusiastic crowd below, she felt certain the Ban Treaty was going to change the world. "I never expected such passionate support," Thurlow said.[41]

The next two days brought no rest, starting with celebrity broadcaster Stephen Sackur's confrontational interview on BBC's *HARDtalk*. When asked her reaction to Donald Trump's threat of "fire and fury," Thurlow shot back, "He doesn't understand that there are millions of human beings who could suffer from this. And I have seen a hundred thousand people melt away. How inhuman can we be?" Did she say "inhuman," instead of "inhumane," on purpose? Probably. Although both words mean lacking in compassion, inhuman also suggests a nonhuman class of beings. "That's totally unacceptable moral behavior," she continued, "and I would tell him that." Her statement made headlines.[42]

On the last evening, Setsuko did not know what to expect when Henrik Syse accompanied her to the Nobel Peace Prize concert. Eight thousand filled the Telenor Arena to honor ICAN with performances, from award-winning Scandinavian artists along with headliner John Legend, who played on a piano saved from the wreckage of Hiroshima. David Oyelowo, the British actor who rose to fame for his portrayal of Martin Luther King Jr. in the movie *Selma*, served as the host.

Setsuko sat between Crown Princess Mette Marit and Henrik Syse. She had never attended a pop concert and knew none of the artists except John Legend. Were she back in Toronto on this December evening, she would be sitting in Roy Thomson Hall, listening to the Toronto Symphony Orchestra play Handel's *Messiah*. Instead she sat in an immense, darkened arena with beams of light flashing across the stage, watching a twenty-year-old Swedish singer, in a miniskirt and high black boots, dance across the stage singing, "Lush Life." Despite the loud music, Setsuko enjoyed the novel experience. Photos showed her clapping, laughing, and waving to acquaintances.

Interspersed with the music, Oyelowo paid tribute to all the members of ICAN, starting with a standing ovation as he avowed, "We believe peace should be as loud as possible." Beatrice Fihn took the stage with a group of ICAN members and told all those listening in the arena and at home, "We are tired of waiting," she said. "If you are not with us, get out of our way." When Oyelowo talked of Setsuko Thurlow's inspirational story, enthusiastic cheers and applause continued longer than for anyone else that evening, even John Legend. The performing artists, most of whom had millions of followers on social media, encouraged young people everywhere to stand up and support the abolition of nuclear weapons. And Legend ended the evening singing "Glory" with the Mosaic Gospel Choir. He urged the audience to rise and join in.[43]

Setsuko may have initially regretted she wasn't attending the Toronto Symphony Orchestra's Christmas concert, yet, by the end of the evening, the passion for peace erupting from so many young people who committed themselves to carrying on ICAN's work was perhaps as uplifting as the *Messiah* would have been.

On the evening of December 12, the celebrations surrounding the 2017 Nobel Peace Prize came to an end. Setsuko never did get to see the sights of Oslo or shop at the Christmas fair or relax with any of her numerous friends who had gathered in Oslo. But she had made citizens of the world take notice, had shaken them up with her story and had thrown down the antinuclear gauntlet.

The next morning she and son Andy flew home. On the plane she was thinking about all the work ahead—the calls and emails to return, interviews to give, invitations to which she must respond, and heads of state she needed to contact—to encourage, and in some cases to coerce, to ratify the Treaty on the Prohibition of Nuclear Weapons. But she was exhausted and in such pain she barely could concentrate. Upon their arrival in Toronto, she was admitted to the hospital in critical condition.

23 The Road to Ratification

> Because everything we do and everything we are is in jeopardy, and because the peril is immediate and unremitting, every person is the right person to act and every moment is the right moment to begin.
>
> –Jonathan Schell, *The Fate of the Earth*

No one in Oslo realized just how ill their honored guest, Setsuko Thurlow, had become. Stones had obstructed her kidneys, causing a severe infection and threatening kidney failure. For an eighty-five-year-old, the prognosis was guarded. Yet, with the expertise of the medical team and her determination, she survived and was discharged from the hospital just before Christmas. When Setsuko returned to her condominium, she found no holiday decorations, no smell of fresh-baked cookies, no carols playing in the background. The Christmas season had been her and Jim's favorite time of the year. Now she was alone. If she felt a bit low, it didn't last long. News of an incoming nuclear attack on Hawaii jolted her.

At 8:07 on Saturday morning, January 13, 2018, while many Hawaiians and holiday vacationers were just waking, enjoying their first cup of Kona coffee, or walking on the beach, an emergency alert flashed across mobile phones: BALLISTIC MISSILE THREAT INBOUND TO HAWAII. SEEK IMMEDIATE SHELTER. THIS IS NOT A DRILL.[1] An urgent message interrupted television and radio programs: "The U.S. Pacific Command has detected a missile threat to Hawaii. A missile may impact on land or sea within minutes. THIS IS NOT A DRILL. If you are indoors, stay indoors. If you are outdoors, seek immediate shelter in a building. Remain indoors well away from windows. If you are driving, pull safely to the side of the road and seek shelter in a building or lay on the floor."[2] North Korea had conducted several missile tests over the year and maintained that it could deliver a nuclear warhead to Hawaii. Panic erupted. Parents grabbed their children and climbed into a bathtub or under a sturdy table; vacationers rushed out into the streets, not knowing where to go or what to do; people called family members to say goodbye, until the phone system jammed; many cried; others prayed. A wave of terror engulfed the islands.

Thirty-eight minutes after the initial warning, another emergency alert flashed on mobile phones across Hawaii: "There is no missile threat or danger to the State of Hawaii. Repeat. False Alarm."[3] People later recalled the anguish they had felt, calling these the longest thirty-eight minutes of their lives. "Now this experience lives inside of me," said one resident, "as a mother, as a human being, and it's never going to go away until we eliminate nuclear weapons."[4]

The error was called a "miscommunication" and a "system failure" by the Hawaii Emergency Management Agency. "Someone pushed the wrong button," officials stated.[5] Fingers were pointed; investigations begun. Whether the cause was related to inadequate management, poor computer-software design, or human error, several things became clear: most civilians had no idea what to do to protect themselves or their families. If missiles had been launched in exchange, a nuclear war likely would have ensued, causing millions of deaths and massive damage to the environment—all the result of a blunder.

This frightful episode, which faded from the news before long, underscored the absolute necessity to eliminate nuclear weapons. And it pressed Setsuko Thurlow back into action. While international news programs played throughout the day on her kitchen-countertop television, she set to work, responding to the hundreds of letters and emails from around the world she had received after ICAN won the Nobel Peace Prize. And she began to answer the calls that had filled her voice mailbox while she was away.

The Treaty on the Prohibition of Nuclear Weapons (TPNW) had been opened for signatures at the UN Headquarters since September 20. Ninety days after the fiftieth state ratified it, the Ban Treaty, as it was also called, would enter into force. So far three states had proceeded through its process of ratification—the Holy See, Thailand, and Guyana. In mid-January Setsuko was pleased, yet not surprised, to learn that Mexico had ratified the treaty. It had been among the first to sign the 1967 Treaty of Tlatelolco, which outlawed nuclear arms in Latin America and the Caribbean. Mexico's confirmation made four states on board, forty-six to go.

ICAN leaders anticipated progress would be slow. After all, it had taken years for the UN ratification of the treaties to eliminate chemical weapons and land mines. And they knew it would be challenging. They had an action plan in place and a host of participants: an international steering group, which included the African Council of Religious Leaders, International Physicians for the Prevention of Nuclear War, Latin America Human Security Network, PAX, Peace Boat, Women's International League for Peace and Freedom, and other distinguished groups; over six hundred partner organizations; and an international team of staff members in Geneva, with Beatrice Fihn as the executive director.

To begin they would support those states proceeding toward ratification. Fifty-six had already signed the Ban Treaty, indicating their intent to validate it. States had different ratification processes, however, some more complicated than others. More difficult would be attempts to persuade the nuclear-umbrella and nuclear-supportive states to sign, then ratify the treaty. ICAN planned to apply the pressure of international laws and norms. Swaying nuclear-armed states would be even more arduous. Coercion might be required. ICAN leaders were prepared to start with reasoning, then proceed to shaming and condemnation.

Defunding could be a powerful approach. ICAN emphasized the extent to which the twenty biggest nuclear-weapon financiers had been funding the current global arms race. If the prohibition of nuclear weapons curtailed their production, investors probably would withdraw, as had been the case with cluster munitions. Through its "Don't Bank on the Bomb" offensive, ICAN urged banks, pension funds, and individuals to divest from companies involved in the manufacture of nuclear weapons or their components. A global report informed the public which specific organizations supported nuclear weapons financially. Deutsche Bank was one of the first to update its investment policies to exclude them.[6]

What would be Setsuko's role? Public education was key. Organizations such as Hibakusha Stories and Peace Boat had been effective yet limited in their audience size. People worldwide needed to comprehend the threat in order to react, rise up, and force their state leaders to sign the Ban Treaty. Although hibakusha could promote action by relating their own stories, many felt uncomfortable doing so, and this population was diminishing in number. Still, ICAN needed the media's attention. That's where Setsuko came in.

Setsuko Thurlow was the most well-known, outspoken hibakusha worldwide. To help keep nuclear weapons front and center in the news, she felt obliged to accept almost every request for an interview, lecture, talk show, graduation speech, or commentary. Furthermore, she needed to help garner support from religious leaders, major civic organizations, and the academic community. That necessitated attending significant conferences, meeting with political figures with whom she had interacted over the years, and contacting state leaders from her homeland, her adopted country, and the United States. At eighty-six she suffered from chronic back pain, high blood pressure, leg numbness, kidney stones, and insomnia. Although her body was telling her "enough," she had vowed to help abolish nuclear weapons. She couldn't flag now.

On January 25 the 2018 Doomsday Clock was reset at 2 minutes to midnight. "Major nuclear actors are on the cusp of a new arms race," stated Rachel Bronson, president and CEO of the *Bulletin of the Atomic Scientists*.[7] In February President Donald Trump announced the first expansion of the United States' nuclear arsenal since the end of the Cold War. At his March 1 annual address, Vladimir Putin boasted about Russia's new nuclear-powered, nuclear-armed cruise missile, capable of delivering a warhead to any point on the earth's surface. India test-fired a long-range nuclear missile that could reach most of Asia, Africa, and Europe. "Where's the outrage?" asked ICAN. "Instead of delivering harsh criticism, states have responded with deafening silence or worse: a renewed focus on rearmament."[8] Then in May President Trump withdrew the United States from the Iran nuclear deal. It had been adopted almost three years earlier, when Iran agreed to dismantle most of its nuclear program in exchange for sanctions relief.

"Airmen charged with protecting a US nuclear missile base busted for taking LSD," reported Robert Burns, the national security writer for the Associated Press, on May 24, 2018.[9] At the humanitarian conferences, Eric Schlosser, author of *Command and Control*, had given hair-raising examples of how miscalculation, miscommunication, and technical lapses engendered by simple human error could have decimated large populations in the United States. And here was yet another frightening incident.

Although the air force had investigated illegal drug use at the Francis E. Warren Air Force Base, near Cheyenne, Wyoming, in 2016, the details of that probe had just come to light. Through the Freedom of Information Act, Burns had obtained records of seven court-martial proceedings and related documents. He found fourteen drug-abusing airmen, six of whom had been tried in a military court. This wasn't the first time a member of the armed forces had been caught using mind-altering drugs. Nevertheless, for this group the stakes were higher than most: these fourteen were members of the air force's nuclear missile corps in charge of Minuteman 3 intercontinental ballistic missiles. They had responsibility for more than four hundred missiles, each capable of delivering a devastating nuclear blow. And it wasn't just marijuana they were using; they had been involved in an LSD (lysergic acid diethylamide) ring that had been ongoing for at least a year. LSD use had not been detected earlier because the Pentagon had eliminated LSD from its standard drug screening.

Initially, the air force spokesperson told Burns and other reporters that the airmen had taken LSD only on off-duty hours, as if that lessened the offense. Once documents of the trial were obtained by the Associated Press, the incidents became more frightening. At the court-martial, prosecutors reviewed the potential reactions to even small amounts of LSD: hallucinations, confusion, distorted perceptions, dreadful thoughts, and rapid mood swings between euphoria and anxiety, all lasting up to twelve hours. These were borne out in the courtroom. "I felt paranoia, panic," Airman First Class Tommy Ashworth said under oath, and it had lasted for hours. Airman Basic Kyle Morrison confessed that if he had been called for a nuclear-security emergency, he could not have responded. There seemed to be an alarming lack of remorse. And the prosecutors found airmen had used not only the hallucinogen LSD but also other mind-altering illegal drugs. Airman First Class Nickolos Harris, the ringleader, who pleaded guilty to using LSD as well as ecstasy, cocaine, and marijuana, told the judge, "I absolutely just loved altering my mind."[10] Six were court-martialed, the other eight disciplined.

The security of U.S. citizens and the safety of the most destructive weapons known to humankind had been entrusted to a group of airmen, many of whom were dishonorable, untrustworthy, and at times mentally unstable. They had the power to obliterate major geographic regions of the world. Veteran Associated Press security reporter Robert Burns's revelation came just as President Trump announced he was planning to spend billions of dollars to upgrade the U.S. nuclear arsenal.

Setsuko Thurlow, along with coauthors Lachlan Forrow and Tilman Ruff, both executives in the International Physicians for the Prevention of Nuclear War, issued a severe warning in the *New England Journal of Medicine*: "The End of Nuclear Weapons or the End of Us." They pointed out that false alarms of impending nuclear attacks in Hawaii, Japan, and Guam, added to the disclosure that the U.S. National Security Agency's computers had been hacked, underscored the increasing risk of a nuclear war started by a mistake or through a cyberattack. The nine nuclear-armed states justified possession of these weapons for security, the authors wrote. That meant assuming "the infallibility of both technical systems and human judgment." They rebutted this stance: "In reality, the fallibility of human and technical systems and the global devastation that would result from a nuclear attack means that any country possessing nuclear weapons is accepting an ever-increasing possibility of self-destruction."[11]

By early summer of 2018, the state of Palestine, Venezuela, Palau, Austria, and Vietnam had submitted documents of confirmation for the TPNW: nine completed, forty-one to go. When a reporter from NHK-World asked ICAN's treaty coordinator, Tim Wright, about the slow pace of ratifications, he replied, "At the ten-month mark, where we are now, the chemical weapons convention had only four ratifications." He explained the complex processes that varied by country. The reporter asked if nuclear-armed states were pressuring states under a nuclear umbrella or NATO members to oppose the treaty. Wright confirmed the insistence by NATO that all members stick together. Yet ICAN knew that some prime ministers and foreign ministers from those states supported the

Ban Treaty. "It's a matter of time before a country breaks from the pack," Wright said.[12] It wouldn't mean leaving NATO, he explained; it would just mean taking a different stance on nuclear weapons. Once one NATO country signed the treaty, he predicted, others would follow. Furthermore, polls indicated a high level of public support for the treaty in many of these states.

When Setsuko's health improved, she traveled to Japan, where she gave invited lectures at Hiroshima Jogakuin University and at the Hiroshima Peace Memorial Museum. While there she enjoyed a banquet with family members. Ahead of her visit to Tokyo, Setsuko requested appointments with Prime Minister Shinzo Abe and Foreign Minister Taro Kono. Both had "scheduling conflicts," she was informed. "Too Busy to Meet? Abe Won't See A-Bomb Activist Thurlow," ran the *Asahi Shimbun* headline. "Is he that busy, or does he not want to meet with me?" she asked the reporter. "Listening to someone who has a different viewpoint from his own is what it takes to be a real leader, doesn't it?"[13]

Instead, she met with the deputy chief cabinet secretary, MP Yasutoshi Nishimura. He thanked Setsuko for speaking out about the inhumanity of nuclear weapons. She replied she found it "heart-wrenching" that Japan, the only atomic-bombed country in the world, would not sign the TPNW.[14] She gave Nishimura a letter addressed to Prime Minister Abe, in which she criticized the government for having declared its opposition to the treaty. "I feel betrayed as an atomic bomb survivor," Thurlow wrote to the prime minister. "I request that Japan break from its dependence on the nuclear deterrent and deepen true conversation and consultation, not as a fake mediator, with atomic bomb survivors and civil society organizations."[15] When he did not reply, she shared her note with the Japanese media. She returned home disappointed. But she'd be back. Setsuko knew how to use the press to inform the public. (She was surprised to be invited to attend the ceremony at the enthronement of His Majesty the Emperor Naruhito a year later.)

By the end of the year, ten more nations had ratified the TPNW. Costa Rica, Nicaragua, Uruguay, and Cuba were also part of the Treaty of Tlatelolco, which prohibited nuclear weapons in Latin America and the Caribbean. New Zealand, the Cook Islands, Vanuatu, and Samoa were also signatories of the Treaty of

Rarotonga, which formalized a nuclear-free zone in the South Pacific. San Marino signed, as well as Gambia, the first African state. Under the Treaty of Pelindaba, Africa had become the world's largest antinuclear zone in 2009. Tim Wright told the media that the African states were being pressured not to ratify the TPNW, especially by the United Kingdom, France, and the United States. "They are sovereign nations," Wright stated, "and they should take direction from their own people, not from foreign powers."[16]

Then, on February 25, 2019, ICAN reported, "Today, the only country that went from developing its own nuclear arsenal to dismantling it and being an outspoken advocate against these weapons of mass destruction, took another critical step towards a nuclear-weapons-free-world."[17] South Africa had just ratified the TPNW. Beatrice Fihn said she applauded the African countries who had "repeatedly challenged the narrative advanced by nuclear-armed states."[18] Twenty confirmations had been completed, thirty remained. They were gaining momentum.

For 2019 the Doomsday Clock remained at 2 minutes to midnight. Unchanged from 2018, this setting was not a sign of stability; it was a stark warning to leaders and citizens around the world. "The current international security situation—what we call the 'new abnormal'—has extended over two years now," wrote John Mecklin, editor of the *Bulletin of the Atomic Scientists*. "It's a state as worrisome as the most dangerous times of the Cold War . . . a state too volatile and dangerous to accept as a continuing state of world affairs."[19] Thurlow agreed. They needed more persons of authority and influence worldwide to raise their voices. The Church of England's ruling body, the General Synod, had voted to support the TPNW in the summer of 2018, joining the Methodists, Baptists, Quakers, United Reformed Church, and the Church of Scotland in calling for the UK government to sign the treaty.

Among the most prominent of religious leaders, of course, was the pope. At the time there were 1.34 billion Catholics worldwide—18 percent of the population. Almost a quarter of U.S. citizens were Catholic and over a third of Canadians. Under Pope John Paul II, the papacy had deemed nuclear deterrence to be morally acceptable if it forwarded the goal of disarmament. This had resulted in three decades of tacit assent. The Catholic Church had stood by and observed the collapse of arms-control treaties, the emergence of more nuclear-armed states, and increased stockpiling of nuclear weapons. That changed after Pope Francis's election as pontiff in 2013.

The Holy See had been the first to ratify the Treaty on the Prohibition of Nuclear Weapons in September 2017. Two months later Pope Francis had convened a disarmament conference at the Vatican. "The threat of their use, as well as their very possession, is to be firmly condemned," he said.[20] Although heartened by his statement, Setsuko thought he should raise his voice even louder. To do so he needed more than just facts and figures; he needed to hear stories from victims to absorb how nuclear weapons affected individuals. That was her role; she was Hiroshima's messenger. The pope likely had heard her passionate Nobel Peace Prize speech. Now she wanted to take her message directly to His Holiness. That opportunity came when Earth Caravan, an interfaith group based in Japan and Canada, asked her to join them.

A delegation of activists, led by Earth Caravan, attended Pope Francis's general audience on March 20, 2019. Among them were Setsuko Thurlow and four thirteen-year-old girls, selected because they were the same age as Thurlow when the atomic bomb had been dropped on Hiroshima. They presented Pope Francis with an oil lamp lit with a flame taken from the burning ashes of the city. The eternal flame of peace, located at the Memorial Cenotaph in the Hiroshima Peace Memorial Park, had been burning continuously. It was to be extinguished when nuclear weapons had been abolished.[21]

Photographers snapped pictures of Pope Francis as he bent down to clasp the hands of Setsuko Thurlow, who gazed up at him from a wheelchair. She gave him a copy of *Hiroshima* by John Hersey with a letter beseeching his help tucked inside: "Your Holiness," it began, "I would like to present to you the very first and original publication of the book entitled Hiroshima, authored by John Hersey. Of 6 survivors who were involved in this book—one was a Catholic priest and one is my own minister of [the] Methodist church." She thanked the Holy See for being the first state to sign and ratify the Ban Treaty and said they were praying for his upcoming journey to Japan. "We Hibakusha desperately hope that your words of peace and justice," she said in ending, "will help the Japanese government to respond to the voice of the majority of the people of Japan to sign and ratify the Treaty on the Prohibition of Nuclear Weapons."[22] Thurlow later received a note from the Vatican expressing His Holiness Pope Francis's appreciation for her message and book. "I have the honor to convey the Holy Father's prayerful good wishes," wrote Monsignor Roberto Cona, Assessor.[23]

At the end of November 2019, Pope Francis visited Hiroshima and Nagasaki to emphasize his call for a global ban on atomic weapons. He spoke at the Hiroshima Peace Memorial Park in front of the renowned Memorial Cenotaph, which holds the names of atomic bomb victims. Just as Setsuko had hoped, the pope spoke with increased passion. He called the use and even possession of nuclear weapons immoral. Then he warned, "We will be judged for this."[24] Setsuko Thurlow had just garnered powerful support. If the 1.34 billion Catholics around the world would rise up, nuclear weapons could be abolished before it was too late.

After ratifications by Panama, as well as Saint Vincent and the Grenadines, Bolivia became the twenty-fifth state to ratify the TPNW. ICAN members rejoiced; they had reached the halfway mark. Meanwhile, cities were taking the lead in increasing public support of the Ban Treaty through ICAN's Cities Appeal. ICAN pointed out that cities would be the probable targets for nuclear attacks, as had been the case in Japan. Since local governments have responsibility for the safety of their citizens, cities must speak up and speak out against nuclear weapons.

The appeal read, "Our city/town is deeply concerned about the grave threat that nuclear weapons pose to communities throughout the world. We firmly believe that our residents have the right to live in a world free from this threat. Therefore, we warmly welcome the adoption of the Treaty on the Prohibition of Nuclear Weapons by the United Nations in 2017, and we call on our national government to join it."[25] Baltimore, Los Angeles, Melbourne, Sydney, and Manchester were among the first to respond while their central governments were idling. By the end of 2019, hundreds of cities, large and small, had joined: Paris, Washington DC, Oslo, Berlin, and Geneva; Yellow Springs, Ohio; Blackshaw Head, England; Gelida, Spain; and Fontvieille, France.

"Majority of millennials support banning nuclear weapons" reported ICAN in January 2020. A new poll, commissioned by the International Committee of the Red Cross, surveyed over sixteen thousand millennials, ages twenty to thirty-five, in sixteen countries. Overall, 84 percent of millennials, even those in nuclear-armed states, opposed the use of nuclear weapons under any circumstance: 73 percent in the United States, 77 percent in Israel, 81 percent in France, 83 percent in the United Kingdom, and 86 percent in Russia. "The next generation has spoken: they don't want nuclear weapons in their future," stated Alicia Sanders-Zakre, ICAN's policy and research coordinator.[26]

Leaders of nuclear-armed and supportive states didn't seem to care. During 2019 those states had spent a total of seventy-three billion dollars on nuclear weapons, the United States having expended almost as much as all the others combined. When asked to explain the variance between the public attitude and the policymakers' actions, Tim Wright replied that many who support nuclear abolition weren't speaking out: "A lot of people don't realize how powerful they themselves are, that they do have agency and capacities to affect change."[27]

"US Deploys New Low-Yield Nuclear Submarine Warhead," revealed the Federation of American Scientists. In 2018 President Trump's administration announced that a new nuclear warhead, the W76–2, had been added to the U.S. nuclear arsenal. With an explosive yield of five kilotons—one-third that of the bomb that destroyed Hiroshima—it could be mounted on a Trident submarine. In December 2019 the U.S. Navy had deployed the USS *Tennessee* from Kings Bay Submarine Base in Georgia, armed with the W76–2 warhead, for a "deterrent patrol" in the Atlantic Ocean.[28]

The 2020 Doomsday clock was reset at 100 seconds to midnight, closer than ever. "Humanity continues to face two simultaneous existential dangers—nuclear war and climate change," wrote John Mecklin in the *Bulletin of the Atomic Scientists*, "that are compounded by a threat multiplier, cyber-enabled information warfare, that undercuts society's ability to respond. The international security situation is dire, not just because these threats exist, but because world leaders have allowed the international political infrastructure for managing them to erode."[29]

By the new year, nine more countries had ratified the TPNW, bringing the number to thirty-four: none of these were nuclear-armed or umbrella states, however. ICAN needed to apply more pressure to the leaders of those states. If one signed, others might follow. To do her part, Thurlow requested a meeting with President Emmanuel Macron in Paris, where she was to give the opening address at the ICAN Paris Forum on February 14. Although the Red Cross poll had revealed that 81 percent of France's millennials considered the use of nuclear weapons as never acceptable, Macron characterized the call for their prohibition as an "ethical debate" that lacked "realism in the strategic context." Not unexpectedly, Thurlow's request for a meeting with the French president was met with "stony silence," the press reported.[30] Setsuko traveled on to Spain, where she spoke to the Spanish Congress. She reminded Prime Minister Pedro Sánchez that membership in NATO did not prohibit him from signing and ratifying the TPNW. And this would be consistent with Spain's stated support for nuclear disarmament.

Back home Setsuko stepped up her pace. To mark the upcoming seventy-fifth anniversary of the atomic bombing of Hiroshima, she joined Tim Wright in writing to the 193 heads of state, warning of the growing threat to humanity and urging those who had not yet signed the historic treaty to do so at once. Kathleen Sullivan assisted them in the effort, although Setsuko insisted on modifying most letters by adding personal comments. Thereupon she received calls and letters from Hungary, Scotland, Turkey, Lebanon, and Ireland. By mid-July four more states ratified the treaty, with Botswana as number forty.

As she expected, Setsuko received no response from Canadian prime minister Justin Trudeau. Her frustration with him, bordering on contempt, was no secret. Initially, he had presented himself as a progressive on foreign affairs, yet his nuclear-weapon policy seemed to refute that assertion. When, in March 2017, he had boycotted the UN meetings to negotiate the TPNW, alongside U.S. ambassador Nikki Haley, Thurlow's ire had increased. She considered Canada's refusal to participate in the UN Ban Treaty negotiations an injustice, given Canada's direct involvement in developing the atom bomb. To make matters worse, Justin Trudeau had ridiculed the negotiations. He told the House of Commons that the treaty was "well-meaning but an ineffective process." Furthermore, he said, "There can be all sorts of people talking about nuclear disarmament, but if they do not actually have nuclear arms, it is sort of useless to have them around talking." Setsuko called the prime minister's comments "callous."[31]

When the TPNW had been adopted by 122 countries on July 7, 2017, Trudeau had fallen into line behind Donald Trump in dismissing its importance. "I am appalled that the Canadian government remains under the nuclear umbrella, and under nuclear deterrence supports threatening people with nuclear annihilation," Thurlow told the *Toronto Star*.[32] He didn't even congratulate Thurlow on her Nobel Peace Prize speech. Angry letters to the editor in major Canadian newspapers followed. A reporter informed Setsuko that the prime minister had posted a tweet saying, "Mrs. Thurlow is a remarkable citizen of Canada and we respect her." He must have thought that was sufficient. Setsuko told the reporter she didn't know what a "tweet" was. Asked if she had received a congratulatory letter from him, she replied, "I am still waiting."[33]

Not dissuaded, Setsuko wrote Trudeau again, as the seventy-fifth anniversary approached. "I am respectfully requesting," it read, "that you acknowledge the direct and extensive Canadian Government involvement in the American Manhattan Project that produced the atom bombs that destroyed Hiroshima and Nagasaki and express a statement of regret for the deaths and suffering inflicted on the two cities."[34] Once more she urged Canada's immediate participation in the TPNW. Although she didn't expect a response, she did make sure her letter reached the public this time. She sent copies to members of the Canadian Parliament, as well as the press. The largest bell in the Peace Tower on Parliament Hill would be ringing on the seventy-fifth anniversary of the bombing of Hiroshima and Nagasaki, she pointed out. "When Mr. Trudeau hears the bell in the Peace Tower strike 75 times on August 6 and 9," she said, "I hope he will not wonder why. As John Donne wrote in his famous poem, 'Any man's death diminishes me . . . never send to know for whom the bell tolls, it tolls for thee.'"[35]

The seventy-fifth anniversary provided additional opportunities for Setsuko to educate the public, to encourage states to ratify the treaty, and to castigate those who had not. By then she had become even more of a public figure. Japanese journalist Yumi Kanazaki had coauthored Thurlow's memoir, titled *Crawl toward the Light,* based on a series of interviews Kanazaki had conducted for *Chugoku Shimbun,* a Hiroshima-based newspaper.[36] *The Vow from Hiroshima,* an award-winning documentary of Thurlow's life journey, had been released.[37] And on August 7 the *New York Times* ran a front-page article on her, titled, "After 'Hell on Earth,' Decades Working for Peace."[38] More reporters contacted her; more people heard Thurlow's plea. Not Donald Trump.

Among the 193 letters she had written to heads of state was one to "Mr. Donald J. Trump." When she did not receive an acknowledgment of its receipt, she released it to the press.

> We atomic bomb survivors are greatly disturbed by the continued modernization of nuclear weapons by the United States and other countries, and your stated willingness to use these instruments of genocide. We are also alarmed by the United States' recent abandonment of arms control agreements and reports that your administration is contemplating a resumption of nuclear testing. Even in this unprecedented time of crisis, nuclear-armed countries, such as yours, continue to hold the world hostage under the threat of nuclear annihilation while squandering billions of dollars on nuclear arsenals instead of meeting human needs. . . . The idea that strategic stability or military dominance could be achieved by detonating a nuclear bomb, irreversibly contaminating our environment and leveraging the instantaneous death of millions of human beings, is intolerable and unacceptable. Nuclear weapons are not a necessary evil, they are the ultimate evil. . . . I urge you to take action to become a state party to the Treaty on the Prohibition of Nuclear Weapons without delay.[39]

Two days after the seventy-fifth anniversary, *Newsweek* published an interview with Thurlow, conducted by their senior editor for foreign policy. When asked what her reaction was to the U.S. withdrawal from the Anti-ballistic Missile Treaty and the Intermediate-Range Nuclear Forces Treaty, she replied she was "horrified" by President Trump's "blatant disregard for treaties and international cooperation." The nuclear age had been characterized by "disinformation, manipulation, secrecy and lies." It astonished her that so many people thought nuclear weapons protected them and maintained peace. Furthermore, Trump seemed to take pride in "de-railing" arms-control agreements and "threatening to use nuclear weapons as a kind of bravado." To that end the level of ignorance regarding nuclear weapons among public servants dismayed her. "My nightmare," she told the senior editor, "is that we might stumble into a nuclear war by accident or . . . due to the blustering egos of men in power who refuse to act on behalf of humanity. It is hard to not shudder at the thought that the likes of Donald Trump and Vladimir Putin have the power to annihilate the planet."

When the *Newsweek* editor asked Setsuko about Trump's consideration of resuming nuclear testing, she exclaimed, "Can you imagine?" Not only would they be breaking a twenty-eight-year taboo, but also it would be in violation of the Nuclear Non-Proliferation Treaty, which the United States had signed. "A return to the past," she emphasized, "as if we do not know the dangers we now face as a world community, is unacceptable." She said she had not lost hope, however, because of the growing antinuclear movement. ICAN had successfully recast the nuclear-weapon conversation "from deterrence credibility and techno-military issues to concerns over their humanitarian and environmental consequences."[40] As they approached ratification of the Treaty on the Prohibition of Nuclear Weapons, nuclear-armed states were getting nervous.

On the seventy-fifth anniversary, three more countries announced their ratifications: Ireland, Nigeria, and Niue. Ireland had played a significant role in the creation of the TPNW. Ireland's position stood in stark contrast to that of the United Kingdom, which was investing billions of pounds to modernize its nuclear arsenal. Although Nigeria had also been a strong advocate for the Ban Treaty, ICAN was having difficulty reaching the right people to make sure their confirmation process went forward. Thurlow's letter proved to be an important impetus. With a population of 206 million, it was the largest nation to join so far. The Pacific Island nation of Niue became the eighth state party from that region to ratify the Ban Treaty. Islanders continued to suffer the health and environmental effects of the more than three hundred nuclear tests conducted in the Pacific. Three days later, on the anniversary of Nagasaki's destruction, Saint Kitts and Nevis endorsed the treaty to honor victims and survivors. Six weeks later Malta added its name, having chosen the anniversary of its independence from the nuclear-armed United Kingdom. Just five more ratifications remained.

The TPNW got one of its biggest boosts when, on September 21, 2020, fifty-six former prime ministers, presidents, and defense ministers from twenty NATO member states, Japan, and South Korea, as well as the former UN secretary-general Ban Ki-moon and two previous NATO secretaries-general, signed an open letter urging all state leaders to sign and ratify the treaty. "The risk of nuclear detonation today," it began, "whether by accident, miscalculation, or design—appears to be increasing with the recent deployment of new types of nuclear weapons, the abandonment of longstanding arms control agreements, and the very real danger of cyber-attacks on nuclear infrastructure." Reflecting on the recent hostile exchanges between North Korea, the United States, and Russia, which prompted a new arms race, they wrote, "It is not difficult to foresee how the bellicose rhetoric and poor judgment of leaders in nuclear-armed nations might result in a calamity affecting all nations and people." Addressing heads of state in their own countries, secured under a nuclear umbrella, they pointed out that these leaders were promoting the "misguided belief" that nuclear weapons heightened their security, thus stymieing progress toward their abolition for fear of upsetting our allies. "Friends can and must speak up when friends engage in reckless behavior that puts their lives and ours in peril," they told their own state leaders, as they urged them to join the Treaty on the Prohibition of Nuclear Weapons before it was too late. "There is no cure for nuclear war," they wrote in conclusion. "Prevention is our only option."[41]

Nine days later Malaysia became the forty-sixth nation to join, when its minister of foreign affairs signed the instrument of ratification at a ceremony in the nation's capital, Kuala Lumpur. He chastised leaders who continued to modernize their weapons because of "power rivalry."[42] The Pacific Island nation of Tuvalu followed on October 12, becoming the forty-seventh nation in the world to join the historic effort.

That's when President Trump became rattled. He never thought so many states would ratify the TPNW and so rapidly. With only three more state ratifications to activate its entry into force, he attempted an ultimate power play to coerce the state leaders who had signed the treaty to withdraw. The Associated Press obtained a copy of the letter he sent to them. It said the five original nuclear powers—the United States, Russia, China, Great Britain, and France—as well as NATO allies "stand unified in our opposition to the potential repercussions of the treaty." Moreover, it contended that the TPNW "turns back the clock" on disarmament and was "dangerous" to the fifty-year-old Nuclear Non-Proliferation Treaty. "We believe that you have made a strategic error and should withdraw your instrument of ratification or accession," the letter strongly suggested.[43]

State leaders, nuclear experts, and antinuclear advocates around the globe condemned the Trump administration's effort to undermine the treaty. As a major spokesperson for the TPNW, ICAN's executive director, Beatrice Fihn, called it "an unprecedented action in international relations." Furthermore, she said, "the increasing nervousness and maybe straightforward panic . . . indicates that they really seem to understand that this is a reality: Nuclear weapons are going to be banned under international law soon." Fihn pointed out that the last time a country withdrew from a multilateral nuclear-weapon treaty was when North Korea left the Nuclear Non-Proliferation Treaty so it could develop nuclear weapons. Denouncing on Twitter the Trump administration's push to block the TPNW as "desperate," she called it "reckless and a new low point."[44]

Other antinuclear leaders joined in, posting tweets—Trump's favorite means of communication. "This is completely outrageous and yet somehow not at all surprising," posted John Carl Baker, the senior program officer for the Ploughshares Fund, a major public foundation that supports antinuclear initiatives. Daryl Kimball, director of Arms Control, called the current leadership of the P5 "arrogant, out of touch, incompetent, divisive, and very wrong." Pointing out that the treaty was three ratifications from entering into force, Ray Acheson, director of the disarmament program for Women's International League for Peace and Freedom, concurred. "When a so-called 'military power' is this afraid of international law," she wrote, "you know you've done it right." She called their purported objections obscure. "Their real concern," she concluded, "is that this treaty, to paraphrase Hiroshima survivor Setsuko Thurlow, makes weapons that are already immoral, now illegal."[45] In the end not one country withdrew its confirmation. And two days after Trump's egregious letter became public, Jamaica and Nauru submitted their documents of ratification at the United Nations.

On October 24, 2020, Honduras became the fiftieth state to endorse the treaty. Setsuko Thurlow was alone at home when she got the news she had been anticipating her entire adult life: the UN Treaty on the Prohibition of Nuclear Weapons had been ratified. She put her head in her hands and, for the first time in her decades-long quest, she wept.

Epilogue

> If history were taught in the form of stories,
> it would never be forgotten.
> –Rudyard Kipling, *Life's Handicap*

On the evening of January 22, 2021, a message was projected on one side of a United Nations Headquarters building: "NUCLEAR WEAPONS NOW ILLEGAL, 22 JAN 2021." Fifty states parties had ratified the UN Treaty on the Prohibition of Nuclear Weapons on October 24, 2020. Now, ninety days later, it had come into force. After decades of work, ICAN, its 607 partner organizations around the globe, the International Committee of the Red Cross, and a host of antinuclear activists celebrated this historic event, joined by diplomats, government officials, religious leaders, scientists, and the general public.

Nuclear weapons were now illegal under international law, making it unlawful for TPNW states parties to possess, develop, deploy, test, use, or threaten to use them. The latter restriction made it difficult to justify employing nuclear arms for deterrence. "These heinous bombs will be on the same legal footing as biological and chemical weapons, as land mines and cluster munitions," wrote Ray Acheson, the director of the Women's International League for Peace and Freedom.[1] UN secretary-general António Guterres called the treaty "an extraordinary achievement and a step towards the eventual elimination of nuclear weapons."[2]

In June 2022 signatories to the UN Treaty on the Prohibition of Nuclear Weapons held their first meeting in Vienna, led by Alexander Kmentt, the

Austrian director of disarmament, arms control, and nonproliferation. By then fifteen additional states had ratified the treaty. To begin they agreed to establish a scientific advisory group on the technical aspects of the treaty, to designate an international authority to monitor treaty implementation and compliance, and to promote further TPNW ratifications. The states parties resolved to start implementing treaty obligations by assisting people affected by nuclear weapons and nuclear tests. Furthermore, they addressed efforts to redress the environmental harms caused by nuclear weapons.

None of the nuclear-armed states were taking serious steps to reduce dependence on these weapons of mass destruction. "The old order is still standing," Thurlow told the group, "and the Doomsday Clock is still ticking."[3] When a news correspondent probed Kmentt about what they hoped to accomplish when nuclear-weapon states were ignoring the Ban Treaty, he replied, "They're not ignoring the TPNW at all. Importantly, some of them are extremely strongly opposed to it." If they were ignoring it, that would mean the treaty was of no consequence. Their strong opposition "demonstrates the transformational potential of the TPNW."[4]

The Second Meeting of States Parties to the Treaty on the Prohibition of Nuclear Weapons took place at the United Nations Headquarters in November 2023. The group agreed that nuclear deterrence still posed a significant security problem and that they would more vigorously "challenge the false narratives of nuclear deterrence."[5] They adopted an action plan to implement the TPNW. Major financial institutions reported on their refusal to invest in and accelerating divestments of companies involved in the production of nuclear arms.

At the time eight billion people lived under the ever-present nuclear menace. The number of nuclear warheads worldwide totaled approximately 12,500, a full 90 percent of which belonged to the United States and Russia. Nuclear-weapon states were spending vast sums to modernize and expand their nuclear arsenals while continuing to emphasize the importance of nuclear weapons in their security doctrines. The saber-rattling was getting louder, resulting in an international political environment that was colder than that during the Cold War. The risk of a nuclear detonation—whether by mistake or intent—was at its highest level in decades. On January 23, 2024, the Doomsday Clock remained where it had been set the prior year—90 seconds to midnight—the closest since the clock was created in 1947, the closest humanity had come to an apocalypse. By April, however, 86 percent of the 193 UN member states had signed or ratified the TPNW. The International Campaign to Abolish Nuclear Weapons had grown to more than six hundred partner organizations. They pledged to keep educating and motivating people around the world until weapons of mass destruction were totally abolished.

When asked on the day the TPNW went into force if she could rest now, Setsuko Thurlow had replied, "I intend to continue until we reach the final goal—the total elimination of nuclear weapons."[6] A tireless advocate, she embodies sacred stubbornness: she has seen something broken in the world, and she will never stop trying to fix it. The apathetic response by citizens of the world regarding the nuclear-arms peril disturbed her, and she took every opportunity to emphasize that humankind stands on a precipice. She persisted in challenging leaders of nuclear-armed states who provoked her with their obstinance. No, she was not ready to rest.

Indefatigable, she continued to fill her days reaching out to government leaders, advocates, and opponents via letters, emails, and phone calls. In an opinion piece for *Newsweek*, she wrote, "As the advent of the Treaty on the Prohibition of Nuclear Weapons shows, for the vast majority of the world's nations and peoples, the atomic destruction of Hiroshima and Nagasaki was not a 'precedent' in Putin's chilling sense of a potentially 'necessary' evil. Nuclear weapons are an abomination, the ultimate evil, an unprecedented blasphemy against creation."[7] Although Setsuko struggled with unresolved anger at U.S. military leaders for the destruction of Hiroshima and Nagasaki, she was able to focus on nuclear disarmament, on saving this precious world, rather than being sidetracked by demanding an expression of apology from the United States.

Meanwhile, among her highest priorities was the younger generation—preparing and encouraging them to accept the antinuclear torch. That's why she enjoyed Hibakusha Stories and Peace Boat. She repeatedly stressed that the youth of the world must strive to free the world from the threat of annihilation. The older generation of antinuclear activists had carried on in spite of indifference and ridicule. Now the younger generation must take the lead. She entrusted them with the responsibility to eliminate nuclear weapons and keep the world safe from self-destruction: "After all," she said, "the future is yours."[8]

Over decades Setsuko accepted almost every request for participation in an antinuclear event. As painful as it was in the telling, she never hesitated to jar audiences with her own story. She was quick to clarify, however, that she did not want their sympathy; she wanted their action. She pointed out that she had been an eyewitness to one of the cardinal events in the birth of the nuclear age. Critical historical events need a personal narrative, and Setsuko Thurlow had become the storyteller for Hiroshima. Just as Elie Wiesel made it his life's work to bear witness to the genocide committed by the Nazis, Setsuko Thurlow vowed, "I am committed to share the warning of Hiroshima until my last breath."[9]

"Hiroshima Survivor Slams G7 Leaders for Embracing War and Rejecting Nuclear Disarmament," read a headline in the international news.[10] It was referring to Setsuko Thurlow. Now ninety-one years old, she had flown from her home in Toronto to Hiroshima for the annual Group of Seven Summit, held on May 19–21, 2023. Setsuko had not been invited to participate in the conference despite being one of the most prominent hibakusha; despite being related to Japanese prime minister Fumio Kishida, who was hosting the summit; and despite having co-delivered the 2017 Nobel Peace Prize lecture on behalf of ICAN. That disregard did not keep her from going. The Japanese press and a team of U.S. filmmakers followed Thurlow's every move, knowing her blunt comments would make good quotations.

On the first day, in an unprecedented move, Prime Minister Kishida arranged for the G7 leaders from the United States, Canada, France, Germany, Italy, Japan, and the United Kingdom to tour the Hiroshima Peace Memorial Museum. They viewed the gruesome consequences of the first atomic bomb, which had killed 140,000, mostly women and children. Setsuko was disappointed not to be one of the hibakusha selected to speak with them afterward, but she wasn't surprised. Kishida was wary of her oftentimes vitriolic remarks.

Like the rest of the public, she could only watch the televised reactions of this group of world leaders as they exited the museum. U.S. president Joe Biden looked stunned and nauseated; French president Emmanuel Macron appeared troubled, his brow furrowed.

Under cloudy skies the somber group climbed the steps to the Memorial Cenotaph, dedicated to all victims of the first atomic bomb. In perfect unison they laid wreaths in their honor. After a moment of silence, an official read the cenotaph inscription: "Let all the souls here rest in peace for we shall not repeat the evil." Those words had been an enduring inspiration for Setsuko Thurlow. She hoped that during the silence, the G7 leaders were reflecting on that statement and would place humanity at the center of their upcoming discussions on nuclear weapons.

"[The G-7 leaders] cannot dare to leave without a plan to end nuclear weapons," ICAN insisted.[11] Later that day the G7 leaders issued their first official statement, titled "Hiroshima Vision on Nuclear Disarmament."[12] When Thurlow read it, she was disgruntled. She had hoped the group would be moved by their visit to the Peace Park. Instead, the statement lacked emotional resonance. The "Vision" seemed to be a regurgitation of past discussions, reaffirming the Treaty on the Non-Proliferation of Nuclear Weapons from 1968 with deterrence at its core. It did not even mention the TPNW, which had entered into force over two years earlier, ratified by the majority of states. It was an insult to atomic-bomb victims, Setsuko opined on the news.

Thurlow knew that nuclear disarmament was only one of nine topics to be covered by the G7 leaders over three days. Yet it infuriated her at the meeting's end when the thirty-five-page summary devoted less than one page to nuclear weapons. "We express our commitment to achieving a world without nuclear weapons . . . through taking a realistic, pragmatic, and responsible approach," it stated, listing no concrete steps for disarmament and relying on deterrence as a major way to accomplish this goal. For years Setsuko had argued that deterrence means threatening the opponent with one's readiness to annihilate masses of human beings. Television audiences around the world heard her call the G7 summit a "disaster."[13] She was not the only one speaking out. Pope Francis, UN secretary-general António Guterres, and leaders of the major antinuclear groups made similar statements. Activists worldwide felt frustrated, angry, even furious—feelings with which Setsuko had struggled throughout her life as she pressed on in her odyssey to eliminate nuclear weapons. But she never quit.

How did the thirteen-year-old girl who crawled out of a burning building to face a field of burned, bloody, mangled people not yield to despair? How could she not languish in sorrow when her cherry blossom life ended in an instant, when she lost so many people she cherished?

Since early times philosophers and clergy have pondered how one can live a meaningful life amid pain and destruction, how the human spirit can rise up in the face of overwhelming adversity and indifference. Holocaust survivor Viktor Frankl wrote in *Man's Search for Meaning* that one can't avoid suffering but can choose how to cope with it and move forward with renewed purpose. Setsuko Nakamura Thurlow did not succumb to her sorrow; she did not turn within to mourn her loss, to heal from her trauma in private. Her indignation and sense of violation generated a moral response: "never again," she had vowed when just a teen. "I profoundly admire her," said Eric Schlosser, author of *Command and Control*, "for her ability to take that trauma and process it and emerge with a remarkably positive life force."[14]

What explains this intense commitment that persisted for her lifetime: early family influence, religious faith, inspiration from and companionship of other dedicated people? Likely it was all of these. She never viewed her effort as self-sacrificial, to which she could credit her wise, devoted husband, Jim. To the contrary, their personal and moral commitments were closely aligned. They were remarkedly realistic yet invariably hopeful.[15]

"Have I made a full psychological recovery from Hiroshima? Am I still haunted?" Setsuko wrote in 1987. "I am having a full, rich life, and I am grateful." She had devoted herself to her antinuclear work with little doubt or agonized reflection, as if she had no choice. "But I suppose that to some extent it is necessary to lead a double life," she reflected, "not just for survivors like myself but for everyone in the world. We make plans for the future assuming that there will be a tomorrow; at the same time, we know that we and everyone dear to us could be incinerated today."[16] In the end, Setsuko Nakamura Thurlow turned her nightmares into a force to impel people to learn from Hiroshima and admit that, yes, it could happen again. She continually rededicated herself to preventing men, women, and children everywhere from suffering a similar fate, as she pursued her near-Sisyphean quest to abolish nuclear weapons.

Acknowledgments

In the spring of 2017, I contacted Hiroshima survivor Setsuko Nakamura Thurlow and proposed that I write her biography. She agreed and, over the next seven years, shared her life story, her files, her photos, and many great meals. I appreciate her honesty and perseverance, along with the kindness of her son Andrew. Setsuko has always been mindful that she represents all hibakusha; her story is theirs.

How fortunate I am to work with literary agent Peter Bernstein. He believed in this biography from the start and devoted more time, wise advice, and patience than I could ever have imagined. I valued Amy Bernstein's reflections as well. Author Scott Seligman called Peter "indefatigable." I agree. Peter's commitment never waned. I am grateful for his expertise and friendship. I feel equally fortunate that Taylor Gilreath, acquisitions editor at Potomac Books (University of Nebraska Press), took the next step in preparing the work for publication, a task that she and her team undertook with such proficiency.

Thanks also go to those who helped me piece together Setsuko's early years and the history surrounding them: Hiroshima guides Taeko Watanabe and Sachi Sakamoto; the chief curator of Hiroshima's Meteorological Observatory, Hiroshi Wakisaka; the Florin Historical Society; Leda Seibert, the Sacramento County Clerk Recorder; Ellen King, who interpreted the legal documents; and Ariel K. Myers, the archivist at the University of Lynchburg. I applaud those who have written extensively on Japanese history, nuclear weapons, and antinuclear activism, as listed in the bibliography. The atomic bombing of Nagasaki is not included, as it is expertly covered in Susan Southard's *Nagasaki: Life After Nuclear War*.

I am grateful to those who spent time talking with me about the antinuclear movement, ICAN, the Nobel Peace Prize, surviving catastrophes, and Setsuko Thurlow. In alphabetical order they include Ray Acheson, Phyllis Creighton, Robert Croonquist, Richard Falk, Stuart Finch, Ralph and Ilene Garber, Peter Gregory, Ira Helfand, Jeffrey Jay, Rebecca Johnson, Annette Kashiwabara, Akira Kawasaki, Peter Kuznick, Zia Mian, William Perry, Eric Schlosser, Susan Strickler, Henrik Syse, Mitchie Takeuchi, Anton Wagner, Elayne Whyte-Gómez, and Tim Wright. Special thanks go to Kathleen Sullivan for her unflagging assistance.

Writing a biography is a long, lonely process. Thank goodness for Biographers International, a vibrant organization that promotes the art and craft of biography. Through BIO I met Anne Boyd Rioux, who critiqued my proposal. I value the company of fellow writers, especially my BIO group, who meet monthly to discuss the joys and heartaches of biography writing. Thanks!

I value beyond measure the unselfish efforts of my devoted, skilled readers: Ellen King, Lucy Berman, Emilie Osborn, and Kenneth Miller. Their careful scrutiny, acumen, and honesty enhanced the book significantly. When it comes to devotion, my husband, Rod, tops the list. For seven years he read draft after draft, took over the household, and boosted me up when I started to flag. I am so blessed.

I have dedicated this story of a woman who spent her life trying to protect people everywhere from nuclear weapons to my dear grandchildren, in hopes that they may live in a more peaceful world. I must end with my immense gratitude to the legions of antinuclear activists worldwide who have devoted much of their lives in attempts to protect our precious world.

Notes

Prologue

1. Tony Robinson, "Interview with Setsuko Thurlow, Hiroshima Bomb Survivor," *Pressenza: International Press Agency*, June 8, 2019; Thurlow, "Nuclear War," 638–40; "Meet Setsuko Thurlow"; "We Learned to Step."
2. Setsuko Thurlow, interview with the author.
3. Till, *Samurai*.

1. Heart of a Samurai

1. Drixler, Fleming, and Wheeler, *Samurai and the Culture*; Turnbull, *Samurai*; Wert, *Samurai*.
2. Drixler, Fleming, and Wheeler, *Samurai and the Culture*, 124.
3. Turnbull, *Samurai*.
4. Thurlow, interview.
5. Annette Kashiwabara to "Auntie Setsuko and Uncle Jim," email message, January 20, 2003.
6. Takaki, *Strangers*, 49.
7. Adachi, *Enemy That Never Was*.
8. "Benkichi Nakamura"; *Directory of Japanese*, 188.
9. Florin Historical Society, *Florin California*, 5.
10. Mills, *Japanese Problem*; Naka, *Social and Economic Conditions*; "Florin."
11. H. E. Kleinsorge to B. Nakamura, November 21, 1907, Sacramento County Recorder, County of Sacramento, State of California.
12. Benkichi Nakamura to T. Miyakawa, November 16, 1908, Sacramento County Recorder, County of Sacramento, State of California.
13. Mills, *Japanese Problem*.

14. Florin Historical Society, *Florin California*, 83.
15. Mills, *Japanese Problem*, 152–71.
16. Thurlow, interview.
17. Quoted in Takaki, *Strangers*, 204.
18. Quoted in "Florin."
19. *Directory of Japanese*, 188.
20. "United States Passport Applications."
21. *Nichibei Shimbun* (Japanese American news), November 30, 1920.
22. *Shin Sekai* (New world), December 7, 1920, 7.
23. *Shin Sekai* (New world), February 6, 1922, 8.
24. Takaki, *Strangers*, 181.

2. Cherry Blossom Life

1. Thurlow, interview; Kanazaki, "My Life," pts. 2–3; "Silent Flash of Light."
2. Thurlow, interview.
3. Takei, *To the Stars*.
4. Thurlow, interview.
5. Kamachi, *Culture and Customs*.
6. Kamachi, *Culture and Customs*; Thurlow, interview.
7. Till, *Samurai*.

3. Raising the Flag

1. Belfi, "Flash of Light."
2. Belfi, "Flash of Light."
3. Mikamo, *Rising from the Ashes*, 1.
4. Yamashita, *Daily Life*, 11.
5. Isaacson, *Einstein*, 474.
6. R. Rhodes, *Making of the Atomic Bomb*, 367–79.
7. Thurlow, interview.
8. Yamashita, *Daily Life*, 33; Brendon, *Dark Valley*, 633.
9. "Executive Order 9066."
10. Takei, *To the Stars*, 11.
11. Takei, *To the Stars*, 24.
12. Takei, *To the Stars*, 41–45.
13. Takei, *To the Stars*, 43–45.

14. Takei, *To the Stars*, 46–57.
15. Takaki, *Strangers*, 55–56.
16. Bill Carey, "Tennessee History for Kids: The Crate, the Crew, and the Secret City," *Rogersville Review*, September 6, 2023.
17. Thurlow, interview.
18. Thurlow, interview.
19. O'Neal, "World War II."
20. Yamashita, *Daily Life*, 35.
21. Yamashita, *Daily Life*, 37–44; Thurlow, interview.
22. Scott, *Black Snow*.
23. Thurlow, interview.
24. Wyden, *Day One*, 201.
25. Lifton, *Death in Life*, 16–17.
26. Thurlow, interview.
27. Thurlow, "Silent Flash of Light"; Thurlow, interview.
28. Zanettin, "Deadliest Error."
29. McCullough, *Truman*, 448.

4. August 6, 1945

1. Ham, *Hiroshima Nagasaki*, 151.
2. Vincent and Vladic, *Indianapolis*.
3. "Hiroshima and Nagasaki Timeline."
4. "USS *Indianapolis* Was Sunk."
5. Wyden, *Day One*, 242–45.
6. Wyden, *Day One*, 245.
7. Thurlow, interview.
8. Wyden, *Day One*, 246.
9. Thurlow, interview; Kanazaki, "My Life," pt. 5; Thurlow, "Silent Flash of Light."
10. Ham, *Hiroshima Nagasaki*, 298.
11. Thurlow, interview; Kanazaki, "My Life," pt. 5.
12. Ham, *Hiroshima Nagasaki*, 316–19; Committee for the Compilation, *Hiroshima and Nagasaki*, 21–66; Liebow, *Encounter with Disaster*, 21–28.
13. Thurlow, interview.
14. Committee for the Compilation, *Hiroshima and Nagasaki*, 87–94; "Destructive Effects."

15. Thurlow, interview.
16. Kamachi, *Culture and Customs*, 40.

5. Necropolis

1. Thurlow, interview; Kanazaki, "My Life," pt. 6.
2. Thurlow, "Award Acceptance Speech."
3. Thurlow interview.
4. Thurlow, interview.
5. Thurlow, interview.
6. "Destructive Effects."
7. Hachiya, *Hiroshima Diary*, 113.
8. Ishikawa, "Continuous Prayers #24," 54.
9. Sekimori, *Hibakusha*, 87–88.
10. Thurlow, interview.
11. Hook, "Censorship and Reportage," 16.
12. "Jewel Voice Broadcast."
13. Minear, *Hiroshima*, 62.
14. Thurlow, "Award Acceptance Speech."

6. Life among the Ruins

1. Thurlow, interview.
2. Hachiya, *Hiroshima Diary*, 171.
3. Hachiya, *Hiroshima Diary*, 166.
4. Wilfred Burchett, "The Atomic Plague," *Daily Express*, September 5, 1945.
5. Ham, *Hiroshima Nagasaki*, 421–24.
6. Donovan, "Military Physicians," 87.
7. W. H. Lawrence, "No Radioactivity in Hiroshima Ruin," *New York Times*, September 13, 1945.
8. Malloy, "Very Pleasant Way," 37.
9. Liebow, *Encounter with Disaster*, 27.
10. Wyden, *Day One*, 262–330.
11. "Survivors."
12. Thurlow, interview; Folkins, "Canadian Hiroshima Survivor."
13. Hachiya, *Hiroshima Diary*, 83.
14. Oe, *Hiroshima Notes*, 12–13.

15. Oe, *Hiroshima Notes*, 126.
16. Thurlow, interview.
17. Hachiya, *Hiroshima Diary*, 200–202.
18. Hiroshi Wakisaka, interview with the author.
19. "Dr. Majimo and Mission Are Victims of Typhoon: Tragedy Befalls Party Dispatched by Kyoto University to Study Atom Damage," *Nippon Times* (Tokyo), September 24, 1945; "Background Information."
20. "More Damage Revealed in Hiroshima Disaster," *Nippon Times*, September 27, 1945.
21. Thurlow, "Silent Flash of Light"; Thurlow, interview.
22. Jungk, *Children of the Ashes: People of Hiroshima*, 80.
23. Thurlow, interview.

7. Occupied

1. "More Landings Announced," *Nippon Times*, October 10, 1945.
2. Jungk, *Children of the Ashes: People of Hiroshima*, 82–83.
3. Liebow, *Encounter with Disaster*, 120.
4. MacArthur, *Reminiscences*, 284.
5. Dower, *Embracing Defeat*, 73–74.
6. Thurlow, interview.
7. Hiroshima Jogakuin High School, *Summer Cloud*, 35.
8. Thurlow, interview.
9. Kurihara, *Black Eggs*, 28–30.
10. Sodei, *Dear General McArthur*, xiii.
11. Thurlow, interview.
12. Thurlow, interview.
13. Thurlow, interview.
14. Mitchie Takeuchi, interview with Masataka Nakamura, August 2015.
15. Dahler, "Japanese Prisoners of War."
16. Thurlow, interview.
17. Schultz, *Hero of Bataan*.
18. Wainwright, *General Wainwright's Story*, 130, 131.
19. Young, *Fall of the Philippines*, 192.
20. Bass, *Judgment at Tokyo*, 127, 132.
21. *Meaning of Survival*, 16.
22. Takei, *To the Stars*, 59.

23. Belfi, "Flash of Light."

24. Thurlow, interview.

25. Kanazaki, "My Life," pts. 7–8.

26. Thurlow, interview.

8. Where Was God?

1. Hiroshima Jogakuin High School, *Summer Cloud*, 2–6.
2. Thurlow, interview.
3. Treglown, *Mr. Straight Arrow*, 146–47.
4. Thurlow, interview.
5. Liebow, *Encounter with Disaster*, 36.
6. Cousins, "Hiroshima," 30.
7. "24 Hours after Hiroshima."
8. Wyden, *Day One*, 336–38.
9. Kurihara, *Black Eggs*, 187.
10. "Meet Setsuko Thurlow."
11. Hiroshima Jogakuin High School, *Summer Cloud*, 13–17.
12. Thurlow, interview.
13. Thurlow, interview.
14. "Jogakuin."
15. Kanazaki, "My Life," pt. 8.
16. Folkins, "Canadian Hiroshima Survivor."
17. Hersey, *Hiroshima*, 2–6, 29–32, 39–40, 50–51, 75–76, 134–36.

9. Born to Serve

1. Cousins, "Hiroshima," 8.
2. Kurihara, *Black Eggs*, 313.
3. Jungk, *Children of the Ashes: Story of a Rebirth*, 237.
4. Thurlow, interview.
5. Jungk, *Children of the Ashes: Story of a Rebirth*, 238.
6. Naono, "Origins of '*Hibakusha*.'"
7. Ham, *Hiroshima Nagasaki*, 440.
8. Committee for the Compilation, *Hiroshima and Nagasaki*, 489–90.
9. Committee for the Compilation, *Hiroshima and Nagasaki*, 259, 251–311.
10. Johnson and Rasche, *Hiroshima*, 189.

11. Thurlow, interview.
12. "Stockholm Peace Appeal."
13. "Korean War."
14. "US Experiment of Atomic Explosion at Bikini Atoll," *Mainichi Shimbun*, March 2, 1954.
15. "Radioactive Dust Hits 264 at Test, Report Says," *Nippon Times*, March 18, 1954.
16. "Fishermen Burned in Bikini Test Blast," *New York Times*, March 16, 1954; Jack Niedenthal, "Paradise Lost: 'For the Good of Mankind,'" *The Guardian*, August 6, 2002.
17. "Radioactive Dust Hits."
18. Robert Sherrod, "The Story of the H-Bomb and the Tuna," *Nippon Times*, July 19, 1954.
19. "U.S., Japan Probing Bikini Bomb Incident," *Nippon Times*, March 17, 1954.
20. "Another Jap Boat Hit by H-Bomb Ash." *Chicago Daily Tribune*, March 27, 1954.
21. "OK Sounded on All Fish," *Nippon Times*, March 19, 1954.
22. "Atom Blast Disrupts Tokyo Fish Diet," *Christian Science Monitor*, March 17, 1954.
23. "OK Sounded."
24. "Radioactive Dust Hits."
25. Sherrod, "Story of the H-Bomb."
26. Strickler, *Vow from Hiroshima*.
27. Thurlow, interview.
28. Military Assistance Act of 1949, H.R. 5748 (81A-D7), Special Collections and University Archives, University of Massachusetts Amherst Libraries, 223–24.
29. Akira Tashiro, "Hiroshima Memo: The Vow of the Inscription on the Cenotaph for the A-Bomb Victims," *Chugoku Shimbun*, July 22, 2011.
30. Cousins, "Hiroshima."
31. Kazuyuki Kawamoto, "U.S. Moral Parents Still Concerned about Their Children," *Chugoku Shimbun*, July 24, 1988.
32. Committee for the Compilation, *Hiroshima and Nagasaki*, 440–41.
33. William Hollingworth, "Hiroshima Hibakusha in London Relates Plight of A-Bomb Orphans," *Kyodo News*, August 6, 2010.
34. Baker, *Hiroshima Maidens*.
35. James 2:14–17 (King James Version).
36. Thurlow, interview.

10. Falling in Love in Bibai

1. Thurlow, interview.
2. Thurlow, interview.

3. Thurlow, interview.
4. "Marriage in Japan."
5. Thurlow, interview.
6. Thurlow, interview.

11. Crossing Borders

1. Robinson, "Interview with Setsuko Thurlow"; Thurlow, interview.
2. Takei, *To the Stars*, 262.
3. "Survivor of Atomic Bomb Is Student at Lynchburg," *Richmond Times Dispatch*, October 3, 1954; Thurlow, interview.
4. "Coed Stirred by H-Bomb Test Tragedy," *Washington Post and Times Herald*, October 11, 1954, 3.
5. Robinson, "Interview with Setsuko Thurlow"; Thurlow, interview.
6. "Living in North America."
7. Thurlow, interview.
8. "Varsity Court Crowning."
9. "Books Collected on LC Campus for Asian Aid," *News* (Lynchburg VA), February 6, 1955.
10. "Observe Amity Week," LC News Bureau, February 24, 1955.
11. "Japanese Girl to Tell Lions of Atom Blast," *News*, October 26, 1954; "Jap Girl in Plea against A-Bomb's Use," *News*, October 28, 1954.
12. Margaret Dowdy, "Japanese Student at LC Survived Hiroshima Blast," *News*, October 3, 1954.
13. "Atomic Experts," *News*, February 11, 1955.
14. "Jap Girl in Plea."
15. "Mike Masaoka."
16. Setsuko Thurlow and Jim Thurlow, letter to family and friends, December 1956.
17. Thurlow and Thurlow, letter to family and friends, December 1956; Thurlow, interview.
18. Thurlow, interview.
19. Thurlow and Thurlow, letter to family and friends, March 14, 1957.
20. "Oath of Citizenship."

12. Blood on Our Hands

1. Hoshino et al., "Leukemia in Offspring."
2. Ozasa, Grant, and Kodama, "Japanese Legacy Cohorts."

3. Thurlow, interview.
4. Thurlow, interview.
5. Miyaji and Lock, "Monitoring Motherhood."
6. "Kwansei Gakuin University."
7. Bass, *Judgment at Tokyo*.
8. Seaton, *Japan's Contested War Memories*.
9. Dixon, *Dark Pasts*.
10. Shin and Sneider, *Divergent Memories*, 249.
11. Foumy Saisho, "The Bridge on the River Kwai," *Japan Times*, December 19, 1957.
12. "Our Own Movie Critics Give Their 'Best 10' List," *Japan Times*, January 16, 1958.
13. Japan Memorial Society, *Listen to the Voices*.
14. "'Ningen No Joken' Last of Epic Three-Part Film," *Japan Times*, January 30, 1961.
15. "Japan War Crime Book Published," *Japan Times*, April 10, 1958.
16. "War Atrocity Book Becomes Legal Issue," *Japan Times*, August 10, 1958.
17. R. Tillerman, "All Captives Slain: Civilians Also Killed as the Japanese Spread Terror in Nanking," *New York Times*, December 18, 1937.
18. Li, Sabella, and Liu, *Nanking 1937*, 89.
19. Lord Russell of Liverpool, *Knights of Bushido*, 52.
20. "Hippocratic Oath."
21. Endo, *Sea and Poison*, 166.
22. Keiichi, "Unit 731"; Powell, "Hidden Chapter in History."
23. Gold, *Unit 731 Testimony*, 11.
24. Bass, *Judgment at Tokyo*, 383–87.
25. *Materials on the Trial*, 437, 530.
26. Powell, "Hidden Chapter in History," 50.
27. Kurihara, *Black Eggs*, 53.
28. Thurlow, interview.
29. "Vivisectionist Recalls His Day of Reckoning," *Japan Times*, October 24, 2007.
30. Kurihara, *Black Eggs*, 226–27.

13. In the Interim

1. Kennedy, "Cuban Missile Crisis."
2. Kennedy, "Cuban Missile Crisis."
3. Kennedy, "Cuban Missile Crisis."
4. Sherwin, *Gambling with Armageddon*, 334.

5. Sherwin, *Gambling with Armageddon*, 9.
6. Sherwin, *Gambling with Armageddon*, 276.
7. Kiger, "Key Moments."
8. "World on the Brink."
9. Thurlow and Thurlow, letter to family and friends, 1963.
10. Thurlow and Thurlow, letter to family and friends, 1972.
11. Joe Cooper, "Canada's Role in Bombing of Hiroshima," *East York Mirror*, August 13, 2015; Edwards, "Canada and the Bomb"; Thurlow, "Silent Flash of Light."
12. McClelland, "Precautions for Workers."
13. Andrew Nikiforuk, "Echoes of the Atomic Age: Cancer Kills Fourteen Aboriginal Uranium Workers," *Calgary Herald*, March 14, 1998.
14. Wagner, *Our Hiroshima*; Cooper, "Canada's Role."
15. Edwards, "Canada and the Bomb."
16. "Canada's Role," *Globe and Mail*, July 30, 2005.
17. Belfi, "Flash of Light."
18. Thurlow, interview.
19. "Timeline."
20. Bernard Weinraub, "India Becomes 6th Nation to Set Off Nuclear Device," *New York Times*, May 19, 1974.
21. "Ripples in the Nuclear Pond," *Desert News*, May 22, 1974.
22. Edwards, "Canada's Nuclear Industry," 127–28.
23. Thurlows et al. to Canadian University Teachers Association, in Thurlow, personal files.
24. "An Appeal for the Total Abolition of Nuclear Weapons," advertisement, in Thurlow, personal files.
25. Thurlow, interview.
26. James Thurlow to Mayor Takeshi Araki, August 24,1975, in Thurlow, personal files.
27. Gentry, "One Voice."
28. Scott Young, "A Bomb Relived," *Globe and Mail*, July 10, 1975.
29. Setsuko Thurlow, "I Told My Hiroshima Story to Warn Others, She Says," letter to the editor, *Toronto Star*, August 26, 1975.
30. Thurlow and Thurlow, letter to family and friends, 1963; Belfi, "Flash of Light."

14. Witness

1. International Forum to End the Arms Race and for World Disarmament, March 28–April 1, 1976, York University, program, in Thurlow, personal files.

2. Thurlow, interview.
3. Setsuko Thurlow, address at the International Forum to End the Arms Race and for World Disarmament, March 1976, York England, in Thurlow, personal files.
4. "Declaration of York," in Thurlow, personal files.
5. Thurlow and Thurlow, letter to family and friends, December 1976.
6. E. Kaye Fulton, "What's This? A Ban-the-Bomb March?," *Toronto Star*, October 18, 1976.
7. Donald Grant, "Ban-Bomb Signs, Protest Songs, Rally Reminiscent of the Sixties," *Globe and Mail*, October 18, 1976.
8. Fulton, "What's This?"
9. Dick Beddoes, "Postscript for the Few," *Globe and Mail*, October 18, 1976.
10. Thurlow and Thurlow, letter to family and friends, December 1976.
11. Gentry, "One Voice," 8.
12. Philip Mascoll, "A-Bomb Terror Recalled on Remembrance Day," *Toronto Star*, November 11, 1987.
13. Meyer, "Pierre Trudeau."
14. Thurlow, interview.
15. U.S. General Accounting Office, "United Nations Special Session."
16. Setsuko Thurlow, "A Survivor Remembers Hiroshima," *Toronto Star*, October 24, 1981.
17. Thurlow, "Survivor Remembers Hiroshima."
18. Thurlow, "Survivor Remembers Hiroshima."
19. Thurlow and Thurlow, letter to family and friends, November 1981.
20. Thurlow, interview.
21. Thurlow, interview.
22. John Bently Mays, "Hiroshima Art Contradicts Exhibit's Optimistic Bent," *Globe and Mail*, June 19, 1982.
23. Thurlow, interview.
24. Paul L. Montgomery, "Throngs Fill Manhattan to Protest Nuclear Weapons," *New York Times*, June 13, 1982.
25. Joyce Wadler and Merrill Brown, "New York Rally Draws Half-Million," *Washington Post*, June 13, 1982.
26. Epstein, "Second Special Session," 138, 146.
27. Thurlow, speech for Toronto Youth Corps, June 27, 1982, in Thurlow, personal files.
28. "Mother Teresa Told a Rally."
29. Schutte, "Here I Am Lord."

30. Paul Majemdie, "Never Too Late to Heal Mental Scars, Hiroshima Survivor Says," Reuters, December 22, 1982.
31. Thurlow and Thurlow, letter to family and friends, December 1982.
32. "Toronto Peace Garden."

15. Watchman

1. Michael K. Frisby, "Demonstration Erupts at 'Avco 7' Trial," *Boston Globe*, December 14, 1983.
2. Bruce DeSilva, "Massachusetts Trial Turns into Emotional Forum on Nuclear Weapons," *Hartford Courant*, December 15, 1983.
3. Frisby, "Demonstration Erupts."
4. Middlesex News Service, "Professor Testifies at N-Protestors Trial," *Telegraph*, December 14, 1983.
5. DeSilva, "Massachusetts Trial."
6. Setsuko Thurlow, summary of Avco trial, in Thurlow, personal files.
7. Middlesex News Service, "Professor Testifies."
8. "Trial of the Avco Plowshares"; Thurlow, personal files.
9. "Court Disrupted in Avco Vandalism Trial," *Sun* (Lowell MA), December 14, 1983.
10. Thurlow, summary of trial, in Thurlow, personal files.
11. John Schuchardt to Setsuko Thurlow, on "The Trial of the Avco Plowshares," March 20, 1986, in Thurlow, personal files.
12. Thurlow, interview.
13. Thurlow, interview.
14. Thurlow and Thurlow, letter to family and friends, December 1984.
15. Setsuko Thurlow to Barbara Eggleston, National Organizer, Christian CND, in Thurlow, personal files.
16. "IPPNW."
17. "Milestones."
18. Lifton, *Death In Life*.
19. Thurlow, "Nuclear War," 640.
20. Thurlow, interview.
21. Thurlow, "Nuclear War," 641.
22. Lifton, *Death in Life*, 481.
23. Jerome D. Frank, "After the Event," *New York Times*, March 31, 1968.
24. Oe, *Hiroshima Notes*, 106.

16. Indifference Is Not an Option

1. Thurlow, interview.
2. Setsuko Thurlow, summary of Japanese Family Services, May 1989, in Thurlow, personal files.
3. "Japanese Family Service Honoured by Consulate General of Japan," *Nikkei Voice*, August 1992.
4. Ralph Garber, interview with the author.
5. Thurlow and Thurlow, letter to family and friends, November 1992.
6. "Japanese Family Service on Verge of Closing Its Doors," *New Canadian*, September 5, 1996.
7. Thurlow and Thurlow, letter to family and friends, December 1997.
8. Office for Disarmament Affairs, "Non-Proliferation of Nuclear Weapons."
9. "Riverside Church."
10. "International Citizens' Assembly to Stop the Spread of Nuclear Weapons," New York, April 21, 1995, in Thurlow, personal files.
11. "International Citizens Assembly."
12. Kurihara, *Black Eggs*, 277–79.
13. "International Citizens Assembly."
14. Thurlow, interview.

17. Reframing the Narrative

1. Thurlow, interview.
2. "About Peace Boat."
3. Belfi, "Flash of Light"; Thurlow, interview.
4. Thurlow and Thurlow, letter to family and friends, January 1995.
5. Wagner, *Our Hiroshima*.
6. "Clock Shifts."
7. Thurlow and Thurlow, letter to family and friends, October 2001.
8. Setsuko to friends, January 2006, in Thurlow, personal files.
9. Thurlow, interview.
10. Governor-General Michaëlle Jean, citation, October 25, 2007, in Thurlow, personal files.
11. Thurlow and Thurlow, letters to family and friends, January 2009, December 2009; Akira Kawasaki, interview with the author.
12. Thurlow, "Atomic Bombing," 234.
13. Kawasaki, interview.

14. Bagnarello, *Flashes of Hope.*
15. Thurlow, interview.
16. Sixty-Third First Committee, "General Debate."
17. Thurlow, "Hibakusha Appeal."
18. George P. Shultz, William Perry, Henry Kissinger, and Sam Nunn, "A World Free of Nuclear Weapons," *Wall Street Journal*, January 4, 2007.
19. Thurlow and Thurlow, letter to family and friends, January 2009.
20. Thurlow and Thurlow, letter to family and friends, December 2009.
21. "Remarks by President Barack Obama."
22. Thurlow and Thurlow, letter to family and friends, December 2009.
23. Thurlow and Thurlow, letter to family and friends, 2010.
24. Thurlow, interview.
25. Thurlow and Thurlow, letter to family and friends, January 2011.
26. Thurlow, interview.

18. Point of No Return

1. "James McKitrick Thurlow," *Toronto Star*, April 28, 2011, https://www.legacy.com/ca/obituaries/thestar/name/james-thurlow-obituary?id=44807863.
2. Strickler, *Vow from Hiroshima.*
3. Setsuko Thurlow, letter to family and friends, December 2011.
4. Elizabeth Renzetti, "In Hiroshima, One August Morning in 1945 Was Dark as Night—and This Woman Can't Forget It," *Globe and Mail*, August 5, 2017.
5. S. Thurlow, letter to family and friends, December 2011.
6. "Mission."
7. Kathleen Sullivan, interview with the author.
8. Norah Robertson, "She Survived an Atomic Bomb. Now She Campaigns against Them," *Christian Science Monitor*, January 2, 2020.
9. Sullivan, interview.
10. S. Thurlow, letter to family and friends, December 2011.
11. Thurlow, interview.
12. "ICAN's Origins."
13. Gibbons, "Humanitarian Turn," 16–18.
14. "General Assembly."
15. Acheson, *Banning the Bomb*, 159–61; Kmentt, *Treaty Prohibiting Nuclear Weapons*, 36–38.

16. Gibbons, "Humanitarian Turn," 20.
17. Fihn, "Open-Ended Working Group."
18. Acheson, *Banning the Bomb*, 171–74; Kmentt, *Treaty Prohibiting Nuclear Weapons*, 38–40; Gibbons, "Humanitarian Turn," 21–22.
19. "Speech by Setsuko Thurlow."
20. Rebecca Johnson, interview with the author.
21. "Speech by Setsuko Thurlow."
22. Lewis et al., "Too Close for Comfort."
23. Kurihara, *Black Eggs*, 277.
24. Acheson, Fihn, and Harrison, "Nayarit Conference."
25. Acheson, Fihn, and Harrison, "Nayarit Conference."
26. "Second Conference."

19. Confronting Truman

1. O'Reilly, "Exchange of Views."
2. Thurlow, "Hiroshima."
3. Thurlow, interview.
4. Sullivan, interview.
5. Johnson, interview.
6. Sullivan interview.
7. "Truman's Decision."
8. Thurlow, "Long Journey," 11, 12.
9. Sullivan, interview.
10. J. Samuel Walker, quoted in "Truman's Decision."
11. Richard Frank, "Bomb! Unbomb," *New York Times*, December 12, 1999.
12. Richard B. Frank, quoted in "Truman's Decision."
13. Wilson Miscamble, quoted in "Truman's Decision."
14. Robert Norris, quoted in "Truman's Decision."
15. Thurlow, interview.
16. Walker, quoted in "Truman's Decision."
17. Setsuko Thurlow, quoted in "Truman's Decision."
18. Frank, quoted in "Truman's Decision."
19. Frank, quoted in "Truman's Decision."
20. "Hiroshima Survivor Setsuko."
21. "Hiroshima Survivor Setsuko."

22. "Hiroshima Survivor Setsuko."
23. Eric Schlosser, interview with the author.

20. Moving toward Zero

1. "Vienna Conference."
2. Kurz, "Opening Remarks."
3. Thurlow, "Remarks at Vienna Conference."
4. Tomasi, "His Holiness Pope Francis."
5. Schlosser, "Most Dangerous Machine."
6. Mueller, "Humanitarian Consequences."
7. Thurlow, interview.
8. Sullivan, interview.
9. Thurlow, interview; Sullivan, interview.
10. Thurlow, interview; Sullivan, interview.
11. *Man Who Saved the World.*
12. Pavel Aksenov, "Stanislav Petrov: The Man Who May Have Saved the World," BBC News, September 26, 2013.
13. Acheson, *Banning the Bomb*, 187.
14. Kurz, "Report and Summary."
15. Linhart, "Pledge Present."
16. Thurlow, interview.

21. Moral Indignation

1. Thurlow, "Nuclear Non-Proliferation Review Conference."
2. Eliasson, "Secretary-General's Message."
3. Kerry, "Treaty Review Conference."
4. Thurlow, "Nuclear Non-Proliferation Review Conference."
5. Feroukhi, "NPT Review Conference."
6. Acheson, *Banning the Bomb*, 193.
7. Kmentt, *Treaty Prohibiting Nuclear Weapons*, 58.
8. Acheson, *Banning the Bomb*, 195.
9. Thurlow, interview.
10. Dan Zak, "U.N. Nuclear Conference Collapses over WMD-Free Zone in Middle East," *Washington Post*, May 22, 2015.
11. S. Thurlow, letter to family and friends, March 2016.

12. Thurlow, "Statement to Open-Ended Working Group."
13. S. Thurlow, letter to family and friends, January 2017.
14. Obama, "Hiroshima Peace Memorial."
15. Thurlow, interview.
16. Obama, "Hiroshima Peace Memorial."
17. Thurlow, "Arms Control Association."
18. Zia Mian, interview with the author.
19. B. Rhodes, "Speaker."
20. Thurlow, "Hiroshima Survivor's Letter."
21. Bauer, "Politics of Empathy."
22. Acheson, "It's Time."
23. Acheson, "Nuclear Weapons."
24. Acheson, "Against All Odds."
25. S. Thurlow, letter to family and friends, January 2017.
26. "Ahmadiyya Prize."
27. Ray Acheson, "Ready, Set, Go: Time to Ban the Bomb," *Nuclear Ban Daily*, March 27, 2017.
28. Acheson, *Banning the Bomb*, 223–83; Kmentt, *Treaty Prohibiting Nuclear Weapons*, 110–32.
29. McCaskill, "Ambassador Haley."
30. Somini Sengupta and Rick Gladstone, "United States and Allies Protest U.N. Talks to Ban Nuclear Weapons," *New York Times*, March 27, 2017.
31. Rick Wayman, "Modernization Violates Every Likely Prohibition in a Ban Treaty," *Nuclear Ban Daily*, March 31, 2017.
32. Beatrice Fihn, quoted in Strickler, *Vow from Hiroshima*.
33. Robinson, "Interview with Elayne Whyte Gómez."
34. "Setsuko Thurlow Speaks."
35. Robinson, "Interview with Elayne Whyte Gómez."
36. Alice Slater, "Democracy Breaks Out at the UN as 122 Nations Vote to Ban the Bomb," *The Nation*, July 13, 2017.
37. Elayne Whyte Gómez, interview with the author.
38. Acheson, *Banning the Bomb*, 281–83; Kmentt, *Treaty Prohibiting Nuclear Weapons*, 110–37.
39. "Setsuko Thurlow Closing Statement."
40. "Conference to Negotiate."

41. Strickler, *Vow from Hiroshima.*

22. Glory

1. "Joint Press Statement."
2. "History Was Made," *Asia News Monitor* (Bangkok), July 13, 2017; "Treaty Is a Milestone," *Asia News Monitor*, July 13, 2017; "We Did It!," *Bath Chronicle* (Bath, England), July 20, 2017, 26.
3. Strickler, *Vow from Hiroshima.*
4. "More Than 120 Nations Adopt Treaty against Nuclear Weapons," *Washington Post*, July 7, 2017, A-7.
5. Rick Gladstone, "The U.N. Adopts Treaty to Ban Nuclear Weapons. Now Comes the Hard Part," *New York Times*, July 8, 2017, A7.
6. "The U.N. Bans Nuclear Weapons: So at Least That Problem Is Solved," *Wall Street Journal*, July 17, 2017, A16.
7. Slater, "Democracy Breaks Out," *The Nation*, July 13, 2017.
8. Nina Tannenwald, "The UN Just Passed a Treaty Outlawing Nuclear Weapons. That Actually Matters," *Washington Post*, July 17, 2017.
9. Einstein, "Emergency Committee."
10. "How to Squeeze North Korea," editorial, *Chicago Tribune*, September 7, 2017.
11. "Chronology."
12. Jonathan Soble, "New Fear in Hiroshima, 72 Years Later," *New York Times*, August 7, 2017.
13. "Nobel Peace Prize Announcement."
14. "Nobel Prize."
15. "ICAN Will Receive."
16. "Secretary-General Applauds."
17. Dmitry Serebryakov, "Ex-Soviet Leader Gorbachev Welcomes Decision to Award Nobel Peace Prize to ICAN," TASS, October 6, 2017.
18. "A Peace Prize That Honors the Quest," *New York Times*, October 9, 2017.
19. Rick Gladstone, "Nobel Peace Prize Goes to Group Opposing Nuclear Weapons," *New York Times*, October 6, 2017.
20. "This Year's Nobel Peace Prize Rewards a Nice but Pointless Idea," *Economist*, October 6, 2017.
21. Saeed Kamali Dehghan and Jon Henley, "Nobel Peace Prize Winner Rebukes Trump over Nuclear Standoff," *The Guardian*, October 6, 2017.

22. "Canadian survivor of Hiroshima."
23. Thurlow, interview.
24. Tim Wright, interview with the author.
25. Sullivan, interview.
26. Wright, interview.
27. Sullivan, interview.
28. Setsuko Thurlow, draft schedule, in Thurlow, personal files.
29. Sullivan, interview.
30. Henrick Syse, interview with the author.
31. Thurlow, interview.
32. Bergland, "Envoys Drop Nobel Ceremony."
33. Reiss-Anderson, "Nobel Peace Prize Award."
34. Reiss-Anderson, "Nobel Peace Prize Award."
35. "Nobel Peace Prize Medal."
36. Legend, "Peace Prize Press Conference."
37. Marley, "Redemption Song."
38. "Nobel Peace Prize Speeches."
39. "Nobel Peace Prize Speeches."
40. Syse, interview.
41. Thurlow, interview.
42. Thurlow, "Hiroshima Survivor's Nuclear Warning."
43. "Nobel Peace Prize Concert."

23. Road to Ratification

1. Nikos Stergiou, "Life in 38 Minutes," *Pressenza* (Athens), January 22, 2018.
2. "Hawaii Missile Alert: False Alarm Warns Residents of 'Ballistic Missile Threat,'" CBS News, January 13, 2018.
3. John Bowden, "38 Minutes Elapse between Hawaii Missile Alert and False Alarm Announcement," *Hill*, January 13, 2018.
4. Stergiou, "Life in 38 Minutes."
5. Amy Wang, "Hawaii Missile Alert: How One Employee 'Pushed the Wrong Button' and Caused a Wave of Panic," *Washington Post*, January 14, 2018.
6. "More Investors Rejecting Nuclear Weapons."
7. Rachel Bronson, "Statement from the President and CEO," *Bulletin of the Atomic Scientists*, January 25, 2018.

8. "India and Russia."
9. Burns, "Security Troops."
10. Burns, "Security Troops."
11. Forrow, Ruff, and Thurlow, "Nobel Peace Prize."
12. Tim Wright, interview, *NHK World-Japan*, July 27, 2018.
13. Masato Tainaka, "Too Busy to Meet? Abe Won't See A-Bomb Activist Thurlow," *Asahi Shimbun*, December 7, 2018.
14. "After Failing to Meet Abe, Hibakusha Activist Setsuko Thurlow Urges PM to Hear Those with Differing Views," *Japan Times*, December 7, 2018.
15. Tainaka, "Too Busy to Meet?"
16. Wright, interview, *NHK World-Japan*.
17. "South Africa."
18. Bosman, "Africa."
19. John Mecklin, "A New Abnormal: It Is Still 2 Minutes to Midnight," *Bulletin of the Atomic Scientists*, January 24, 2019.
20. Davenport, "Pope Condemns."
21. Toko Tanaka, "Peace Advocates Will Hand Flame from A-Bomb to Pope Francis," *Asahi Shimbun*, March 18, 2019.
22. Setsuko Thurlow to "Your Holiness," in Thurlow, personal files.
23. Monsignor Roberto Conan to Setsuko Thurlow, October 28, 2019, in Thurlow, personal files.
24. "Pope Brings Anti-nuclear Message to Nagasaki Hiroshima," *Bloomberg News*, November 24, 2011.
25. "ICAN Cities Appeal."
26. "Majority of Millennials."
27. Wright, interview, *NHK World-Japan*.
28. Kristensen and Arkin. "US Deploys."
29. John Mecklin, "It Is 100 Seconds to Midnight," *Bulletin of the Atomic Scientists*, January 27, 2021.
30. Kunal Gaurav, "French President Emmanuel Macron Warned European Nations That They Cannot Remain Spectators in the Nuclear Race and Called for Disarmament Efforts," *Republic*, February 7, 2020.
31. Laura Stone, "Canadian Woman Who Survived Hiroshima Bombing Urges Change of Heart from Trudeau," *Globe and Mail*, October 27, 2017.

32. Setsuko Thurlow, "Canada Needs to Embrace Peace and Sign Nuclear Ban Treaty," *Toronto Star*, July 26, 2017.
33. Thurlow, interview.
34. S. Thurlow, letter to Justin Trudeau, June 22, 2020, Thurlow, personal files.
35. Setsuko Thurlow, "Canada Must Acknowledge Our Key Role in Developing the Deadly Atomic Bomb," *Globe and Mail*, August 1, 2020.
36. Keiji Hirano, "Autobiography Depicts Hibakusha's Long Struggle," *Kyodo News*, November 7, 2019.
37. Strickler, *Vow from Hiroshima*.
38. "After 'Hell on Earth,' Decades Working for Peace," *New York Times*, August 7, 2020.
39. Setsuko Thurlow, "Setsuko Thurlow: 'Nuclear Weapons Are the Ultimate Evil,'" *Daily Hampshire Gazette*, August 3, 2020.
40. Tom O'Connor, "Hiroshima, Nagasaki Survivors Fear Trump Policies Could Bring about New Nuclear Attacks," *Newsweek*, August 8, 2020.
41. "56 Former Leaders."
42. "Malaysia Brings Treaty on the Prohibition of Nuclear Weapons a Step Closer to Reality," *Malay Mail*, September 30, 2020.
43. Jessica Corbett, "'Unprecedented and Desperate': As Nuclear Weapon Ban Treaty Nears Entry into Force, Trump Administration Urges Withdrawals," *Common Dreams*, October 21, 2020.
44. Lederer, "US Urges Countries."
45. Corbett, "Unprecedented and Desperate."

Epilogue

1. Ray Acheson, "Nuclear Weapons Have Always Been Immoral. Now They're Illegal," *The Nation*, October 27, 2020.
2. "Treaty on the Prohibition."
3. Thurlow, "Survivor's Journey."
4. Gakushi Fujiwara, "Interview/TPNW Signatories Meeting Chair: Reminding World of Threat as Nuke Danger 'Gravest' in Decades," *Asahi Shimbun*, June 20, 2022.
5. "Second Meeting of States."
6. Strickler, *Vow from Hiroshima*.
7. Setsuko Thurlow, "The Hell of Hiroshima: Let's Get Real about Nuclear Weapons," *Newsweek*, November 4, 2022.

8. Quoted in Aiko Doda, "Visionary for a Nuclear-Free World," *Tokyo News*, January 8, 2019.
9. "Meet Setsuko Thurlow."
10. Amy Goodman, "Hiroshima Survivor Slams G7 Leaders for Embracing War and Rejecting Nuclear Disarmament," *Democracy Now!*, May 22, 2023.
11. "Briefing Paper."
12. "G7 Hiroshima Summit."
13. "ICAN Closing Press Conference."
14. Schlosser, interview.
15. Colby and Damon, *Some Do Care*, 262–84.
16. Thurlow, "Silent Flash of Light."

Bibliography

Personal Interviews

Acheson, Ray. Video conference. February 28, 2023.

Creighton, Phyllis. Telephone conference. June 5, 2015.

Croonquist, Robert. Telephone conference. July 8, 2019.

Falk, Richard. Video conference. April 25, 2023.

Finch, Stuart. San Mateo CA. February 7, 2019.

Garber, Ralph, and Ilene. Toronto. August 19, 2019.

Gregory, Peter. Palo Alto CA. August 14, 2018.

Helfand, Ira. Video conference. January 12, 2023.

Jay, Jeffrey. Video conference. November 2, 2022.

Johnson, Rebecca. Video conference. March 1, 2023.

Kashiwabara, Annette. Telephone conference. August 30, 2023.

Kawasaki, Akira. Video conference. April 4, 2023.

Kuznick, Peter. Telephone conference. September 11, 2020.

Mian, Zia. Video conference. June 19, 2023.

Perry, William. Stanford CA. June 26, 2018.

Schlosser, Eric. Video conference. May 20, 2021.

Strickler, Susan. Video conference. April 13, 2023.

Sullivan, Kathleen. New York City. May 17, 2019.

———. Telephone conference. August 27, 2019; November 24, 2020; February 10, 2022.

Syse, Henrik. Oslo. August 11, 2019.

Takeuchi, Mitchie. Video conference. February 20, 2023.

Thurlow, Setsuko. Telephone conference. March 8, 2017; September 1, 2018; January 18, 2019; April 19, 2019; July 5, 2019; December 7, 2019; May 8, 2020; June 8, 2024.

———. Toronto. May 6–8, 2017; March 24–26, 2018; February 12–14, 2019; August 19, 2019; April 20–25, 2022.

———. Video conference. May 31, 2022; April 11, 2024; April 22, 2024; May 23, 2024.

Wakisaka, Hiroshi. Hiroshima. November 11, 2018.
Whyte Gómez, Elayne. Video conference. August 8, 2023.
Wright, Tim. Video conference. April 27, 2021.

Published Sources

"24 Hours after Hiroshima." *National Geographic*. YouTube. August 11, 2010. www.youtube.com/watch?v=6_v3y9NQKos.

"56 Former Leaders and Ministers of US Allies Urge States to Join the Nuclear Weapon Ban Treaty." ICAN. September 21, 2020. https://www.icanw.org/56_former_leaders.

"About Peace Boat." Peace Boat. Accessed October 20, 2024. http://peaceboat.org/english/about-peace-boat.

Acheson, Ray. "Against All Odds." *First Committee Monitor*, October 3, 2016. https://reachingcriticalwill.org/images/documents/Disarmament-fora/1com/FCM16/FCM-2016-No1.pdf. Acheson, Ray.

———. *Banning the Bomb, Smashing the Patriarchy*. Lanham MD: Roman and Littlefield, 2021.

———. "It's Time." *First Committee Monitor*, October 24, 2016. https://reachingcriticalwill.org/images/documents/Disarmament-fora/1com/FCM16/FCM-2016-No4.pdf.

———. "Nuclear Weapons." *First Committee Monitor*, October 17, 2016. https://reachingcriticalwill.org/images/documents/Disarmament-fora/1com/FCM16/FCM-2016-No3.pdf.

Acheson, Ray, Beatrice Fihn, and Katherine Harrison. "Report from the Nayarit Conference." Reaching Critical Will. Accessed October 21, 2024. https://www.reachingcriticalwill.org/disarmament-fora/hinw/nayarit-2014/report.

Adachi, Ken. *The Enemy That Never Was: A History of Japanese Canadians*. Toronto: McClelland and Stewart, 1976.

"After the USS *Indianapolis* Was Sunk, the Sailors Had to Survive the Worst Shark Attack in History." War History Timeline. March 25, 2018, https://www.warhistoryonline.com/world-war-ii/uss-indianapolis-worst-shark-attack.html.

"Ahmadiyya Prize for the Advancement of Peace 2016." Al Islam. Accessed October 21, 2024. https://www.alislam.org/video/setsuko-thurlow-ahmadiyya-prize-for-the-advancement-of-peace-2016/.

"Background Information on Monument to Typhoon Victims from Kyoto University Atomic Bomb Disaster Research Team." Hiroshima for Global Peace. Accessed October 18, 2024. https://hiroshimaforpeace.com.

Bagnarello, Erika. *Flashes of Hope: Hibakusha Traveling the World*. Tokyo: Peace Boat, 2009.

Baker, Rodney. *The Hiroshima Maidens*. New York: Penguin, 1985.

Bass, Gary J. *Judgment at Tokyo: World War II on Trial and the Making of Modern Asia*. New York: Knopf, 2023.

Bauer, Gary. "Obama and the Politics of Empathy." Politico. April 7, 2010. https://www.politico.com/story/2010/04/obama-and-the-politics-of-empathy-035499.

Beck, John Jacob. *MacArthur and Wainwright: Sacrifice of the Philippines*. Albuquerque: University of New Mexico Press, 1974.

Belfi, Rory. "A Flash of Light: The Setsuko Thurlow Story." SiriusXM. August 6, 2018. https://soundcloud.com/mmfrancis/a-flash-of-light-the-setsuko-thurlow-story#:~:text=Stream%20A%20Flash%20Of%20Light%20%2D%20The,320%20million%20tracks%20for%20free%20on%20SoundCloud.

"Benkichi Nakamura." FamilySearch. October 16, 2024. https://familysearch.org/ark:/61903/1:1:MHWQ-36V.

Bergland, Nina. "Some Envoys Drop Nobel Ceremony." News in English. November 30, 2017. http://www.newsinenglish.no/2017/11/30/some-envoys-drop-nobel-ceremony/.

Bosman, Isabel. "Africa: Nuclear Disarmament; What the World Can Learn from Africa." September 3, 2021. https://allafrica.com/stories/202109030801.html.

Brendon, Piers. *The Dark Valley: A Panorama of the 1930s*. New York: Knopf, 2000.

"Briefing Paper on G7 Hiroshima Summit, 19–21 May." ICAN. April 2023. https://www.icanw.org/g7_briefing_paper.

Brown, Alice Margaret. *Japanese in Florin, California*. Berkeley: University of California Berkeley Bancroft Library, 1913.

Burns, Robert. "Security Troops on US Nuclear Missile Base Took LSD." Associated Press. May 24, 2018. https://apnews.com/article/98f903367b50404cb3c9695bcabefa5a.

"California, San Francisco Passenger Lists, 1893–1953." FamilySearch. October 16, 2024. https:familysearch.org/ark:/61903/1:1:KX4R-6QF.

"Canadian Survivor of Hiroshima Nuclear Bombing to Accept Nobel Peace Prize." Canadian Press. October 27, 2017. https://toronto.citynews.ca/2017/10/27/canadian-survivor-of-hiroshima-nuclear-bombing-to-accept-nobel-peace-prize-2/.

"Chronology of U.S.-North Korean Nuclear and Missile Diplomacy." Arms Control Association. Accessed October 21, 2024. https://www.armscontrol.org/factsheets/dprkchron.

"The Clock Shifts." *Bulletin of the Atomic Scientists*. Accessed October 20, 2024. https://thebulletin.org/doomsday-clock/.

Colby, Anne, and William Damon. *Some Do Care*. New York: Free Press, 1992.

Committee for the Compilation of Materials on Damage Caused by the Atomic Bombs in Hiroshima and Nagasaki. *Hiroshima and Nagasaki: The Physical, Medical, and Social Effects of the Atomic Bombings*. Translated by Eisei Ishikawa and David L. Swain. New York: Basic Books, 1981.

"Conference to Negotiate Legally Binding Instrument Banning Nuclear Weapons Adopts Treaty by 122 Votes in Favour, 1 Against, 1 Abstention." United Nations. July 7, 2017. https://press.un.org/en/2017/dc3723.doc.htm.

Cousins, Norman. "Hiroshima: Four Years Later." *Saturday Review of Literature*, September 17, 1949, 8–10, 30–31.

Dahler, Richard. "The Japanese Prisoners of War in Siberia, 1945–1956." *Internationales Asienforum* 34 nos. 3–4 (2003): 285–302.

Davenport, Kelsey. "Pope Condemns Having Nuclear Weapons." December 2017. www.armscontrol.org/act/2017-12/news/pope-condemns-having-nuclear-weapons.

"Destructive Effects." Atomic Bomb Museum. Accessed October 18, 2024. https://atomicbombmuseum.org/3_social.shtml.

Directory of Japanese in Sacramento. Vol. 7. N.p.: 1916.

Dixon, Jennifer M. *Dark Pasts: Changing the State's Story in Turkey and Japan*. Ithaca NY: Cornell University Press, 2018.

Donovan, Aine. "Military Physicians: The Myth of Divided Loyalties." *International Journal of Applied Philosophy* 24, no. 1 (2010): 87–91.

Dower, John W. *Embracing Defeat: Japan in the Wake of World War II*. New York: Norton, 1999.

Drixler, Fabian, William D. Fleming, and Robert George Wheeler. *Samurai and the Culture of Japan's Great Peace*. New Haven: Yale University Press, 2015.

Edwards, Gordon. "Canada and the Bomb: Past and Future." Coalition for Canadian Responsibility. Accessed October 20, 2024. http://www.ccnr.org/opinion_ge.html.

———. "Canada's Nuclear Industry and the Myth of the Peaceful Atom." In *Canada and the Nuclear Arms Race*, edited by Ernie Regehr and Simon Rosenblum, 127–28. Toronto: Lorimer, 1983.

Einstein, Albert. "Emergency Committee of Atomic Scientists Incorporated." FAS Project on Government Secrecy. January 22, 1947. https://sgp.fas.org/eprint/einstein.html.

Eliasson, Jan. "Secretary-General's Message to the Opening Plenary of the Treaty on the Non-Proliferation of Nuclear Weapons." United Nations. April 27, 2015. https://www.un.org/sg/en/content/sg/statement/2015-04-27/secretary-generals-message-opening-plenary-treaty-non-proliferation.

Endo, Shusaku. *The Sea and Poison* (*Umi to dokuyaku*).Translated by Michael Gallagher. London: Owen, 1972.

Epstein, William. "The United Nations Second Special Session on Disarmament: A Reassessment." *Bulletin of Peace Proposals* 14 (1983): 137–46.

"Executive Order 9066: Resulting in the Relocation of Japanese (1942)." National Archives. Accessed October 16, 2024. https://www.archives.gov/milestone-documents/executive-order-9066.

Feroukhi, Taous. "2015 NPT Review Conference Outcome Is the Humanitarian Pledge." Reaching Critical Will. Accessed October 21, 2024. https://www.reachingcriticalwill.org/news/latest-news/10048-2015-npt-review-conference-outcome-is-the-humanitarian-pledge.

Fihn, Beatrice. "The Open-Ended Working Group Concludes." Reaching Critical Will. September 6, 2013. www.reachingcriticalwill.org/disarmament-fora/oewg/2013/reports/8004-the-open-ended-working-group-concludes.

"Florin." California Japantowns. Accessed September 6, 2024. www.californiajapantowns.org/florin.html.

Florin Historical Society. *Florin California*. Sacramento CA: Florin Historical Society, 2018.

Folkins, Tali. "Canadian Hiroshima Survivor and Anti-nuclear Activist Says Faith a Motivator." *Anglican Journal*, October 27, 2017.

Forrow, Lachlan, Tilman Ruff, and Setsuko Thurlow. "The 2017 Nobel Peace Prize and the Doomsday Clock: The End of Nuclear Weapons or the End of Us?" *New England Journal of Medicine* 378, no. 24 (June 14, 2018) 2258–61.

Frank, Richard B. *Downfall: The End of the Imperial Japanese Empire*. New York: Random House, 1999.

Frankl, Viktor E. *Man's Search for Meaning*. Boston: Beacon, 2006.

"G7 Hiroshima Summit Fails to Deliver Progress on Nuclear Disarmament." ICAN. Accessed November 2, 2024. www.icanw.org/g7_hiroshima_summit_fails_to_deliver_progress_on_nuclear_disarmament.

"General Assembly, Sixty-Seventh Session, First Committee." Reaching Critical Will. October 19, 2012. https://www.reachingcriticalwill.org/images/documents/Disarmament-fora/1com/1com12/resolutions/L46.pdf.

Gentry, Bryan. "One Voice." *Lynchburg Magazine*, April 13, 2018, 4–9.

Gibbons, Rebecca D. "The Humanitarian Turn in Nuclear Disarmament and the Treaty on the Prohibition of Nuclear Weapons." *Nonproliferation Review* 25 (July 5, 2018): 1–2, 11–36.

Ginn, John L. *Sugamo Prison, Tokyo: An Account of the Trial and Sentencing of Japanese War Criminals in 1948, by a U.S. Participant*. Jefferson NC: McFarland, 1992.

Gold, Hal. *Unit 731 Testimony*. Tokyo: Yenbooks, 1996.

Hachiya, Michihiko. *Hiroshima Diary: The Journal of a Japanese Physician*. Translated by Warner Wells. Chapel Hill: University of North Carolina Press, 1955.

Ham, Paul. *Hiroshima Nagasaki: The Real Story of the Atomic Bombings and Their Aftermath*. New York: Picador, 2015.

Harris, Sheldon H. *Factories of Death: Japanese Biological Warfare, 1932–45, and the American Cover-Up*. New York: Routledge, 1994.

Hersey, John. *Hiroshima*. 1946. Reprint, New York: Knopf, 1985.

"Hippocratic Oath." *Britannica*. Accessed October 20, 2024. https://www.britannica.com/topic/Hippocratic-oath.

"Hiroshima and Nagasaki Timeline." American Heritage Foundation. April 26, 2016. https://www.atomicheritage.org/history/hiroshima-and-nagasaki-bombing-timeline.

Hiroshima Jogakuin High School. *Summer Cloud: A-Bomb Experience of a Girls' School in Hiroshima*. Rev. ed. Tokyo: Sanyusha Shuppan, 1976.

"Hiroshima Survivor Setsuko." YouTube. October 21, 2024. https://www.youtube.com/watch?v=cre8SDTZP4s.

Hook, Glenn D. "Censorship and Reportage of Atomic Damage and Casualties in Hiroshima and Nagasaki." *Bulletin of Concerned Asian Scholars* 23, no. 1 (January–March 1991): 13–25.

Hoshino, Takashi, Hiroo Kito, Stuart Finch, and Zdenek Hrubec. "Leukemia in Offspring of Atomic Bomb Survivors." *Blood* 30, no. 6 (1967): 719–30.

"ICAN Cities Appeal." ICAN. Accessed October 20, 2024. https://cities.icanw.org/appealtext.

"ICAN Closing Press Conference with Setsuko Thurlow." ICAN. May 21, 2023. https://www.icanw.org/g7_ican_closing_press_conference_setsuko_thurlow.

"ICAN's Origins." ICAN. October 21, 2024. https://www.icanw.org/ican_origins.

"ICAN Will Receive Nobel Peace Prize on Sunday, December 10." Concerned Citizens for Nuclear Safety. December 8, 2017. https://nuclearactive.org/ican-will-receive-nobel-peace-prize-on-sunday-december-10th/.

"India and Russia Are Testing Nuclear Missiles: Where Is the Global Outcry?" ICAN. June 6, 2018. https://www.icanw.org/india_and_russia_are_testing_nuclear_missiles_where_is_the_global_outcry.

"IPPNW: A Brief History." International Physicians for the Prevention of Nuclear War. Accessed October 20, 2024. https://www.ippnw.org/.

Isaac, Mac. *Strategic Bombing in World War Two: The Story of the United States Strategic Bombing Survey*. New York: Garland, 1976.

Isaacson, Walter. *Einstein: His Life and Universe*. New York: Simon and Schuster, 2007.

Ishikawa, Itsuko. "Continuous Prayers #24." In *White Flash/Black Rain: Women of Japan Relive the Bomb*, edited by Lequita Vance-Watkins and Mariko Aratani, 53–54. Minneapolis: Milkweed, 1995.

Japan Memorial Society for the Students Killed in the War. *Listen to the Voices from the Sea: Writings of the Fallen Japanese Students*. Translated by Midori Yamanouchi Rynn and Joseph L. Quinn. Scranton PA: University of Scranton Press, 2000.

"Jewel Voice Broadcast." American Heritage Foundation. October 16, 2024. https://ahf.nuclearmuseum.org/ahf/key-documents/jewel-voice-broadcast/.

"Jogakuin." Hiroshima Jogakuin Junior and Senior High School. Accessed October 19, 2024. www.hjs.ed.jp.

Johnson, Katherine, and John F. Rasche. *Hiroshima: Chronicles of a Survivor*. Weston MA: Branden, 1994.

"Joint Press Statement from the Permanent Representatives to the United Nations of the United States, United Kingdom, and France Following the Adoption of a Treaty Banning Nuclear Weapons." Global Public Affairs. July 7, 2017. https://2017-2021-translations.state.gov/2017/07/07/joint-press-statement-from-the-permanent-representatives-to-the-united-nations-of-the-united-states-united-kingdom-and-france-following-the-adoption-of-a-treaty-banning-nuclear-weapons/.

Jungk, Robert. *Children of the Ashes: The People of Hiroshima after the Bomb*. London: Paladin Books, 1985.

———. *Children of the Ashes: The Story of a Rebirth*. New York: Harcourt, Brace and World, 1961.

Kamachi, Noriko. *Culture and Customs of Japan*. Westport CT: Greenwood, 1999.

Kanazaki, Yumi. "My Life: Interview with A-bomb Survivor Setsuko Thurlow." *Chugoku Shimbun*. September 1, 2018. https://www.hiroshimapeacemedia.jp/?p=87650.

Keiichi, Tsuneish. "Unit 731 and the Japanese Imperial Army's Biological Warfare Program." *Asia Pacific Journal* 3 (2005): 1–9.

Kennedy, John F. "Address during the Cuban Missile Crisis." John F. Kennedy Presidential Library and Museum. Accessed October 20, 2024. https://www.jfklibrary.org/learn/about-jfk/historic-speeches/address-during-the-cuban-missile-crisis.

Kerry, John. "Remarks at the 2015 Nuclear Nonproliferation Treaty Review Conference." United Nations. May 1, 2015. https://www.un.org/en/conf/npt/2015/statements/pdf/US_en.pdf.

Kiger, Patrick J. "Key Moments in the Cuban Missile Crisis." History. June 17, 2019. www.history.com/news/cuban-missile-crisis-timeline-jfk-khrushchev.

Kmentt, Alexander. *The Treaty Prohibiting Nuclear Weapons: How It Was Achieved and Why It Matters*. New York: Routledge, 2021.

"Korean War." History.com. May 11, 2022. https://www.history.com/topics/asian-history/korean-war.

Kristensen, Hans, and William M. Arkin. "US Deploys New Low-Yield Nuclear Submarine Warhead." Federation of American Scientists. January 29, 2020. https://fas.org/publication/w76-2deployed/.

Kurihara, Sadako. *Black Eggs*. Translated by Richard H. Minear. Ann Arbor MI: Center for Japanese Studies, University of Michigan, 1994.

Kurz, Sebastian. "Opening Remarks." Federal Ministry Republic of Austria. Accessed October 21, 2024. https://www.bmeia.gv.at/fileadmin/user_upload/Zentrale/Aussenpolitik/Abruestung/HINW14_Opening_remarks_by_Sebastian_Kurz.pdf.

———. "Report and Summary of Findings of the Conference." Federal Ministry Republic of Austria. Accessed October 30, 2024. https://www.bmeia.gv.at/fileadmin

/user_upload/Zentrale/Aussenpolitik/Abruestung/HINW14/HINW14_Chair_s_Summary.pdf.

Kuznick, Peter. *Rethinking the Atomic Bombings of Hiroshima and Nagasaki: Japanese and American Perspectives*. Kyoto: Horitsu Bunkasha, 2010.

"Kwansei Gakuin University." Kwansei Gakuin University. Accessed October 20, 2024. https://www.kwansei.ac.jp/.

Lederer, Edith M. "US Urges Countries to Withdraw from UN Nuke Ban Treaty." Associated Press News. October 21, 2020. https://apnews.com/article/nuclear-weapons-disarmament-latin-america-united-nations-gun-politics-4f109626a1cdd6db10560550aa1bb491.

Legend, John. "Nobel Peace Prize Press Conference." Renaissance Charity. December 9, 2017. www.youtube.com/watch?v=LL4H6-21e54.

Lewis, Patricia, Heather Williams, Benoît Pelopidas, and Sasan Aghlani. "Too Close for Comfort: Cases of Near Nuclear Use and Options for Policy." Chatham House. April 28, 2014. https://www.chathamhouse.org/2014/04/too-close-comfort-cases-near-nuclear-use-and-options-policy.

Li, Fei Fei, Robert Sabella, and David Liu, eds. *Nanking 1937: Memory and Healing*. Armonk, NY: Sharpe, 2002.

Liebow, Averill A. *Encounter with Disaster: A Medical Diary of Hiroshima, 1945*. New York: Norton, 1970.

Lifton, Robert Jay. *Death in Life: Survivors of Hiroshima*. New York: Random House, 1967.

Linhart, Michael. "Pledge Present at the Vienna Conference on the Humanitarian Impact of Nuclear Weapons." Federal Ministry Republic of Austria. Accessed October 21, 2024. https://www.bmeia.gv.at/fileadmin/user_upload/Zentrale/Aussenpolitik/Abruestung/HINW14/HINW14_Austrian_Pledge.pdf.

"Living in North America as a Nuclear Weapon Survivor: Setsuko Thurlow Shares Her Experience." DiaNuke.org. March 12, 2019. https://www.dianuke.org/living-in-north-america-as-a-nuclear-weapon-survivor-setsuko-thurlow-shares-her-experience-video/.

Lord Russell of Liverpool. *The Knights of Bushido: A Short History of Japanese War Crimes*. 2nd ed. London: Greenhill Books, 2002.

MacArthur, Douglas. *Reminiscences: General of the Army Douglas MacArthur*. New York: McGraw-Hill, 1964.

MacIsaac, David. *Strategic Bombing in World War Two: The Story of the United States Strategic Bombing Survey*. New York, Garland, 1976.

"Majority of Millennials Support Banning Nuclear Weapons." ICAN. January 17, 2020. https://www.icanw.org/majority_of_millennials_support_banning_nuclear_weapons.

Malloy, Sean L. "'A Very Pleasant Way to Die': Radiation Effects and the Decision to Use the Atomic Bomb against Japan." *Diplomatic History: The Journal of the Society for Historians of American Foreign Relations* 36 (2012): 515–45.

The Man Who Saved the World. IMBd. Accessed October 21, 2024. https://www.imdb.com/title/tt2277106/.

Marley, Bob. "Redemption Song." AZ Lyrics. October 20, 2024. https://www.azlyrics.com/lyrics/bobmarley/redemptionsong.html.

"Marriage in Japan: History, Love, Arranged Marriages, Interracial Marriages." Facts and Details. Accessed October 19, 2024. http://factsanddetails.com/japan/cat18/sub117/item619.html.

Masaoka, Mike. *They Call Me Moses Masaoka: An American Saga.* New York: Morrow, 1987.

Materials on the Trial of Former Servicemen of the Japanese Army Charged with Manufacturing and Employing Bacteriological Weapons. Moscow: Foreign Languages, 1950.

McCaskill, Noland D. "U.N. Ambassador Haley Opposes International Ban on Nukes." *Politico,* March 27, 2017. https://www.politico.com/story/2017/03/nikki-haley-united-nations-nuclear-weapons-ban-236544.

McClelland, W. R. "Precautions for Workers in the Treating of Radium Ores." Canada Department of Mines. February 8, 1932. http://www.ccnr.org/radium_warning.html.

McCullough, David. *Truman.* New York: Simon and Schuster, 1992.

The Meaning of Survival: Hiroshima's 36 Year Commitment to Peace. Hiroshima: Chugoku Shimbun and Hiroshima International Cultural Foundation, 1983.

"Meet Setsuko Thurlow." Hibakusha Stories. Accessed October 16, 2024. www.hibakushastories.org/meet-the-hibakusha/meet-setsuko-thurlow/.

Meyer, Paul. "Pierre Trudeau and the 'Suffocation' of the Nuclear Arms Race." *International Journal* 71 (2016): 393–408.

Mikamo, Akiko. *Rising from the Ashes: A True Story of Survival and Forgiveness from Hiroshima.* Morrisville NC: Lulu, 2013.

"Mike Masaoka." *Densho Encyclopedia.* October 20, 2024. https://encyclopedia.densho.org/.

"Milestones: IPPNW's First Decade." International Physicians for the Prevention of Nuclear War. Accessed October 20, 2024. https://www.ippnw.org/.

Mills, Harry A. *The Japanese Problem in the United States: An Investigation for the Commission on Relations with Japan, Appointed by the Federal Council of the Churches of Christ in America.* New York: Macmillan, 1915.

Minear, Richard H., ed and trans. *Hiroshima: Three Witnesses.* Princeton NJ: Princeton University Press, 1990.

Miscamble, Wilson D. *The Most Controversial Decision: Truman, the Atomic Bomb, and the Defeat of Japan.* Cambridge: Cambridge University Press, 2011.

"Mission." Hibakusha Stories. October 21, 2024. https://hibakushastories.org/.

Miyaji, Naoko, and Margaret Lock, "Monitoring Motherhood: Sociocultural and Historical Aspects of Maternal and Child Health in Japan." *Daedalus* 123 (1994): 87–112.

"More Investors Rejecting Nuclear Weapons." ICAN. Accessed October 20, 2024. https://www.icanw.org/109_investors_rejecting_nuclear_weapons_dont_bank_on_the_bomb_policies_report.

"Mother Teresa Told a Rally of 20,000 People Sunday." United Press International. June 27, 1982. https://www.upi.com/Archives/1982/06/27/Mother-Teresa-told-a-rally-of-20000-people-Sunday/7079948831390/.

"Mother Teresa Visited Toronto's Varsity Stadium in 1982." CTV Toronto. Accessed October 20, 2024. https://twitter.com/CTVToronto/status/772481988515270656.

Mueller, Rudolph. "Responding to the Humanitarian Consequences of Nuclear Weapon Use in Populated Areas." Federal Ministry Republic of Austria. Accessed October 21, 2024. https://www.bmeia.gv.at/fileadmin/user_upload/Zentrale/Aussenpolitik/Abruestung/HINW14/Presentations/Rudolf_Muller_for_Vienna_Meeting.pdf.

Naka, Kaizo. *Social and Economic Conditions among Japanese Farmers*. Berkeley CA: R and E Research Associates, 1913.

Naono, Akiko, "The Origins of '*Hibakusha*' as a Scientific and Political Classification of the Survivor." *Japanese Studies* 39, no. 3 (2019): 333–52.

"Nobel Peace Prize Announcement, 2017." YouTube. Accessed October 21, 2024. https://www.youtube.com/watch?v=vNQ8CuFKvfo.

"Nobel Peace Prize Concert, 2017." YouTube. October 24, 2024. https://www.youtube.com/watch?v=F5IIkBxcEZA.

"The Nobel Peace Prize Medal." Nobel Peace Prize. October 21, 2024. https://www.nobelpeaceprize.org/nobel-peace-prize/about-the-nobel-peace-prize/the-medal.

"Nobel Peace Prize Speeches." Nobel Prize. December 10, 2017. https://www.nobelprize.org/prizes/peace/2017/ican/lecture/.

"The Nobel Prize." Nobel Prize.org. Accessed October 24, 2024. https://www.nobelprize.org/about-the-nobel-prize/.

Norris, Robert S. *Racing for the Bomb: General Leslie R. Groves, the Manhattan Project's Indispensable Man*. South Royalton, VT: Steerforth, 2002.

"Oath of Citizenship and Ceremony." Government of Canada. Accessed October 19, 2024. https://www.canada.ca/en/immigration-refugees-citizenship/services/canadian-citizenship/become-canadian-citizen/citizenship-ceremony.html.

Obama, Barack. "Remarks by President Obama and Prime Minister Abe of Japan at Hiroshima Peace Memorial." Office of the Press Secretary. May 27, 2016. https://obamawhitehouse.archives.gov/the-press-office/2016/05/27/remarks-president-obama-and-prime-minister-abe-japan-hiroshima-peace.

Office for Disarmament Affairs. "Treaty on the Non-Proliferation of Nuclear Weapons." Accessed October 20, 2024. https://treaties.unoda.org/t/npt.

Oe, Kenzaburo. *Hiroshima Notes*. Translated by David Swain and Goshi Yonezawa. New York: Grove, 1996.

O'Malley, Gerald F. "The Grave Is Wide: The Hibakusha of Hiroshima and Nagasaki and the Legacy of the Atomic Bomb Casualty Commission and the Radiation Effects Research Foundation." *Clinical Toxicology* 54, no. 6 (July 7, 2016): 526–30.

O'Neal, Michael J, "World War II, United States Breaking of Japanese Naval Codes." Encyclopedia.com. Accessed October 18, 2024. http://www.encyclopedia.com/politics/encyclopedias-almanacs-transcripts-and-maps/world-war-ii-united-states-breaking-japanese-naval-codes.

O'Reilly, Breifine. "Exchange of Views, Remarks by the Delegation of Ireland." Reaching Critical Will. Accessed October 30, 2024. https://www.reachingcriticalwill.org/images/documents/Disarmament-fora/nayarit-2014/statements/Ireland.pdf.

Ozasa, Kataro, Eric J. Grant, and Kazunori Kodama. "Japanese Legacy Cohorts: The Life Span Study Atomic Bomb Survivor Cohort and Survivors' Offspring." *Journal of Epidemiol* 28 (2018):162–69.

Powell, J. W. "A Hidden Chapter in History." *Bulletin of the Atomic Scientists* 37 (1981): 44–52.

"Questions 27 and 28." *Densho Encyclopedia*. Accessed October 23, 2024. http://encyclopedia.densho.org/Questions_27_and_28/.

Reiss-Anderson, Berit. "Nobel Peace Prize Award Ceremony." YouTube. December 10, 2017. www.youtube.com/watch?v=P1daV8n6fTY.

"Remarks by President Barack Obama in Prague as Delivered." Office of the Press Secretary. April 5, 2009. https://obamawhitehouse.archives.gov/the-press-office/remarks-president-barack-obama-prague-delivered.

Rhodes, Ben. "Speaker: Ben Rhodes, Deputy National Security Adviser for Strategic Communications." Arms Control Association. October 21, 2024. https://www.armscontrol.org/events/2016-06/june-6-annual-meeting-global-nuclear-challenges-solutions-next-us-president.

Rhodes, Richard. *The Making of the Atomic Bomb*. New York: Simon and Schuster Paperbacks, 1986.

"The Riverside Church." Riverside Church. Accessed October 20, 2024. https://www.trcnyc.org.

Robinson, Tony. "Interview with Elayne Whyte Gómez, Costa Rican Ambassador to the UN in Geneva." Pressenza. July 30, 2019. https://www.pressenza.com/2019/07/interview-with-elayne-whyte-gomez-costa-rican-ambassador-to-the-un-in-geneva/.

———. "Interview with Setsuko Thurlow, Hiroshima Born Survivor." Pressenza, International Press Agency. June 8, 2019. https://www.pressenza.com/2019/08/interview-with-setsuko-thurlow-hiroshima-bomb-survivor/.

Schlosser, Eric. *Command and Control: Nuclear Weapons, the Damascus Accident, and the Illusion of Safety*. New York: Penguin, 2013.

———. "The Most Dangerous Machine." Federal Ministry Republic of Austria. Accessed October 21, 2024. https://www.bmeia.gv.at/fileadmin/user_upload/Zentrale/Aussenpolitik/Abruestung/HINW14/Presentations/HINW14_S2_Presentation_Eric_Schlosser.pdf.

Schultz, Duane. *Hero of Bataan: The Story of General Jonathan M. Wainwright*. New York: St. Martin's Press, 1981.

Schutte, Dan. "Here I Am Lord." Oregon Catholic Press. Accessed October 20, 2024. https://www.ocp.org/en-us/songs/1523/here-i-am-lord.

Scott, James M. *Black Snow: Curtis LeMay, the Firebombing of Tokyo, and the Road to the Atomic Bomb*. New York: Norton, 2022.

Seaton, Philip A. *Japan's Contested War Memories: The 'Memory Rifts' in Historical Consciousness of World War II*. New York: Routledge, 2007.

"Second Conference on the Humanitarian Impact of Nuclear Weapons: Chair's Summary." Reaching Critical Will. October 21, 2024. http://www.reachingcriticalwill.org/disarmament-fora/hinw/nayarit-2014/statements.

"Second Meeting of States Parties Agrees Nuclear Deterrence Is the Problem.'" ICAN. December 1, 2023. https://www.icanw.org/tpnw_2msp_conclusion.

"Secretary-General Applauds International Campaign to Abolish Nuclear Weapons on Winning Nobel Peace Prize, Hailing Determined Efforts of Civil Society." United Nations. October 6, 2017. https://press.un.org/en/2017/sgsm18734.doc.htm.

Sekimori, Gaynor. *Hibakusha: Survivors of Hiroshima and Nagasaki*. Tokyo: Kosei, 1986.

"Setsuko Thurlow Boosts Campaign to Acknowledge Canada's Role in Atomic Bomb Development." ICAN. July 27, 2020. https://www.icanw.org/setsuko_thurlow_boosts_campaign_to_acknowledge_canada_role_in_atomic_bomb_development.

"Setsuko Thurlow Closing Statement at Nuclear Ban Conference." YouTube. July 8, 2017. https://www.youtube.com/watch?v=8QOOXRCdkHU.

"Setsuko Thurlow Speaks at the Nuclear Ban Treaty Negotiations." Hibakusha Stories. March 28, 2017. https://hibakushastories.org/meet-the-hibakusha/meet-setsuko-thurlow/.

Sherwin, Martin J. *Gambling with Armageddon: Nuclear Roulette from Hiroshima to the Cuban Missile Crisis, 1945–1962*. New York: Knopf, 2020.

Shin, Gi-Wook, and Daniel Sneider. *Divergent Memories: Opinion Leaders and the Asia-Pacific War*. Stanford CA: Stanford University Press, 2016.

Sixty-Third First Committee. "General Debate." October 7, 2008. https://www.reachingcriticalwill.org/disarmament-fora/unga/2008/statements.

Sodei, Rinjiro. *Dear General McArthur: Letters from the Japanese during the American Occupation*. Lanham MD: Rowan and Littlefield, 2001.

———. *Were We the Enemy? American Survivors of Hiroshima.* Boulder CO: Westview, 1998.

"South Africa: From Nuclear Armed State to Disarmament Hero." ICAN. February 25, 2019. https://www.icanw.org/south_africa_from_nuclear_armed_state_to_disarmament_hero.

"Stockholm Peace Appeal." In *W. E. B. Du Bois: An Encyclopedia*, edited by Gerald Horne and Mary Young, 301–2. Westport CT: Greenwood, 2001.

Stone, Oliver, and Peter Kuznick. *The Untold History of the United States.* New York: Gallery Books, 2012.

Strickler, Susan, dir. *The Vow from Hiroshima.* Produced and written by Mitchie Takeuchi, 2019. Aired May 1, 2024, on PBS. https://www.pbs.org/video/the-vow-from-hiroshima-awxbyw/.

"The Survivors." Atomic Bomb Museum. Accessed October 18, 2024. https://atomicbombmuseum.org/3_social.shtml.

Takaki, Ronald. *Strangers from a Different Shore: A History of Asian Americans.* Boston: Little, Brown, 1998.

Takei, George. *To the Stars: The Autobiography of George Takei.* New York: Pocket Books, 1994.

Thurlow, Setsuko. "Arms Control Association Annual Meeting: Welcome Remarks and Morning Keynote with Setsuko Thurlow." Arms Control Association. October 21, 2024. https://www.armscontrol.org/events/2016-06/june-6-annual-meeting-global-nuclear-challenges-solutions-next-us-president#Thurlow.

———. "The Atomic Bombing of Hiroshima and Nagasaki: The Role of Women in the Japanese Peace Movement." In *Women and Peace: Theoretical, Historical and Practical Perspectives*, edited by Ruth Roach Pierson, 225–34. London: Croom Helm, 1987.

———. "Hibakusha Appeal for a Nuclear Free World." Reaching Critical Will. Accessed October 21, 2024. https://www.reachingcriticalwill.org/disarmament-fora/unga/2008/statements.

———. "Hiroshima: A Survivor's Testimony." *Irish Studies in International Affairs* 25 (2014): 13–16.

———. "Hiroshima Survivor's Letter to President Obama." Nuclear Age Peace Foundation. August 8, 2016. https://www.wagingpeace.org/hiroshima-survivor-letter-president-obama/.

———. "Hiroshima Survivor's Nuclear Warning." BBC. December 11, 2017. www.bbc.co.uk/programmes/p05qr3tp.

———. "A Long Journey." *SGI Quarterly* 81 (July 2015): 10–12. https://sgi-peace.org/resources/a-long-journey.

———. "Nuclear Non-Proliferation Review Conference NGO Presentation to the Delegates United Nations." Reaching Critical Will. May 1, 2015. https://www.reachingcriticalwill.org/images/documents/Disarmament-fora/npt/revcon2015/statements/1May_S.Thurlow.pdf.

———. “Nuclear War in Human Perspective: A Survivor’s Report.” *American Journal of Orthopsychiatry* 52 (October 1982): 638–45.

———. “Remarks at Vienna Conference.” Federal Ministry Republic of Austria. Accessed October 21, 2024. https://www.bmeia.gv.at/fileadmin/user_upload/Zentrale/Aussenpolitik/Abruestung/HINW14/HINW14_Speech_Setsuko.pdf.

———. “Setsuko Thurlow’s Award Acceptance Speech.” Nuclear Age Peace Foundation. November 15, 2015. https://www.wagingpeace.org/setsuko-thurlows-award-acceptance-speech.

———. “A Silent Flash of Light.” In *Your Voice and Mine 2*, edited by Joan M. Green, Natalie Little, and Brenda Protheroe. Toronto: Holt, Rinehart and Winston of Canada, 1987.

———. “Speech by Setsuko Thurlow.” Reaching Critical Will. Accessed October 21, 2024. http://www.reachingcriticalwill.org/disarmament-fora/hinw/nayarit-2014/statements.

———. “Statement to the Open-Ended Working Group on Nuclear Disarmament.” Reaching Critical Will. May 4, 2016. https://www.reachingcriticalwill.org/images/documents/Disarmamenfora/OEWG/2016/Satements/4May_SetsukoThurlow.pdf.

———. “A Survivor’s Journey.” ICAN Civil Society Forum. June 18, 2022. https://vienna.icanw.org/live.

Till, Barry, *Samurai: The Cultured Warrior*. Victoria BC: Sano Nis, 1984.

“Timeline.” *Bulletin of the Atomic Scientists*. Accessed October 20, 2024. https://thebulletin.org/doomsday-clock/.

Tomasi, Silvano. “Message from His Holiness Pope Francis.” Federal Ministry Republic of Austria. Accessed October 21, 2024. https://www.bmeia.gv.at/fileadmin/user_upload/Zentrale/Aussenpolitik/Abruestung/HINW14/HINW14_Message_from_His_Holiness_Pope_Francis.pdf.

“Toronto Peace Garden.” Hiroshima Nagasaki Day Coalition. Accessed October 20, 2024. http://hiroshimadaycoalition.ca/peacegarden.

“Treaty on the Prohibition of Nuclear Weapons: The Support of Arab League States.” ICAN. May 2023, https://assets.nationbuilder.com/ican/pages/3748/attachments/original/1683184213/LAS_-_TPNW.pdf?1683184213.

Treglown, Jeremy. *Mr. Straight Arrow: The Career of John Hersey, Author of Hiroshima*. New York: Farrar, Straus and Giroux, 2019.

“Trial of the Avco Plowshares.” Media Burn. Accessed October 20, 2024. https://mediaburn.org/video/trial-of-the-avco-plowshares/https://mediaburn.org/video/trial-of-the-avco-plowshares/.

“Truman’s Decision to Use the Atomic Bomb.” C-SPAN. May 17, 2014. www.c-span.org/?319305-1/trumans-decision-atomic-bomb.

Turnbull, Stephen R. *The Samurai: A Military History*. New York: Macmillan, 1977.

"United States Passport Applications, 1795–1925." FamilySearch. Accessed October 16, 2024. https://familysearch.org/ark:/61903/1:1:QKDF-Y6P3.
U.S. General Accounting Office. "United Nations Special Session on Disarmament: A Forum for International Participation." General Accounting Office. July 3, 1979. https://www.gao.gov/products/id-79-27.
"Varsity Court Crowning." University of Lynchburg Library Photo Archive. November 15, 1954. https://digitalshowcase.lynchburg.edu/archive_photos/.
"Vienna Conference on the Humanitarian Impact of Nuclear Weapons." Federal Ministry Republic of Austria. December 8–9, 2014. https://www.bmeia.gv.at/en/european-foreign-policy/disarmament/weapons-of-mass-destruction/nuclear-weapons/2014-vienna-conference-on-the-humanitarian-impact-of-nuclear-weapons/.
Vincent, Lynn, and Sarah Vladic. *Indianapolis: The True Story of the Worst Sea Disaster in U.S. Naval History and the Fifty-Year Fight to Exonerate an Innocent Man*. New York: Simon and Schuster, 2019.
Wagner, Anton. *Our Hiroshima*. YouTube. Accessed October 20, 2024. https://www.youtube.com/watch?v=MnLk8eczE34.
Wainwright, Jonathan M. *General Wainwright's Story: The Account of Four Years of Humiliating Defeat, Surrender, and Captivity*. Garden City NY: Doubleday, 1946.
Walker, J. Samuel. *Prompt and Utter Destruction: Truman and the Use of Atomic Bombs against Japan*. Chapel Hill: University of North Carolina Press, 1997.
"We Learned to Step over the Dead: Hiroshima Survivor and Anti-nuclear Activist Recalls U.S. Bombing." *Democracy Now!* May 27, 2016. https://www.democracynow.org/2016/5/27/we_learned_to_step_over_the.
Wert, Michael. *Samurai: A Concise History*. New York: Oxford University Press, 2019.
"The World on the Brink, John F. Kennedy and the Cuban Missile Crisis, Thirteen Days in October 1962." John F. Kennedy Presidential Library and Museum. Accessed October 20, 2024. https://microsites.jfklibrary.org/cmc/.
Wyden, Peter. *Day One: Before Hiroshima and After*. New York: Simon and Schuster, 1984.
Yamashita, Samuel Hideo. *Daily Life in Wartime Japan, 1940–1945*. Lawrence: University Press of Kansas, 2015.
Young, Donald J. *The Fall of the Philippines: The Desperate Struggle against the Japanese Invasion, 1941–1942*. Jefferson NC: McFarland, 2015.
Zanettin, Federico. "The Deadliest Error: Translation, International Relations and the News Media." *Translator* 22, no. 3 (2016): 303–18.

Index

Atomic bombs: decision to use, 194–99; Nagasaki and, 53, 120–21, 137; production of, 25–26, 31, 33, 35; radiation illness from, 55, 56–59, 69, 80–83, 89, 92–94. *See also* Hiroshima; nuclear weapons